AF324112

The challenge of microprocessors

**SELECTED READINGS
FOR ENGINEERING EDUCATORS**

Papers from a special issue of the
International Journal of electrical engineering education,
augmented by additional material

Edited by **Michael G. Hartley** and **Anne Buckley**

MANCHESTER UNIVERSITY PRESS

© Manchester University Press   1979

Whilst copyright in the volume as a whole is vested in Manchester University Press,
copyright in individual chapters belongs to the respective author, and no part of any chapter
may be reproduced or utilised in any form or by any means, electronic or mechanical, including
photocopying, recording, or by any information storage and retrieval system, without the express
permission in writing of both author and publisher

Published by
Manchester University Press
Oxford Road, Manchester M13 9PL
ISBN 0 7190 0757 7

British Library Cataloguing in Publication Data

The challenge of microprocessors.
    1. Microprocessors — Addresses, essays, lectures
    I. Hartley, Michael George
    II. Buckley, A.
    001.6'4044   QA76.5
ISBN 0-7190-0757-7

Printed in Great Britain
by H Charlesworth & Co Ltd, Huddersfield

CONTENTS

GLOSSARY OF ABBREVIATIONS

ACIA	asynchronous communication interface adapter.
ADC	analog to digital converter.
ALU	arithmetic and logic unit.
BA	bus available.
CPE	central processor element.
CPU	central processor unit.
CR	control register.
DAC	digital to analogue converter.
DDR	data direction register.
DIL	dual-in-line.
DILIC	dual-in-line integrated circuit.
DMA	direct memory access.
EPROM	erasable programmable read only memory.
I/O	input/output.
IOR	input/output register.
LED	light-emitting diode.
LSI	large-scale integration.
MCU	microprogram control unit.
MOS	metal oxide semiconductor.
MPU	microprocessor unit.
MSB	most significant bit.
MSI	medium scale integration.
NC	numerical control.
NMI	non maskable interrupt.
NMOS	N-channel metal oxide semiconductor.
PIA	peripheral interface adapter.
PROM	programmable read only memory.
RALU	register-arithmetic logic unit.
RAM	random access memory.
ROM	read only memory.
R/W	read/write.
S/H	sample and hold.
TTL	transistor-transistor logic.
TTY	teletypewriter.
UPI	universal peripheral interface.
USART	universal synchronous asynchronous receiver transmitter.
UV-PROM	ultra-violet erasable programmable read only memory.
VDU	visual display unit.
WAI	wait for interrupt.

The word 'microprocessor' is now unknown to few in Britain, and indeed
unknown to few in the western world. Seldom has a scientific and technological
advance had such publicity from the media, with emphasis on the hope for
widespread new industrial opportunities that the enormous potential of
microelectronics should bring; but there comes also the creation of a fear that
great unemployment may follow the large-scale incorporation of the techniques
of microelectronics into so many aspects of our everyday life — redundancy is
another word not unknown in the western world.

Some of the technological aspects of microprocessors are already clear, since
they fit into a continuum of computing power; at present they lie between hard-
wired logic and the minicomputer, but the scope and potential increase daily.
For example, in the editorial of the special issue of the *International Journal of
Electrical Engineering Education* on Microprocessors, from which most of the
contents of the book *The Challenge of Microprocessors* is taken, Dr. Martin
Healey discusses the rapidly escalating power of the microcomputer and quotes
specific examples, but such is the speed of progress that appreciable further
enhancement of computing power will occur by the time his editorial has been
read. Whilst the microprocessor of the single-chip microcomputer is cheap, and
daily becomes cheaper, the effective cost is determined by its specific application. In a one-off role, the development of robust applications software leads
to a unit price system not far short of that which applies when a conventional
minicomputer is used. By contrast a mass market spreads the software development costs and enables full advantage to be taken of the low unit cost for
hardware; transducer and data transmission costs are for some time unlikely to
be negligible. Whilst the fully instrumented car may have publicity value, it is
likely to remain at the top price end of the market for some appreciable time.

There will certainly be many new opportunities, but what about the fear that
our social structure may be affected at a rate too great for the changes to be
assimilated without enormous human problems and inadequately thought-
through changes in our society? It seems likely that for many people free
(leisure) time will be increased to such an extent that it will require hard effort
to fill it in a satisfying way; can we adjust to this unusual challenge? How valid
is the fear that robots may become more important than men in an industrial
workforce? Whilst these and other social effects may well be major in type, it is
important to get them into perspective, since even with the present speed of
technological change, an overnight automation revolution is just not possible.
There has to be enormous capital investment in terms of plant and human
resources, but additionally it requires time for new ideas to be accepted,
developed into programmes, and finally applied to production. During this
breathing space the necessary redeployment and massive retraining of people,
and the steady adjustment of us all to a different way of life becomes possible,
but we must not linger or the opportunity will be lost.

With sensible planning and efficient execution of the plans we look forward to a situation where this positive use of localised computing power leads to a more efficient economy and where limited resources may be used to the best advantage. For example, a microprocessor-based controller for a domestic central heating plant is not going to reduce employment opportunities, and will, in fact, open up new markets given adequate design and competent manufacture; it also requires highly trained service personnel. The domestic market is one of the largest of the mass markets, and many aspects of it will be affected: dishwashers, office machines, information retrieval systems with access via TV and telephone, are but a few of the areas of rapid change.

In the commercial field banking transactions already employ significant amounts of centralised computing power, and provide a base-load overnight for the telephone service as customers' accounts are brought up-to-date; microcomputers at the branch level enhance the possibilities still further by providing local intelligence, but without loss of employment. Examples such as this refer to the urban areas of industrialised countries where both batch-orientated and real-time process control are well established, and where the use of microprocessor technology is made feasible via an extension of an already existing situation. By contrast, the position in rural areas, and especially in the developing countries is very different, and labour-intensive technology for local small industries will remain the most sensible approach for some time to come.

Change there must be, and change there will be, and our human task is to ensure that the undoubted increase in production and industrial efficiency which can be achieved is carried out with the minimum of social disturbance, and the complete exclusion of the social disasters wildly predicted by some. The microprocessor can do much to enhance the quality of life, and this, as always, will be the acid test.

What we have therefore is a marvellous new opportunity. One that we can use in a way that can enhance happiness and the full enjoyment of life by the human race. It requires wise teachers, inspired research workers, receptive industry, and long-range thinking and planning by government. I have full confidence that continual and intelligent appraisal of the developing situation will not only enable advanced technological work to proceed apace, but will also ensure that the fragile human being, so full of fears and worries, is not damaged by this pulse of exciting development. It is our job as scientists and technologists to advance the area as rapidly as we can; it is our job as human beings to ensure that this is done without loss of human dignity. This we can do.

I believe that this volume is timely and of scholarly quality; I commend it to you.

R. N. HASZELDINE, *Principal, U.M.I.S.T.*

THE SOCIAL EFFECTS OF THE SEMICONDUCTOR REVOLUTION — AN ENGINEER'S VIEW

M. G. HARTLEY
Digital Processes Group, Department of Electrical Engineering and Electronics, University of Manchester Institute of Science and Technology, England

INTRODUCTION

This special issue of the International Journal of Electrical Engineering Education is devoted to many aspects of microprocessor technology as viewed by the engineering educator. Careful attempts have been made by the Editors to provide balanced coverage of all relevant topics. One area alone seemed to have been in danger of omission. This is the vitally important subject of the effects which the new technology is likely to have on the population generally. The first reaction to the possible omission was to speak to the sociologist, the economist and the economic historian. Those approached, naturally enough, were reluctant to offer firm opinions as to the probable effects of semiconductor technology and microprocessors in particular. Under these circumstances it falls to the Editor to hazard some comment and suggestions. At first sight the idea seems foolhardy in the extreme, but this is not necessarily the case. Those who were leaving school about 1950 and who are now beginning to admit to the onset of middle-age have witnessed all the changes brought about by the computer and indeed electrical engineers and computer personnel have participated in the changes. They have seen the situation about which Lord Bowden, the former Principal of U.M.I.S.T. and one of the very first responsible for marketing commercial computers was able to write in the Preface to *Faster than Thought*[1] published in 1953:

> A rough count showed that about 150 digital computers are being built at this moment, most of them in universities and other research establishments. It will be interesting to see if these machines play in the next decade the part of the cyclotrons and high voltage generators in the 'thirties'. In those days every university had to have a cyclotron on the campus; they were mysterious and expensive and they gave tone to the place; they impressed distinguished visitors and attracted endowments; their construction gave the whole of the physics department plenty of healthy exercise, and kept them happy, out of mischief and covered in oil; the united efforts of the staff were required to keep the machine on the verge of operation, and those who so wished could postpone into the indefinite future the embarrassing decision as to what was to be done with the machines when they actually started to work.

What an interesting observation and how typical of that exciting time a quarter of a century ago. Thereafter we have watched the circumstances develop dramatically and in a very different direction. All our everyday lives have been affected profoundly by changes in banking procedures and communications. Our professional lives have responded to technological change, sometimes via involvement in inovative techniques and at other times we have watched virtually helpless while such change has seen a loss of jobs — in some cases our own. Under these circumstances it is perhaps not so inappropriate after all for an engineer, albeit now in the university sector, to offer some comments and suggest some pointers for the future.

The article begins with some historical background relating both to the Industrial Revolution of the 19th century and equally importantly to the Computer Revolution of the last twenty-five years. The later suggestions as to the probable effects of the Microprocessor Revolution are set against these historical precedents.

EARLY DAYS

It is appropriate, when considering the impact of computers on society, to start with Charles Babbage (1792–1871), the father of digital computing. Babbage, as early as 1834, began work on his Analytical Engine. The project was conceived in mechanical engineering terms and employed decimal arithmetic. It was beyond the resources of the age, but nevertheless incorporated most of the basic principles included in modern machines, be they main-frame or microcomputers. There were three motivations for the work, apart from its intrinsic interest. These have remained unchanged as motivations for computer development and use until the present day and comprise commercial applications, scientific computation and the stimulus of defence projects. With Babbage, the military incentive was tabulations of the trajectories of cannon balls. At the latter end of the 20th century, military interest relates to real-time tracking of intercontinental ballistic missiles and surveillance systems generally. The work of Babbage took place during a period of rapid technological change in Western Europe and North America. Indeed, much of the innovation occurred in Britain, not least in Manchester and the north-west region generally. A recent book, *Science in Victorian Manchester*[2], captures the flavour of the time extremely well.

By the latter part of the century, the electric telegraph permitted both domestic and business communication efficiently and comparatively cheaply. The railway network in Western Europe, with the exception of Spain and Portugal, was complete before 1870 and mechanical power was abundant with coal as well as water as the motive force. It was the age of the entrepreneur. Names such as Brunel, Marconi, and Simon spring to mind. The case of Ferranti who, in his twenties raised very substantial capital with which to design and build the first London power station and a 10 kV transmission-line to the city centre, with the object of lighting the Strand, and this in the 1890's, is a case in point. Single-handed he saw an entrepreneurial situation and used both financial skill and technological expertise to achieve success. Today such an approach is scarcely possible.

The Victorian age, though many people experienced great poverty, was nevertheless an age of conspicuous spending both on what we now call consumer durables and on inessentials. Both were made possible by a cheapening of basic manufacturing techniques due to advanced technology in the processing of ferrous and other metals and by reduction of costs as a result of mechanisation. Kitchen equipment, often of the most ingenious sort, proliferated, while clothes and household furnishings among the newly-emergent middle classes took on the most extravagant aspects. Even the lot of the artisan improved, through enhanced sanitation, street lighting and the like.

Perhaps the worst social effects of the Industrial Revolution came in the textile field, where there was a transition from small-scale labour-intensive activity, typically in the home, to the factory environment. Here a handful of machine-minders were able to look after a large number of spindles in the case of spinning, and an equally small number of operatives could handle weaving machines for which patterns were pre-programmed using Jacquard cards. The same Jacquard cards provided inspiration to Babbage and Hollorith alike. The scale of industrialisation in the textile field was very considerable.

The modern welfare state had not emerged to provide financial help, re-training schemes and the like. Even today, economic forces are imperfectly understood. In the second half of the 19th century comprehension was slight. This first transition from a rural to an urban industrial society was probably the largest upheaval to be experienced. The semi-conductor revolution is likely to be small in comparison — but more of this later.

THE FIRST COMPUTER REVOLUTION

Through the Victorian age, and indeed well into the 20th century, the pioneer work of Babbage was exploited to only a limited extent. Indeed, progress in that direction was restricted to two areas only. One was the simplest sort of data processing such as that required for census work and first carried out by Herman Hollorith for the U.S. census of 1890[3]. The other was small-scale technical calculation performed using mechanical desk calculators. It was not until the advent of the Second World War that the impetus came for substantial progress. Initially this was via electro-mechanical computation using machines such as the Harvard Mark I Automatic Sequence Controlled Calculator (ASCC) which came into service by 1944 in the U.S.A. Significant progress did not take place until the late 1940's and this only with the aid of surplus electronic equipment, suddenly available cheaply and on a large scale.

By the mid 1950's computers were becoming well-established. By modern standards they were of limited power, expensive and unreliable. They made huge demands on programmers since programs were written exclusively in what are now called low-level languages. However, they awakened popular interest. Books appeared with titles such as *Giant Brains — Machines that Think* and one experienced what was a reflection, though only faint, of the religion-versus-science controversies of the previous century which related to fundamental views as to exegesis particularly in respect to the Old Testament and centred on Charles Darwin's *Origin of the Species*. Thus there were earnest discussions as to the relationship between computer and brain, the nature of freewill, 'could computers be said to think', and an automation revolution seemed just around the corner. But the expected revolution never quite came off. With hindsight some of the reasons are clear enough.

By the early 1950's the first computers incorporated many of the features of modern machines. Thus they included hard-wired micro-programming units. The importance of storage hierarchy was well understood, as was the trade-off between hardware and software features. Input/output facilities were increasingly available. On the software side the importance of sub-routines was appreciated. However, higher-level languages were unavailable and indeed in certain quarters were regarded as 'unsporting'[4]. As a result, programmers were specialist personnel requiring long and expensive training, and individual programs were not written lightly. Programs took a long time to write and as a result were expensive to produce. Peripheral interface presented problems, especially since bussing systems were yet to be developed to a high level.

Thus the introduction of a computer system to handle commercial data processing or in process control was not lightly undertaken. Machines were expensive in hardware costs, staff training was also expensive, while extensive programming time was necessary. The changeover to computer data bases was painful but certainly caught the popular imagination. Witness the situation portrayed even in popular contemporary novels such as John Braine's *Life at the Top*.

As a result of all these factors the immediate and universal automation revolution never occurred. Instead, during the period mid 1950's–mid 1960's came more gradual developments. Various trends can be identified. A distinction was gradually drawn between main-frame and minicomputers. The former developed into general-purpose machines with provision for multi-programming. High-level languages (autocodes) were developed and sophisticated operating systems appeared to take most of the burden of 'housekeeping' work within and outside the computer from the programmer or latterly the installation manager. The minicomputer, on the other hand, adopted initially a role as a process-controller involving on-line real-time work in many cases. Low-level languages were retained for efficiency, though the price paid was substantial expertise demanded of the programmer.

Since then, mini's have become increasingly powerful and have incorporated high-level languages and multi-programming facilities. Multi-user working, often interactive, has become possible. With the advent of the more comprehensive operating systems, today's mini often looks remarkably like yesterdays main-frame machine, apart from reduced physical size and cost. Though traditionally the mini was thought of in terms of scientific computing, often in the process-control field, it is used increasingly for banking transactions, wages calculations, as the heart of airline and theatre-booking systems, as well as in such applications as road-traffic control and motorway monitor and warning systems.

By the present time — mid 1979 — the mini is to be found everywhere. It is used for handling data bases large and small. Thus it might be found in commercial offices of all sizes. It is used for stock or inventory control in factories and warehouses. It is found in a printing firm or is used to control an electric typewriter used in typesetting. It even finds a place in micro-teaching in a classroom.

One important aspect must not be overlooked. This is the degree to which young people, and others too, take the computer completely for granted. Thus, school pupils of all ages will respond to the computer. Even primary school children will not flinch at the idea of a simple program. For example in Britain one of a series of books for the youngest readers devotes a volume to computers (the *Ladybird Book* series). Rumour has it that this particular book, in plain covers, is used to provide a basic introduction to computers for senior military personnel. Teachers, too, take the computer for granted. The annual chore, often devolving upon a deputy head and taking weeks of painstaking effort, of producing the school timetable is now achieved within minutes — once the relevant data has all be entered via the VDU.

The importance of this aspect of computer education should not be minimised. Increased knowledge brings with it increased confidence, and as a result, a substantial reduction in the fear of the machine. It is this fear, largely of the unknown, which is now transferred to semiconductor technology generally, and the microprocessor in particular. Hence we must be clear as to what the microprocessor really offers — or fails to offer.

THE MICROPROCESSOR IN REALITY

The myth, projected to a large extent by the media intent on a spectacular approach, is of a new device providing substantial computing power on a single chip of minute proportions. This power is available readily, and at extremely low cost. The performance of a wide range of existing devices will be enhanced very substantially through the incorporation of such chips. Applications will extend from the automatic dishwasher, through the domestic central heating plant and the family car to commercial operations such as banking transactions and the like. In industry generally, microprocessors will make possible the totally automated factory at an early date. As a result, many people will lose their jobs while a general reduction of working hours will make for substantial problems as to how best to employ new-found leisure.

What is the reality? It would be true to say that the microprocessor is part of the overall spectrum of computing power extending from hard-wired logic through to main-frame machines of substantial power and high cost. At present, microcomputers based on the microprocessor, and constituting one or several IC chips, depending on circumstances, find a place in the hierarchy between hard-wired logic and the minicomputer. The unit cost of the microcomputer itself is probably not more than a few hundred pounds. Certainly the price would appear to be less than that of a small minicomputer configuration comprising CPU and store alone, while the computing power might well be comparable — especially if a 16-bit microcomputer were involved.

With conventional computers the hardware expense is only the 'tip of the iceberg' as so many have come to appreciate — sometimes the hard way. The same is likely to be true of the microcomputer based on the microprocessor. An illustrative example should serve to make this clear.

The microprocessor is often held out as the device which will make for safer and more efficient motoring. We have a mass market. Why not incorporate a microprocessor-based hazard and instrumentation system? Work in these areas is already in progress[5]. However the problem is not so easy of solution.

For example, we require reliable, cheap and accurate transducers. Take fuel consumption. An opportunity to display fuel consumption — short and longer term, provides an excellent index of car performance A little reflection reveals that a flow meter of requisite performance and appropriate price and which incorporates digital read out suitable for interface to a microprocessor involves formidable problems. When the further environmental and interface problems associated with the automobile are remembered, the solution at an economic price becomes even more difficult. Such a situation may be repeated for each of the various parameters to be monitored for the vehicle.

The overall development costs are likely to be considerable. Production costs, even when spread over a substantial volume, will be far from trivial. Similar considerations apply to the provision of an effective display.

Quite apart from hardware considerations, which will involve bussing arrangements in addition to the above, robust applications software capable of handling all the various inputs, together with appropriate systems software must be provided. This too is a formidable exercise involving extensive development systems and substantial staff time.

From the above considerations it becomes clear that for our example, unit costs are inevitably significant even if the cost of the microprocessor itself fell to zero. But the above considerations are not all. Schemes for maintenance must be set up and training arrangements for staff organised. As a result of all these factors, it is perhaps not so surprising that the impact of the microprocessor so far is in the area of heavy bus and truck operation rather than in the domestic passenger car where, so far, it fails to appear even at the top end of the market.

This example is not intended to belittle the contribution which the microprocessor has and will make in industry generally. The purpose of the example is to show that an instant and low-cost impact cannot be expected. Where are the real contributions likely to occur? One way to help predict the answer is to look at the current roles of the minicomputer and to project these forward. Thus we may expect to see an increasing use of interaction with data bases via VDU where the role of the central minicomputer is augmented with local 'intelligence' at the VDU terminal provided by a microcomputer installed within the VDU. Bank, stock control, theatre ticket booking and the like spring to mind. For the educationalist, computer-assisted learning becomes more of a real possibility — though we must recall the very limited scope of programmed learning so far. Local libraries already have limited facilities for access to larger collections. The microprocessor will accelerate the process.

However we must not be carried away with too much enthusiasm. The hire of data-links and terminal equipment such as Modems constitutes a considerable fraction of overall cost of many installations. There seems little chance of spectacular breakthrough in hire charges, though terminal equipment is being re-engineered in semiconductor terms.

Process control has always been a typical application for minicomputers. Considerable advantage and economies have resulted in such industries as the chemical industry. With the microprocessor, further advantage will accrue, and the somewhat reduced system costs with the microprocessor should result in further exploitation, in situations for which economics prevented adoption of computer control in the past.

The low unit cost of microprocessors and microcomputers themselves has one considerable advantage in process control and on-line real-time applications generally. Highly reliable systems incorporating multi-microprocessor configurations are now both practically realisable and economically viable. Thus on-board computer systems for aircraft may expect to have a hardware reliability at least one order of magnitude better than that of the aircraft structure itself[6]. Low unit cost also permits distributed computing power. Suitably configured, this may be regarded as an aspect of reliability. Alternatively if the system is geographically dispersed, weak serial data links operating at low speed may replace more expensive and faster parallel links. For example, in an urban road-traffic network where the signals are computer controlled, local microprocessor-based controllers may exhibit local control with only limited data transfer to and from a central processor. Such a procedure would not have been viable in terms of the provision of a minicomputer at each intersection.

So far, the vast majority of microprocessor activity has been supported by software written at low level. There are several consequences. Most obviously program development has been time-consuming, and expensive development systems and/or cross-product software has been necessary to assist the programmer. The cost of such aids is far from negligible. Thus a development system up to the level of floppy-disk support may cost up to £10K and attract substantial overheads while the salaries of programmers together with their overheads are considerable. Accordingly the re-writing of applications software is not undertaken lightly. Only if applications software is of wide use are unit costs in this direction reduced to manageable proportions.

THE ANALOGY WITH THE 1950's
How does all this, which is more realistic than the media image, relate to the social effects of the microprocessor? It seems to the writer that the present position has some similarities to the initial computer revolution of the 1950's and 1960's. At the very beginning of the period there was scepticism. The view was expressed that a very few computers would suffice for the nation's needs. Thereafter came euphoria with increasingly widespread applications of computers large and small. Both main-frame and minicomputers have had substantial impacts on the lives of everyone. It is important to distinguish between

those situations where enhanced efficiency has been the result and others where jobs have been lost. An example of the former is the speed and cheapness of banking transactions. Here the proportion of the population with bank accounts has increased very greatly over the decades but nevertheless all accounts are updated overnight. While people are very quick to criticise on the basis of occasional spectacular blunders, the banking revolution has been very significant. An example where jobs have disappeared is in respect of the generation and distribution of electricity in Britain. Here the number of employees per megawatt of output capacity has shrunk over the decade 1964–65 to 1974–75 by about half[5]. Much of this reduction can be attributed to automation in which computer technology has played a significant role. This process, which was gradual, has been achieved without undue trauma.

Many other examples of enhanced efficiency and production without reduction in labour force can be cited. A few might be mentioned; the manufacture of detergents and soap powders, bakeries and biscuit production, chemical plant generally, consumer durables including radio and TV, automated typesetting for books and newspapers, stock control, structural design, automatic test gear for a very wide range of components. The list is almost endless. Indeed it is difficult to think of any manufacturing process or service industry which is untouched by the computer.

We now turn to the microprocessor. With increasingly large integrated circuits (in terms of components per chip) came a reduction in size of the minicomputer. In the earlier 1970's fabrication reached the stage where a CPU might be placed on a single chip at reasonable cost while semiconductor memory also became available. The first significant result for the general public was the pocket calculator. With ever decreasing cost, the volume of sales expanded beyond belief, providing the opportunity for the microprocessor. At first microprocessors comprised the CPU in respect of 4-bit machines, but rapidly 8-bits became the norm. Now 16-bit machines are increasingly popular. However it is true that most of the microprocessor systems installed and working belong to the simpler of the 8-bit categories, e.g. Intel 8008 and Motorola 6800.

On first appearance the microprocessor was little known and little appreciated. More recently the euphoria surrounding the device is comparable to that of the early and mid 1950's in respect of computers. The computer revolution proceeded more slowly than was expected. Constraints included conservative attitudes on the part of government, management and labour. Some of the conservatism sprang from suspicion of the new equipment, the fear of the unknown. However some reflected a genuine reluctance to make a premature commitment during a period of rapid change in computer technology. Lack of suitably trained staff and venture capital also played a part. Many of these motivations are equally true today and represent valid reasons why change in respect of microprocessors cannot occur overnight.

IMPLICATIONS OF THE PRESENT REVOLUTION

The microprocessor has been with us for several years already. Much of the automation revolution expected of the microprocessor has been achieved with minicomputers already. Contrary to popular belief the real costs associated with the use of microprocessors are not negligible though for situations where many identical configurations can be deployed there is reasonable hope of substantial cost saving.

The use of higher-level languages has begun. With the minicomputer this promoted significantly wider exploitation. The same is likely to be true for the microprocessor with the result that the 'one-off' microprocessor installation achieved at moderate real cost becomes feasible.

All this activity will be achieved within a time scale. The problems of training of programmers alone will ensure that progress will be gradual — though this is a relative term. The time scale has the valuable result that adjustments to the changes can be made. This is true not merely in respect of management and workforce but equally importantly in respect of government and educationalists.

The fear at the back of everyone's mind is that the microprocessor will lead to the loss of jobs on the grand scale. The considered view of the present writer is that such a situation is not likely to develop, and for two principal reasons.

The *first* is that the automation revolution is with us already. Across the widest range of industry and commerce the computer is widely deployed. Even the hope of further reduction in computing costs is unlikely to bring very many further large sectors within computer monitor and control. Almost all are there already. Naturally there remain small industrial and commercial enterprises which will now be able to install a microcomputer with VDU and keyboard. Small economies will be made as a result. The office employing three clerks may manage with two. However the need to make provision for holidays, sickness, telephone switchboard duties, etc. will ensure that the two are unlikely to become one. The larger companies have made their basic economies in terms of staff long ago.

Indeed a study of the unit costs of computing reveals enormous reductions both in hardware and software over the last two decades. The advertising program of the largest American computer company, IBM, makes this abundantly clear. It is likely that the reduction-in-computing costs/year will never again be exceeded.

The *second* reason for cautious optimism is that the side effects of the new and enhanced computing power will in fact create new jobs in two categories. The first relates to the use of microprocessors to enhance current industrial and commercial situations. Here there will be demands for a new generation of programmers, system analysts and hardware designers to implement schemes. These people will require support from designers of transducers, data-links and the like. Systems will require manufacture, test, installation and thereafter maintenance. Industrial techniques previously too expensive to implement will become realisable for the first time. The services of those enumerated above will be much in demand. Over and above this, however, will come entirely new developments. The current limited use of data transmission systems via domestic TV (Ceefax etc.) in the U.K. give some inkling of one range of possibilities. While some of the other applications will be as ephemeral as TV games, others will doubtless prove more valuable and indeed may 'enhance the quality of life'. Based on previous experience, exaggerated claims for computer-aided instruction are likely to prove unsucessful though the microprocessor will prove a boon to more soundly-based schemes. The analogy with the Victorian era should not be forgotten. The first Industrial Revolution enhanced production, lowered unit costs, increased prosperity (though unevenly) and as a result new markets opened up.

It is often maintained that unskilled labour has the most to lose from the automation revolution. This is probably true but again I would contend that the worst effects of the automated factory in this respect are already behind us. The service industries and the domestic scene remain. Attempts to devise domestic and industrial robots capable of clearing tables and sweeping floors have not so far proved very successful. The capital costs of automated and central waste disposal systems for cities are such that the municipal refuse collectors are likely to be with us for the forseeable future. Accordingly employment in service industries such as these is not likely to disappear as a result of the advent of the microprocessor.

CONCLUSIONS
On balance, a fairly optimistic prognosis is suggested for the developed countries. Here, the bulk of the computer revolution has happened already. For the future, the three pressures for computing power which motivated Babbage 150 years ago are likely to remain as spurs to further progress. But what about the Third World? The position there is much more difficult. The various revolutions, agricultural, industrial, computer and now microprocessor are likely to be telescoped into one huge amalgam. For oil-rich countries with small populations like Libya, the position is not so very difficult and the situation appears from personal observation to be developing reasonably well in spite of what detractors might imagine. This is not to say that huge blunders are not made, but lessons are learnt even if painfully. Perhaps for such countries the biggest problems revolve round the training locally within a very limited time scale of every type of professional engineer and skilled tradesman and the need to realise that the expatriate educator must be given freedom of action and status to assist in this process. The expatriate, for his part, must be sensitive to local susceptibilities and well aware that his key rôle has a very limited time span.

But in the case of many Asian and African countries, particularly the poorer ones with large populations, the position is very different. Indeed, it is analogous to the European situation on the eve of the first Industrial Revolution. For such countries the provision of labour-intensive agricultural and industrial activity is a short-term palliative but national pride and external forces do not respond favourably to such ideas. The irony is that the countries which provided the mass markets and raw materials for 19th century Europe, and as a result helped its prosperity, without necessarily much local benefit, are now likely to suffer a second time as a result of the importation of high-level technology. All that can be suggested is a leisurely adoption of intermediate technology before high-level technology makes an appearance, but this is not the advice that the developing countries are anxious to hear. The African in his kraal has his transistor radio already and will not be content with his span of oxen much longer. He wants a diesel-powered tractor too and all the modern aids to agriculture, with a share in consumer durables. Indeed, in very many cases he wants to leave the land for the big city where all these desirable things should be found. If, as is the case, there is no work for him therein, the resulting situation is to be deplored. How these dilemmas may be resolved lies outside the competence of the writer.

ACKNOWLEDGEMENTS
While the author's views are his own, he wishes to acknowledge with thanks the discussions with staff and students at U.M.I.S.T. which have helped to shape those views.

REFERENCES
[1]   Bowden, B. V., ed., *Faster than Thought*, Pitman, (1953).

[2]   Kargon, R. H., *Science in Victorian Manchester*, Manchester University Press, (1977).

[3]   Randell, B., ed., *The Origins of Digital Computers*, ch. 3, Springer-Verlag, (1973).

[4]   Wilkes, M. V. Wheeler, D. J. and Gill, S., *The Preparation of Programs for an Electronic Digital Computer*, Addison-Wesley, (1957).

[5]   Shepard, B., 'Vehicle instrument displays', *Electronics and Power, I.E.E.*, pp. 809–811, (Nov./Dec. 1978).

[6]   Depledge, P. G. and Hartley, M. G., 'Fault tolerant microcomputer systems for aircraft', *Institute of Radio and Electronic Engineers, Conference Proceedings 36 on Computer Systems and Technology*, pp. 205–220, (March 1977).

[7]   *C.E.G.B. Statistical Yearbook*, p. 17, (1974–5).

INTRODUCTION TO MICROPROCESSOR SYSTEMS — PART 1[1]

E. T. POWNER, M. A. ESCUDER and P. G. DEPLEDGE
Department of Electrical Engineering and Electronics, University of Manchester
Institute of Science and Technology, England

STRUCTURE OF MICROPROCESSOR SYSTEMS

Introduction

The semiconductor fabrication of 16–20 transistor and resistor components organized to realize four separate logic functions or gates integrated onto a single microcircuit has developed in both manufacturing and technological innovation to the present day state where the availability of devices containing 14,000 active devices or a few thousand gate equivalencies per integrated circuit are commonplace. The electronic calculator is perhaps the most widely known example of a complex logic circuit being available at a reasonable cost. Calculators, although capable of storing and processing digital information, are severely limited in both the number and types of operation they can perform since they are inherently fixed at the design stage and remain unalterable.

Microprocessors have evolved from calculators but are essentially different in both their functional capability and mode of operation. Often a microprocessor is erroneously referred to as a 'computer on a chip'. In actual fact it is the central processing unit (C.P.U.) of a microcomputer system and requires several additional external components before it can function in a realistic manner. It is now possible, however, to integrate these 'external' components on to the same silicon slice to form a single-chip micro computer.

The revolutionary difference between the calculator and the microprocessor is that the latter is programmable by the user, enabling the same basic system configuration to solve problems and applications which are apparently unrelated. A microcomputer system based on a microprocessor is shown in Fig. 1 consisting of:

(i)   memory with a read/write capability for the storage of data in the form of both numbers and instructions.

(ii) a controllable input-output interface for the communication of data to and from external devices or users.

(iii) the microprocessor or C.P.U. which performs all control and timing functions according to a repertoire of instructions which govern:

    (a) arithmetic, logical and transfer operations by the manipulation of data stored in the memory.

---

[1]   This article and Parts 2 and 3 which follow it, are reprinted, with slight modifications, from *IJEEE*, Vol. 14 (1977), pp. 73, 173 and 269.

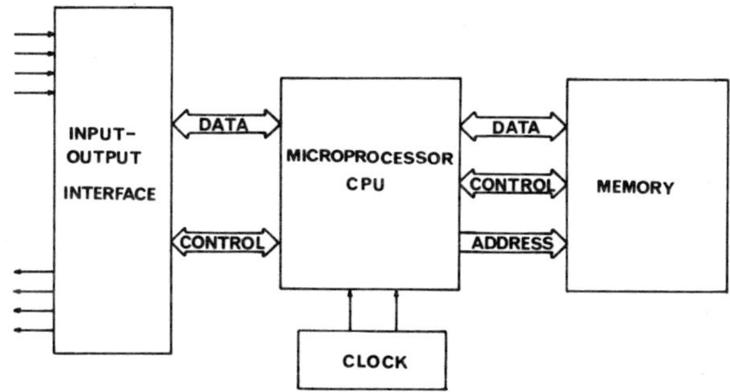

FIG. 1   Basic microcomputer system.

(b) modification of instructions and data.

(c) decision making to transfer program control as a result of an inherent or calculated data condition.

(d) interrupt facility in order to either control or respond to an external equipment demand.

The microprocessor is thus the kernel of any small computer system. Prior to the advent of the microprocessor the choice of a system having limited computational capability lay between the use of fairly complex hard-wired logic systems using small and medium-scale integrated circuits or a minicomputer which would be underemployed. Advances in semiconductor technology have led to a spectrum of microprocessors ranging from cheap and relatively crude devices which can compete economically with hard-wired systems to the more expensive, fast devices which equal the computing power provided by minicomputers.

Microprocessors are usually classified according to word length, 4, 8, 12 or 16 bits, and the semiconductor technology and process used in their manufacture. First generation microprocessors used P.-M.O.S. technology, which has been superseded in second generation devices by N-M.O.S. having greater speed and higher packing density (giving inherently a more powerful processor in functional terms) or C.M.O.S. which has the advantage of low power dissipation and wide supply voltage tolerance. High-speed M.O.S. (H.M.O.S.) and bipolar Integrated-Injection Logic (I^2L) technology is now being used for third-generation microprocessors. These characteristics and other important ones such as execution times, instruction repertoire, etc. lead to an almost bewildering proliferation of available microprocessors on the market. Whatever the pedigree of the device *all* microprocessors have basic functional similarities to be explained in this article. The actual selection of a particular device is too dependent on its intended use or application: only general comment and guidance will be given although specific examples of realization are quoted in a later article.

Microprocessor structure
A simplified diagram of the internal organization is shown in Fig. 2. The most important feature of the microprocessor is the arithmetic and logic unit (A.L.U.).

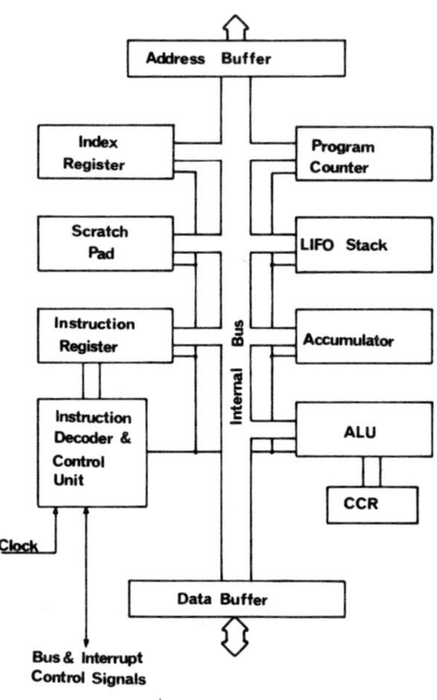

FIG. 2   Simplified microprocessor block diagram.

This provides the computational and logical power of the device and is capable of performing simple functions such as add, add with carry, subtract, subtract with borrow, shifting, AND, OR etc. etc. The A.L.U. usually operates between the accumulator register and an internal register or a memory location, the result being placed in the accumulator. Associated with the A.L.U. is a condition code register which consists of several flip-flops showing, for example, whether the previous operation caused a carry to be generated, gave a zero result or gave a negative result.

The internal registers mentioned previously are often called scratch-pad registers and their function is, as their name suggests, to hold temporary data during a computational process. These registers are supplied because they can be accessed faster and more conveniently than external memory locations.

A distinguishing feature of microprocessors is the internal data highway or 'bus'. This is connected and hence shared by all the internal registers and A.L.U., the precise timings and connections governed by the control (microprogram) unit. The data highway is usually bidirectional with three-state logic being utilized to control routing and isolation of the sub-units.

The program counter (P.C.) enables the instructions to be addressed and brought down from external memory in the correct sequence. The P.C. contains the address of the next instruction that is to be loaded into the instruction register and is normally incremented after each instruction fetch. However, certain classes of instruction can modify the program counter so that the programmer can provide branches away from the normal program flow. Often the branch a program takes depends upon the result of some previous computation, and this is where the

14

condition code registers are employed. For example a typical conditional branch instruction may be 'Branch if the carry flip-flop is set — otherwise carry on.' Another class of instructions that are allowed to modify the P.C. are the 'call subroutine' group. Subroutines are small programs that carry out specific functions which may be required several times during the main program execution. Thus, unlike a branch instruction, the program counter value at the time the call subroutine was made must be incremented and stored so that, at the end of the subroutine, the main program will be re-entered at the correct position. The stack is used to store the P.C. value at subroutine calls. The stack is usually a 'last in, first out' type so that addresses are 'pushed' on and 'popped' off the stack as the subroutine is entered and left. By having a multiple stack, subroutines can be nested; i.e. one subroutine can call another subroutine which can call another etc. etc. up to the limits of the stack depth. In addition, with many microprocessors, the programmer can manipulate the stack by pushing and popping addresses or data on or off the stack.

In addition to addressing the program instructions the machine must, of course, be able to address the appropriate program data. Several addressing methods are commonly used, e.g.

(i)   Direct — the word(s) following the instruction form the address of the data.
(ii) Immediate — the data are continued in the word immediately following the instruction.
(iii) Indexed —the data contained in the word following the instruction are added to the contents of the index register to form the address.
(iv) Relative — the data contained in the word following the instruction is added to the program counter contents to form the address.

The instruction decoder and control unit decodes each instruction and under the supervision of the external clock controls the external and internal data paths and registers ensuring the correct logical operation of the processor. The control unit can also accept control signals from outside the device. These are known as interrupts and cause a call to an interrupt service routine. This feature is particularly important in 'real-time' applications as it allows synchronization with an external process.

System architecture
As indicated earlier the microprocessor is only one component in a working system and it must be connected to memory and input/output devices to make it into a practical system.

Due to the pin limitation on standard I.C. packages it is necessary to multiplex memory and interface devices onto a common bus structure. The bus is usually split into an address and a data part, although some devices have a common data and address bus. The data and addresses are demultiplexed using signals provided by the microprocessor. Typically, outputs such as memory read, memory write, data bus ready are supplied together with synchronization signals.

The external components required to realize a system depend greatly upon the type of microprocessor being used and, of course, on the application. However, most manufacturers supply standard 'chip-sets' which are simply connected to the appropriate bus and timing lines to provide the basis of a working system. Specialized user-devices may then be connected either straight onto the bus system or to the interface chips provided. A typical system configuration is shown in Fig. 3. This clearly again illustrates the bi-directional bus-system concept and is almost a natural reflection of the internal bus structure for both compatibility and efficiency.

The program memory is in most cases required to be non-volatile (i.e. the programs are not lost when power is removed) and is therefore usually semiconductor read-only-memory (R.O.M.). There are four main classes of R.O.M., namely:

(i) Mask programmable — this is best suited to applications where the program has been 'debugged' and verified and where a large production run is anticipated. This is because the R.O.M. is programmed during its manufacture; this is an expensive process and once programmed the R.O.M. cannot be altered.

(ii) Fusible link/shorted junction — these are programmed by applying high-voltage pulses to the data 'output' of the device. This action either blows a fusible link or breaks down the base-emitter junction of a transistor changing it into a diode, dependent upon the type. These types are best suited to proven program applications with small production runs.

(iii) Electrically reprogrammable — U.V. erasable (E.P.R.O.M.) — These again are programmed by applying a high-voltage pulse to the device. They have the advantage that they may be erased by shining a U.V. light upon them and then subsequently reprogrammed. These devices are therefore very useful in proto-type systems.

(iv) Electrically erasable — electrically reprogrammable (E.A.P.R.O.M.) — These

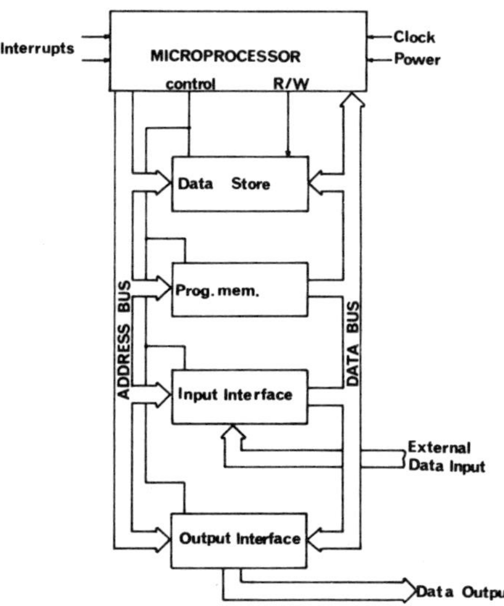

FIG. 3   A typical microprocessor system architecture.

operate as their name suggests, however they have the disadvantage over
E.P.R.O.M. that they are slow to program. Their main advantage is that they
are usually word-alterable and so the whole program does not have to be re-
written to make a single change. Again these devices are used in prototype
systems.

The data storage is usually required to be changed during the process and so
read/write (often called random-access) memory is used for this purpose. Again
semiconductor types are generally used. This can either be bipolar or M.O.S., static
or dynamic. Bipolar read/write memory is faster than M.O.S., but consumes much
more power; dynamic memory is faster than static but has the disadvantage that
refresh circuitry must be incorporated to periodically refresh the charge holding
the memory cell at '1' or '0'. For most microprocessor applications memory access
times are not too critical and the simpler static M.O.S. type is generally satisfactory.

Input and output facilities are generally provided by logically flexible interface
packages. Programmable interface circuits are available which control the transfer
of data, its direction and timing, together with the generation of interrupt and
status signals to the microprocessor when required. Thus each port may be either
an input or an output under user control and program specification.

In addition to the memory devices most manufacturers also supply special-
purpose devices such as clock and timing generators, communications interface
(parallel to serial converters and M.O.D.E.M.S.), programmable delay generators
and system controllers. Hardware multiply chips, direct memory access controllers,
and even more comprehensive input/output devices, for example, 'intelligent'
peripheral controllers, are now available, which permit direct interfaces to floppy
disk drives, keyboards, C.R.T.'s etc.

Available microprocessors
At the present time microprocessors are available, together with memory, input/
output devices etc. in compatible families for incorporation into microcomputer
or special purpose systems. Table 1 lists a few of the devices current early in 1977.

Single chip microcomputers, containing the basic microprocessor, a limited
amount of R.A.M. (~64 bytes), R.O.M./P.R.O.M. (~1K bytes) and input/output
ports, are readily available but are generally limited to 4 or 8 bit word-lengths.

Other types of available microprocessors include the so-called 'bit-slice' microprocessors which unlike the types described in this article are effectively 2 or 4
bit slices of an A.L.U. which can be coupled together to form a multiple length
A.L.U. for a central processor. They are fabricated using bipolar transistor technology, and hence have very fast operational speeds, but since they have little
in common with single chip microprocessors/microcomputers, will not be discussed.

Parts 2 and 3 which follow discuss the programming of microprocessors and
the general hardware and software design. Development aids and applications
produced at U.M.I.S.T. are covered.

TABLE 1 *A selection of the microprocessors available at the beginning of 1977*.*

MANUFACTURER	MODEL	TECHNOLOGY	DATA WORD SIZE	MEMORY CAPACITY	INSTRUCTIONS	STACK LEVELS	INTERRUPTS	REGISTER CYCLE TIME
AMERICAN MICROSYSTEMS	9209	PMOS	4	64K	28	–	NONE	
BURROGHS	MINI-D	PMOS	8	256		–	NONE	
FAIRCHILD	F8	NMOS	4/8	64K	101	64	MULTILEVEL	2μS
FAIRCHILD	PPS-25	PMOS	4	12K	32	4	NONE	
GENERAL INSTRUMENT	CP1600	NMOS	16	64K	68	8	MULTILEVEL	400nS
INTEL	4004	PMOS	4	4K	47	3	NONE	12μS
INTEL	4040	PMOS	4	4K/8K	60	7	MULTILEVEL	10.8μS
INTEL	8008	PMOS	8	16K	48	7	MULTILEVEL	12.5–30μS
INTEL	8080	NMOS	8	64K	78	RAM	MULTILEVEL	2μS
INTERSIL	6100	CMOS	12	4K	40	–	1	5μS
MOS TECHNOLOGY	6501	NMOS	16	65K	55	RAM	1	
MOSTEK	5065	PMOS	8	32K	51	RAM	3	
MOTOROLA	6800	NMOS	8	64K	72	RAM	2	1μS
NATIONAL SEMICONDUCTOR	PACE	PMOS	8/16	64K	45	10	MULTILEVEL	2μS
NATIONAL SEMICONDUCTOR	SCAMP	PMOS	8	64K	46			
RCA	COSMAC	CMOS	8	64K	91	RAM	MULTILEVEL	
ROCKWELL	PPS 4	PMOS	4	4K	50	3	NONE	5μS
ROCKWELL	PPS 8	PMOS	8	16K	90	2	MULTILEVEL	6μS
SIGNETICS	2650	NMOS	8	32K	75	8	MULTILEVEL	2.4μS
TEXAS INSTRUMENTS	TMS1000	PMOS	4	8K	43	1	NO	15μS
TEXAS INSTRUMENTS	9900	NMOS	8/16	64K	69	RAM	16	4.67μS
TOSHIBA	TLCS-12	NMOS	12	4K	18	RAM	MULTILEVEL	1μS
WESTERN DIGITAL	MCP1600	NMOS	8	64K	VARIABLE	–	4	
ZILOG	Z-80	NMOS	8	64K	158	RAM	2	0.4μS

*See 'A Review of Available Microprocessors' pp. 44–53 below, for an up-to-date list.
A comparison illustrates the pace of change.

INTRODUCTION TO MICROPROCESSOR SYSTEMS – PART 2

E. T. POWNER, M. A. ESCUDER and P. G. DEPLEDGE
Department of Electrical Engineering & Electronics, University of Manchester
Institute of Science & Technology, England

1   SYSTEM COMPONENTS

Introduction

In the previous article[1] the general features of microprocessors and their integration
into a working system were discussed. We shall now consider in more detail the
external circuitry that is required, particular attention being paid to interface and
special function devices.

Microprocessors may be used to advantage in simple measurement, process
control and data logging systems and, in such applications, it is important that
efficient microcomputer – peripheral data transfers are achieved. The microcomputer must therefore include interface devices which are capable of carrying
out the data transfer and also provide control signals such that the peripheral
device is able to receive or send the data as appropriate. This data transfer or
input/output (I/O) as it is commonly called, can fall into three broad type
classifications:

(i)   Programmed data transfers (I/O), in which the microprocessor program
        controls and initiates all data transfers to or from a specific peripheral
        device.

(ii)   Interrupt data transfers (I/O), in which the peripheral devices generate
        an interrupt to the microprocessor and so demand attention.

(iii)   Direct memory access (D.M.A.), in which the peripheral devices directly
        transfer data to and from memory without any program intervention.

The operation and implementation of these three classes of I/O will now be
discussed in more detail.

Programmed data transfers

A programmed data transfer is achieved by an I/O instruction; i.e. during the
program execution data is read from or written to a specified device by, for
example, an INPUT from device 1 or OUTPUT to device 2. Some processors,
such as the Motorola M6800, do not have specific I/O instructions but use a
technique called 'Memory-Mapped-I/O' in which the interface device is assigned a
'memory' location. Thus normal memory read-write instructions may be used to
access the device. This scheme has the advantage that the data does not have to be
explicitly loaded into the microprocessor since it is treated as an operand in

memory e.g. by comparison:

(a)	INPUT/OUTPUT INSTRUCTION SYSTEM	(b)	MEMORY MAPPED I/O
(1)	Load one operand into register B from memory	(1)	Load one operand into register A from memory
(2)	INPUT data from peripheral 1 to register A	(2)	Add peripheral 1 data to register A
(3)	Add A + B	(3)	Store result to memory
(4)	Store result to memory		

Thus for case (b) one instruction is saved, in this simple example. These techniques can, of course, be applied to all processors even if they have explicit I/O instructions.

In the simplest case the interface device will be an n-bit register, where n is the length of the processor data word (Figs. 1 and 2). The input interfaces will have tri-state buffers at their connection to the system data bus, which are enabled as

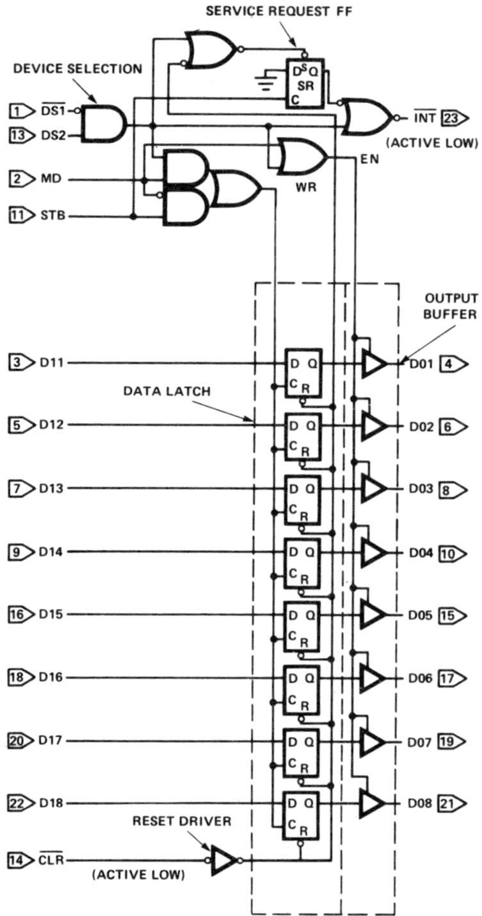

FIG. 1   Simple latch-type interface device (Intel. 8212).
(Courtesy Intel Co.)

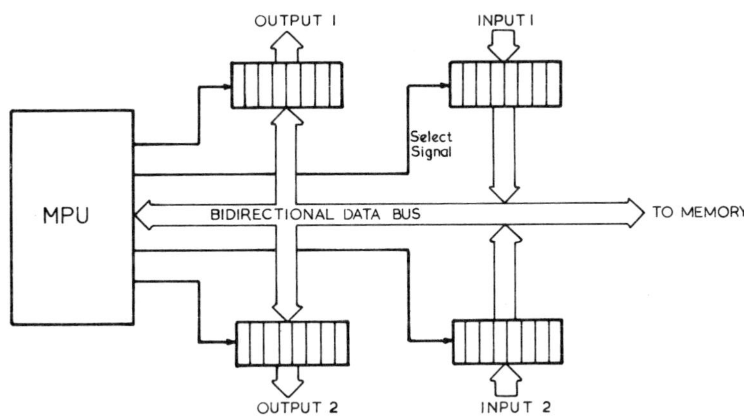

FIG. 2   Simple programmed data input-output.

the input is selected. The output interfaces latch the information on the data-bus
under the control of the select signal. Many applications will not require an n-bit
input or output for each peripheral device; for example, single line status inputs
and outputs are often used. For output, the solution is simply to latch the
appropriate bit of the data-bus in a single flip-flop. However, for input it is
convenient to read an n-bit port as usual and use a software mask to pick out the
state of the input. The masking operation consists of logically ANDing a data
word with the appropriate bit(s) set to the input data, i.e.

Input word	01101011
Mask	00100000
Result of AND	00100000

           ⌐— input bit set.

The conditional jump/call instructions may then be used to determine program
flow according to the state of the input bit. Thus the n-bit input port can be used
to provide any combination of n-inputs as required.

Most microprocessor chip-sets now contain a more sophisticated multi-port
programmable interface device. Typically 2—3 ports are available in each package
and the data direction of each port may be changed under program control. This is
achieved by having internal registers, accessible by the processor, which specify
the functional configuration of the peripheral interface, Fig. 3. The flexibility of
devices varies from manufacturer to manufacturer but, generally for an 8-bit
device the peripheral data lines can be specified as input or output in blocks of
8, 4, 2 or individually. Thus the masking operation required for the simple register
type interface is not needed. In addition, some devices also contain program
controlled interrupt and interrupt disable functions and 'handshaking' lines. The
handshaking lines or status outputs can be used in conditional data transfers;
i.e. the processor only reads (or writes) to the port if the port is ready. The data
transfer routine would thus consist of: a status read; check status and if ready,

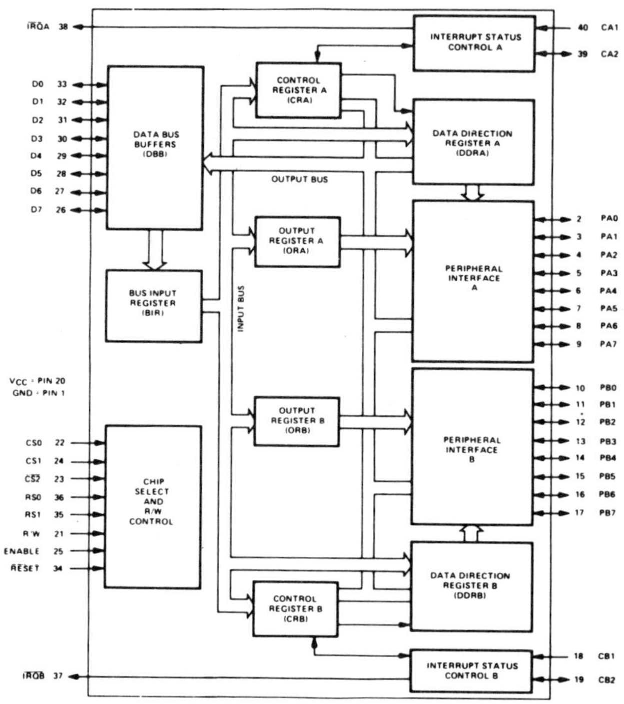

FIG. 3 *Motorola MC 6820 programmable interface adapter.*
(Courtesy Motorola Inc.)

input or output the data. If the port is not ready the processor can either cycle round checking the status until it is valid or alternatively carry out another operation and recheck later.

So far we have discussed parallel I/O but, of course, many applications require serial I/O and thus the manufacturers have produced communications interface devices. Thes have a parallel I/O bus, compatible with the microprocessor, but a serial I/O to the peripheral device. Again these are programmable and normally include all the features to be found in universal synchronous/asynchronous receiver/transmitter (U.S.A.R.T.) chips. Compatible MODEMS are also available which provide all functions required to implement 0-600 b.p.s. frequency shift keying (F.S.K.) systems. Typical applications are shown in Fig. 4.

Interrupt Data Transfers
Interrupt driven data transfers are used in cases where the processor is, for most of the time, carrying out a background program independent of the peripheral device. When the peripheral is ready it will attempt to interrupt the job currently being executed. The processor generally has an interrupt enable/disable flag which can be set or reset by the background program thus protecting

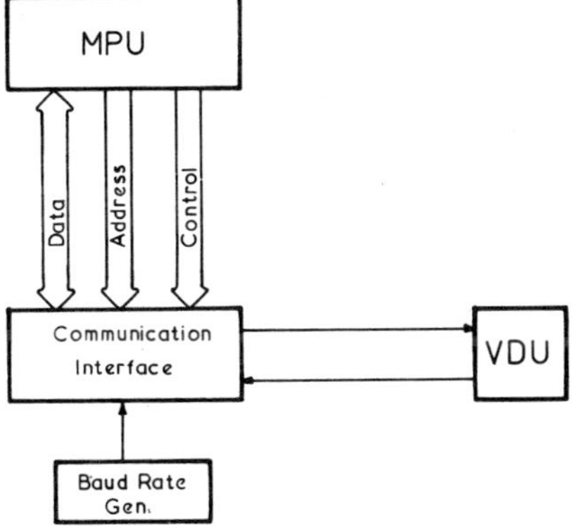

[A] Asynchronous Serial Interface to VDU

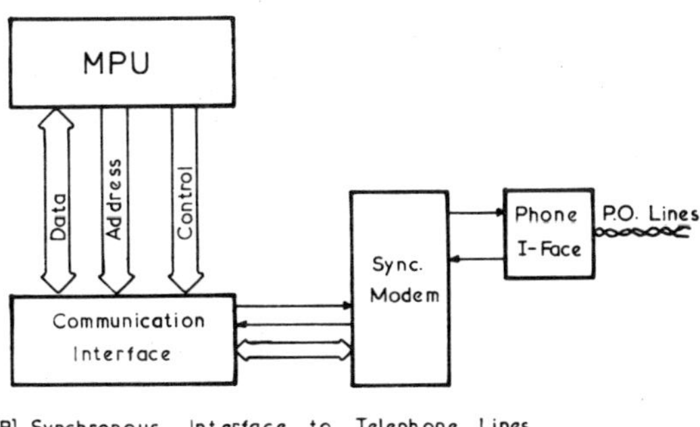

[B] Synchronous Interface to Telephone Lines

FIG. 4   Communications interface device applications.

any critical routines. On detecting the interrupt the microprocessor then executes a subroutine for the data transfer (Fig. 5). Since, when the interrupt occurs, the processor status flags, program counter and registers may contain important data and it follows that these must be stored away before the data transfer is carried

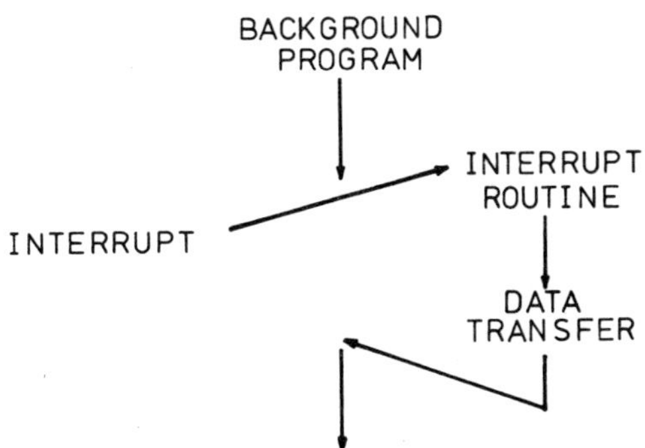

FIG. 5   Interrupt data transfer program flow.

out. For most microprocessors, during an interrupt, it is usual to save the current contents of the internal registers of the C.P.U., which define its status, by transferring this data into a predefined temporary storage location. This temporary storage of C.P.U. status is often referred to as the stack. It has the additional property that it is organised as a last-in, first-out, (LIFO), or push-down store[1].

Such status-saving transfers can be achieved automatically by the processor (as in the Motorola M6800) or by an interrupt service routine written by the user (as in the Intel 8080). An enhancement of the Intel 8080, the Zilog Z-80, has two banks of identical registers so that when servicing an interrupt the processor switches to the bank not in use and hence does not have to store the registers' data away. This makes for very fast interrupt servicing. After the register contents have been stored away, using one of the above methods, the data transfers are identical to programmed I/O, except that after the transfer the processor must, of course, be restored to its former state.

Priority control devices are available as LSI circuits so that more important inputs and outputs are attended to first. Some processors also have a non-maskable interrupt (N.M.I.) line which always interrupts the processor no matter what the state of the interrupt enable is. This is often used in power failures or other critical situations so that the system can be shut down in an orderly fashion, or data can be transferred and preserved in non-volatile memory.

Direct memory access

The previous two I/O methods become inefficient if large amounts of data are required to be transferred at relatively high speeds, e.g. to floppy disks. For these applications a direct memory access system can be used. During a D.M.A. the processor has its control of the system bus removed so that the auxiliary D.M.A. controller can manage the data transfers. A simple method is to halt the processor forcing its system bus into the high impedance state, and then carry out the transfer under the D.M.A. controller. However, several other alternatives such as cycle stealing, i.e. inserting the transfers in instruction cycles, may be used. Both these methods are available for certain processors in L.S.I. chip form.

Special function devices

From the above I/O systems description, it should be apparent that in order to speed up overall system responses more and more 'intelligence' is being provided within the interface devices. Similarly some functions which may be carried out less effectively in software are also being delegated to L.S.I. hardware devices. For example, a hardware multiplier is available which is intended to be used with an 8-bit microprocessor and carries out an 8-bit by 8-bit multiplication in $5\ \mu s$ compared with, say, $300\ \mu s$ for its software equivalent. The multiplier is treated as 4 ports (or memory locations) and so multiplication involves simply writing the operands to and reading the result from the device. Another function that is commonly required in microcomputer systems is the generation of a delay. These are required where there is an interface to a mechanical device so that the peripheral has time to respond to a system command, before the next command occurs. The delays

can be achieved in software by using timing loops that, for example, decrement
a register until it reaches a certain value. However, if more than one timing loop
is required the program can become complex and unmanageable. To solve this
problem counter/timer circuits have been developed which are basically groups
of programmable independent counters. The user can initialise and start the
counters under program control — when the count reaches zero i.e. the end of
the delay, the processor is interrupted. Multiple delays can be achieved by
assigning different interrupt levels to different counters, using a priority interrupt
controller. Again the counters are treated as parts of memory locations and thus
software overheads are very low.

Manufacturers are also beginning to integrate some of these features onto
a single multi-function chip. One example has 2 programmable I/O ports, one
programmable interval timer, 1 K bytes of R.O.M. and 64 bytes of R.A.M. plus
an interrupt request line in a single 40 pin package.

2   MICROPROCESSOR SYSTEM DESIGN

Having surveyed the available devices, their functional characteristics, methods of
programming and software structures, it becomes necessary to integrate the
hardware and the software techniques into a coherent unit for the microprocessor
and its components in order that it may operate as a practical and useful system.

A system designed around a microprocessor is inherently more difficult to test
and debug than a more conventional minicomputer or hardwired-logic system:
internal registers cannot be accessed, single-step facilities are limited or non-existent,
programming is usually done at a low-level and the final program is difficult to
examine when committed to P.R.O.M. Hardware and software aspects of the
design can be kept separate to a certain extent and this is a satisfactory way of
designing most systems. However, in some cases this is not possible and a unified
systems approach is necessary where the hardware and the software designs modify
and affect each other. The basic interfacing between the microprocessor and its
peripherals and memory is now regarded as standard. Most of the design effort
will be spent on timing considerations, the Input-Output interface between the
microprocessor ports and the external process being controlled. The software
design has become a major aspect and a large percentage of the design effort will
be spent in program writing, testing and debugging. This is no easy task and
in all but the simpler cases, the designer will find it essential to use some of the
powerful design aids now available. The design process is of necessity an iterative one
(Fig. 6) and several changes may be required before a satisfactory solution is
obtained. Hardware and software functions may be defined at an early stage, but
the designer must be prepared to alter them in the light of experience. The software
can then be written and tested using assemblers and simulators. Then, once a
prototype becomes available, emulators and logic analyzers will help to verify
the finer timing and other considerations under real-time conditions. Such tests
may result in modifications to either the hardware, the software or both. Design
development aids in almost all cases shorten the design time and in many cases are

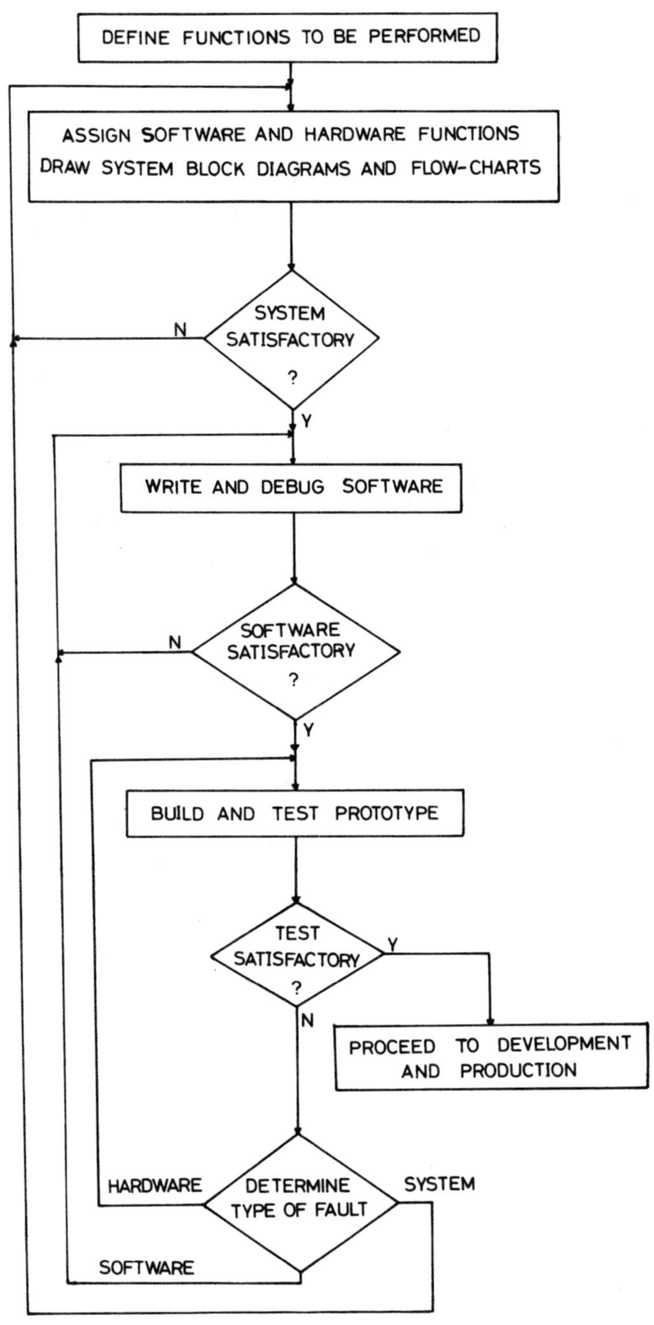

FIG. 6 Microprocessor system design procedure.

essential if the design process is to be practically feasible. The following is a short account of the main features of such aids.

Software design aids
Although these are aids in program writing, it is difficult sometimes to establish a distinction between purely software and purely hardware aids since some can be used as both.

(a) *Cross-products*
These are truly software aids, they are software packages written in some high-level language like Fortran which run on large computers with interactive facilities.
(i) *Cross compilers* – these allow the designer to write the software in a high-level language which makes it independent of the microprocessor being considered; the compiler converts the high level language program (source code) into binary code suitable for loading in the microprocessor system memory (object code). Fig. 7 is an example of a section of a program written in P.L.M. a popular high level language for microprocessors.
(ii) *Cross-assemblers* – these are basically translators which converts from a symbolic notation to binary code; it produces a one-to-one conversion of the source code. Programs written in assembler code are dependent on the microprocessor for which they are written. Most small-system software is written at this level since it produces smaller and faster programs, but as the complexity of the system increases, the effort and possibility of error also increase; and for a program of about 2 K or more, a high-level language approach becomes essential. Fig. 8 shows an equivalent assembly level routine for part of the P.L.M. program shown in Fig. 7.
(iii) *Simulators* – as the name implies this is a software testing aid; the object code produced by a cross-assembler or cross-compiler is used by the simulator which performs the corresponding operations the microprocessor would, but providing the designer with a large number of facilities which enable him to follow the running of the program and to verify the operations being performed.

```
/** PROGRAM WEIGHT MEASUREMENT **/
/** ENTER VIA CALL FROM MAIN PROGRAM **/
/* "COUNTER" IS TIMER-COUNTER SERVICE ROUTINE   */
/* IT RETURNS FREQUENCY VALUE FROM SYSTEM INPUT PORT */
COUNTER (FREQUENCY)        /* FREQUENCY MEASURED */
/* "SQRT" IS A SQUARE ROOT ROUTINE */
WEIGHT=K/SQRT(FREQUENCY)
/* FORMULA ACCOUNTS FOR TRANSDUCER CHARACTERISTICS */
/* UP-DATE PARAMETERS WITH NEW VALUES */
PREVIOUS = PRESENT         /* PREVIOUS WEIGHT VALUE */
PRESENT = WEIGHT           /* PRESENT WEIGHT VALUE */
RETURN                     /* RETURN TO MAIN PROGRAM */
```

FIG. 7   *Section of a high-level language program (P.L.M.).*

```
; ****************************************
; SECTION TO UP-DATE PARAMETERS
; ****************************************
LXI  H, PRESENT      ; MEMORY ADDRESS WHERE VALUE
                     ; OF PRESENT WEIGHT IS STORED
LXI  D, PREVIOUS     ; MEMORY ADDRESS WHERE VALUE OF
                     ; PREVIOUS WEIGHT IS STORED
MOV  A, M            ; ACCUMULATOR = PRESENT WEIGHT
STAX D               ; PREVIOUS = PRESENT
LXI  D, WEIGHT       ; MEMORY ADDRESS WHERE VALUE OF
                     ; ACTUAL WEIGHT IS TEMPORARILY STORED
LDAX D               ; ACCUMULATOR = ACTUAL WEIGHT
MOV  M, A            ; PRESENT = ACTUAL WEIGHT
RET                  ; RETURN TO MAIN PROGRAM
```

FIG. 8   Section of an 8080 assembly-level program.

This aid is clearly dependent upon the particular microprocessor being used.

(iv) *Interpreters* — these are software aids which resemble the action of a simulator in that a program is actually run under operator control; however, an interpreter operates directly on high-level language statements and it does not produce a binary code suitable for loading in the microprocessor (a cross-compiler could be used for this purpose). As such, it is machine-independent and its use is not limited to the microprocessor being considered; most computer installations running BASIC are in fact running an interpreter. A microprocessor system could benefit from this aid by either having a resident interpreter which would execute the high-level language program stored as such in its memory, or by using the interpreter and a compiler package — resident or cross products — to test the program at the high-level stage and produce suitable binary code for loading in the microprocessor memory. The first option is very wasteful of memory and would be extremely slow in operation. The second seems a most satisfactory solution but such systems are not commonly available. Research in this subject is presently being carried out at U.M.I.S.T. and preliminary results suggest a highly sophisticated and powerful software design package.

(b) *Resident software*

All the aids previously discussed need large computer installations for their operation. It is possible to benefit from their counterparts which run on the microprocessor in use rather than on a different machine. For this purpose, most microprocessor manufacturers offer what are basically dedicated microcomputers with associated peripherals, known euphemistically as microprocessor development systems (Fig. 9). These microcomputers provide the designer with similar facilities to those previously discussed: compilers, assemblers, and interpreters; simulation facilities are trivial since the microprocessor used as the centre of the micro-computer will directly execute the software written for it. These development

28

FIG. 9   A typical microprocessor development system (MDS-80).
(Courtesy Intel Co.)

aids also provide the basis for hardware design aids since they overcome the
inherent inability of a software simulator to test a program under actual real-time
conditions.

Hardware design aids

The microprocessor development system facilities described above as a software
aid also have a limited capability for the proving and testing of prototype systems.
Their power as hardware development systems is greatly increased by the use of
additional facilities such as:

(a) *Emulators* − these are perhaps the most useful debugging aid currently
available; basically, an emulator is a facility provided by special-purpose hardware
incorporated in a microprocessor development system. It will connect to the
memory and input-output interface being developed, physically replacing the
microprocessor and performing its software and hardware tasks under real-time
conditions. All the facilities associated with a simulator are usually available. It is
at this point that the distinction between a hardware and a software development
aid becomes almost impossible to make. The emulator does not need to use the memory or input-output of the system under development since the microcomputer
facilities can be used for this purpose. Thus the designer can, in the extreme
case, use the emulator with no connection to an external system and consequently
use it as a simulator, testing the software only. It is clear that this is a highly
flexible aid and it could well replace the simulation step, making the use of

cross-products quite redundant, and concentrating the whole design effort around the facilities offered by a microprocessor development system fitted with an emulator for the microprocessor under consideration.

(b) *Logic analyzers* — although these are not aids specifically for microprocessor systems, their use for this purpose is widely recognized. Since they provide storage and display of a large number of digital signals, they are ideal for any system using a bus structure, hence their suitability for microprocessor systems. They are truly hardware aids and in many situations, an essential tool.

(c) *Limited power development aids* — several manufacturers have produced relatively low cost development aids ($\sim$ £1000) which do not have the full capability of the microprocessor development systems described above. However, they enable the user to create microprocessor software for the entry, running, testing, debugging display, etc. of programs with the comparable ease of a calculator. They also allow the connection of equipment via I/O channels and some have self-contained P.R.O.M. programming facilities. Typical of such aids is the autonomous development system shown in Fig. 10.

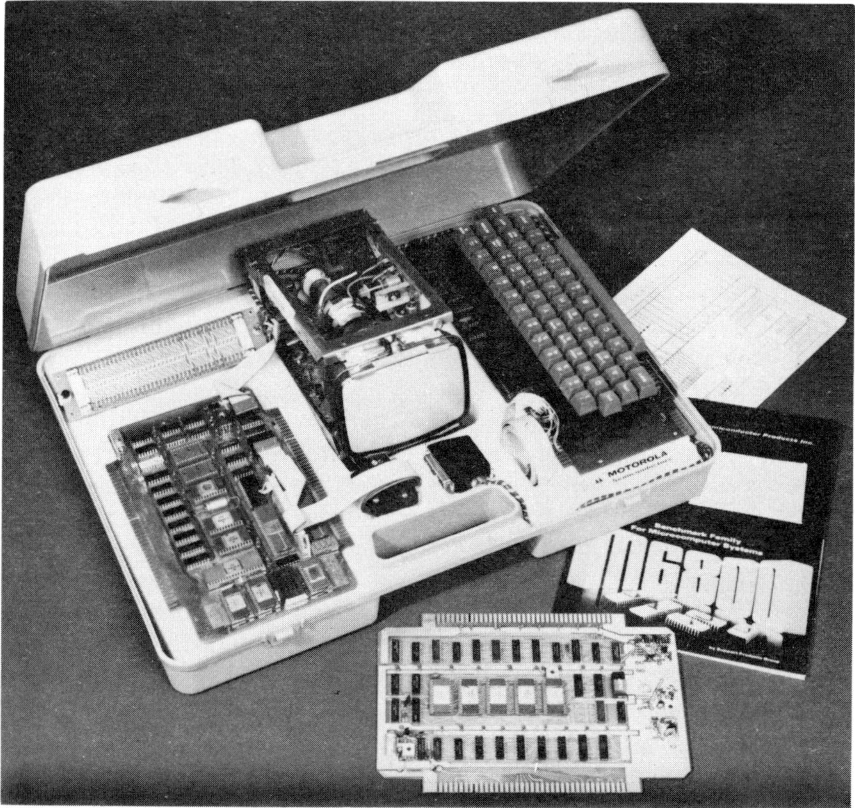

FIG. 10   A limited-power microprocessor development aid (M68 ADS).
(Courtesy Motorola Inc.)

(d) *Ready-built systems* — also known as one-board microcomputers (Fig. 11); they provide a certain amount of R.A.M., P.R.O.M., Input-Output and resident software. They allow some simple operations to be performed via a teletype interface, providing an inexpensive although limited development facility. These systems shorten design time considerably since the hardware design is cut down to a minimum and, in fact, some industrial users have considered using such general-purpose systems as production units.

3 SUMMARY OF SYSTEM DEVELOPMENT OPTIONS

The actual realisation of complete facilities for both hardware and software development for microcomputer use is predominantly governed by two major factors:

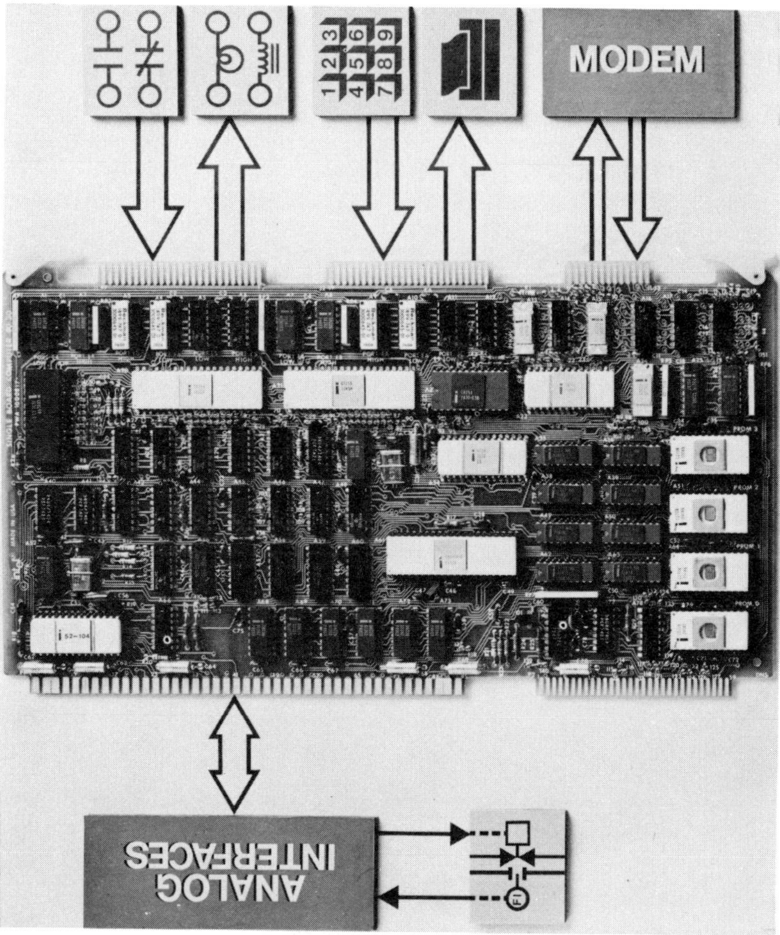

FIG. 11   A typical one-board ready-built system, showing some input-output peripherals.
(Courtesy Intel Co.)

(i) the computing resources available to user, e.g. access to time-sharing network, laboratory minicomputer equipped with disc, printer, punch etc. in-house batch computing service, etc., on which programs can be developed, tested and simulated runs performed.

(ii) the financial resources to purchase independent development systems and test equipment for hardware evaluation in addition to the chosen mode of software production.

Low-cost, low-volume microprocessor systems can be developed economically with access to a time-sharing network computer terminal and limited power development aid. Conversely, the higher cost, larger volume, generally more complex system can often justify the purchase of powerful stand-alone development systems with in-circuit emulators, monitors and simultaneous access to computing resources available locally.

4   REFERENCES

[1]   Powner, E. T., Escuder, M. A. and Depledge, P. G. 'Introduction to microprocessor systems – Part 1' *Int. J. Elect. Enging. Educ.*, **14**, No. 1, (1977). Reprinted here pp. 12–18.

[2]   Nauful E, S. 'Software support for microprocessors poses new design choices' *Computer Design*, pp. 93–98, (October 1976).

INTRODUCTION TO MICROPROCESSOR SYSTEMS – PART 3

P. J. BEST, P. G. DEPLEDGE, M. A. ESCUDER, and E. T. POWNER
Department of Electrical Engineering and Electronics, University of Manchester Institute of Science and Technology, England.

1   SYSTEM CONFIGURATIONS

Introduction

The previous two articles[1,2] discussed the general features of microprocessors, their integration into working systems and, subsequently, the interface, special-function devices and software facilities which are available as adjuncts to the main components. In this the third and final article, we will now consider the process of establishing a microprocessor evaluation environment suitable both for a research and teaching situation and, to conclude, we will cite three applications projects, the diversity of which underlines the versatility of the microprocessor as a system component. The three projects have been chosen from research in the Microprocessor Engineering Unit and Digital Processes Group at U.M.I.S.T.

The key to the versatility of the microprocessor lies in its use of stored program code to define the task sequence which it executes. Unlike committed hard-wired logic assemblies, the microprocessor places fewer initial constraints on the system-designer in his approach to a working solution for a given problem. In the hard-wired technology, the solution, of necessity, has to be clearly specified at the outset before the hardware can be configured and tested. In the present technology, the preparation of software and the algorithms which it must implement are in every way as important as the final hardware system. Indeed, it is generally more expedient for the designer to consider his software requirements by evaluating preliminary test programs on a suitable general-purpose system. This done, he may then consider the precise hardware requirements needed to support his application program and so move his design towards the final, dedicated configuration.

Clearly, the availability of development aids is essential for the preparatory stages of microprocessor applications and the provision of such aids is an important exercise for a research and teaching group. To simplify the process of establishing a general microprocessor facility, it is useful to consider the following cost-orientated categories into which the development systems fall:

(i)	Single-board evaluation kits	£100 ~ £500
(ii)	Limited-power development systems	£300 ~ £3,000
(iii)	Extended development systems	£3,000 ~ £15,000
(iv)	Cross-software aids	£500 and upwards.

Single-board evaluation kits
Available from most manufacturers, these kits represent a minimum hardware
configuration which typically consists of a printed circuit board (P.C.B.), the
microprocessor chip and any essential supporting chips for the master-clock and
I/O ports together with locations for R.O.M. and R.A.M. memory. Such kits are
rarely supplied with extensive software but a USART chip provides for the serial
interface to a teletype. With the use of the teletype, it is possible to prepare
object-code programs; a process which may be tedious and time-consuming but
which is quite adequate for a preliminary evaluation of an application.

Limited-power development systems
As an elaboration on the single-board computer kits, the systems which fall into
the present category are usually complete multi-board development systems with
an increased memory capacity and a simple terminal device such as a basic keyboard and monitor display. Limited expansion of these systems is possible through
the inclusion of further memory and other peripherals e.g. a fast paper-tape reader
and punch. Given sufficient R.A.M. storage, these systems may be supported by the
simpler software aids so that user programs can be prepared in mnemonic rather
than object form.

Extended development systems
In contrast to the previous categories, the systems which may be considered to be
'extended' are those which are configured around a pre-wired 'mother-board' with
connectors for many functionally-complete P.C.B.s. Their facilities are often comparable with the minicomputers and, when enhanced with mass storage devices like
the floppy disc, they may be supported by the full spectrum of software aids. With
these facilities, the user may prepare programs in a high-level language and introduce P.R.O.M.-programmer modules and diagnostic aids together with emulator
cards to test his application system. The software items are licenced material
provided by the system vendor but, like the optional cards, these too may be
purchased as and when required.

Cross-software aids
In a teaching and research environment where minicomputers are already available,
much can be done to alleviate the cost of a full development system. In place of a
commitment to extensive memory, I/O facilities and the more advanced software
items, the user may prepare cross-product software on the minicomputer. Additionally, he may make use of the features of the 'mini' in preparing and editing his
programs, simulating a run and tracing its activity. The excercise of preparing such
software not only results in facilities which may be specifically tailored to the
requirements of a particular applications group, but it also ensures a proper understanding of the system architecture by the writer.

Although there can be no 'hard-and-fast' rules for the establishment of a microprocessor facility, it is generally realized that a limited-power development system is
a useful base from which to start. It has been shown that this level is a sufficient

commitment for subsequent improvement and, indeed, much can be achieved by contributions from the users themselves.

To reinforce this observation and to conclude our series on the microprocessor, we now offer summary descriptions of three diverse application projects. Separately, they represent the use of microprocessors in:

(a)   Teaching Aids
(b)   Automotive Control
(c)   Augmented Data-Logging.

2   A COMPUTER ARCHITECTURE TEACHING AID (S.M.I.C.)

Teaching requirements

A knowledge of the theory and operation of digital systems is becoming an increasingly important prerequisite for all electronic engineers regardless of their eventual industrial placement. Thus, to satisfy this requirement, universities and colleges are placing greater emphasis on digital techniques in their undergraduate and postgraduate syllabuses and, to augment the lecture courses, there is a need to provide practical work to reinforce the theoretical concepts.

To satisfy this demand, at U.M.I.S.T., a careful study has been made of the requirements of a digital teaching laboratory and, from it, an integrated series of *teach-aids* has been developed. The first aids in the series are used to introduce the student to the fundamentals of combinational and sequential logic, such experiments being undertaken towards the end of the first year and in the early terms of the second year. Second in the series, the student uses computer arithmetic tutors to study the full spectrum of binary addition and multiplication techniques. Until recently, the final stage in the series was the use of a Minimal Instruction Computer (M.I.C.) which, being an updated and modified version of the system proposed by Heath and Grubb[3], emphasises the decoding of instructions and the controlled routing of data in the computer C.P.U. Although M.I.C has proved to be a very successful element in the series, its inability to store programs and its necessarily limited instruction set proved to be excessive limitations for the third-year student who might wish to specialize in digital systems. It was therefore agreed to provide a machine of greater sophistication to illustrate more fully the idea of an order-code, the techniques for memory addressing and the problems inherent in simple machine-code programming.

One obvious solution at this level would be to offer 'hands-on' experience with a minicomputer although this would be a significant departure from the philosophy underlying the *teach-aids.*

As an alternative, the solution which was adopted uses a microprocessor as the system kernal to offer an attractive emulation of computer architecture features. The resulting aid, known as Super-M.I.C. (S.M.I.C.)[4], was developed to the following specifications:

(i)   The operation of the machine should be clear to the user. Thus the contents and state of the accumulator, program counter and instruction register should be permanently displayed.

(ii)   The machine should be capable of operation at one of several speeds ranging from step-by-step to full logic speeds.

(iii)   To illustrate the stored program concept and the notion that instructions and data are held in a common store, the aid must provide a limited amount of read/ write memory.

(iv)   Instructions should be input in binary form with the word split into order, address and control fields. (Two's complement notation has been used).

(v)   Branch instructions should be provided and, to make the range of programs more interesting, a multiply instruction should be included.

(vi)   Two addressing modes should be available; direct and indirect, to allow two basic levels of experiment to be carried out.

Finally, since the aid is to be based on a microprocessor it may also be used to introduce students to these devices. To this end, a spare instruction has been provided to enable the student to write his own microprocessor program and use the linking instruction in his teach-aid programs.

Microprocessor Implementation

An eight-bit Intel i8008-1 microprocessor was chosen as the heart of the machine. At the time of S.M.I.C.'s conception and design this was in fact the most commonly available and best supported microprocessor on the market even though it is now crude by comparison with the current generation of devices. To keep the aid simple, the 8-bit word-length of the i8008-1 was retained as the word-length of S.M.I.C. For single byte instructions, the instruction format uses a 3-bit order-code and a 5-bit address field; thus providing the machine with 8 instructions and an address range of thirty-two. By sacrificing one of the address bits for use as an indirect address bit, the store capability may be extended to 256 locations, i.e. 16 pages of 16 locations each.

The Super-M.I.C. hardware consists of the M.P.U., our input ports, five output ports, 1,024 bytes of read/write memory and 768 bytes of U.V. P.R.O.M. The input ports allow instructions, timing signals, addresses, interrupt instructions and memory data to be set on the i8008 data bus. The output ports drive L.E.D. indicators to display the accumulator, the program counter and the current instruction together with 'program-complete' and 'next-instruction' signals to the user. (Fig. 1). Basically, S.M.I.C. is interrupt driven i.e. each depression of the ACT button (Fig. 2) causes the M.P.U. to execute the operation defined by mode switches on the aid. Thus, to load a user program, the machine is set to 'program load' and the instruction is set up on the input switches. Programs are entered instruction-by-instruction with each depression of the ACT button causing the sequential instructions to be loaded into contiguous memory locations. A correction feature is included to allow the contents of memory locations to be changed. Program execution is achieved by simply selecting 'execute' and depressing the ACT button, the rate of execution being determined by timing switches which may be varied during execution if required. The internal execution of the program, within S.M.I.C., consists of reading the next S.M.I.C.-instruction from memory,

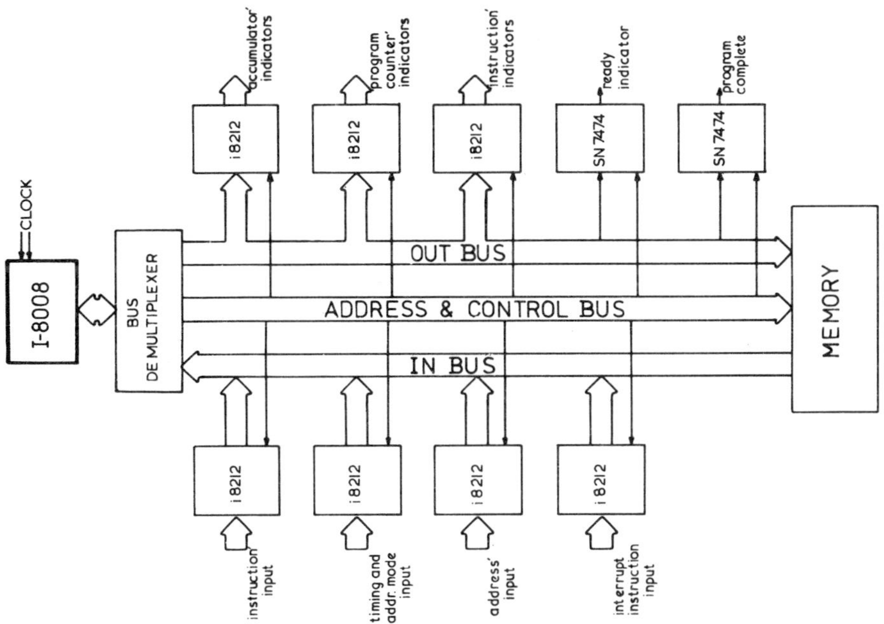

FIG. 1   Block diagram of Super-M.I.C. hardware.

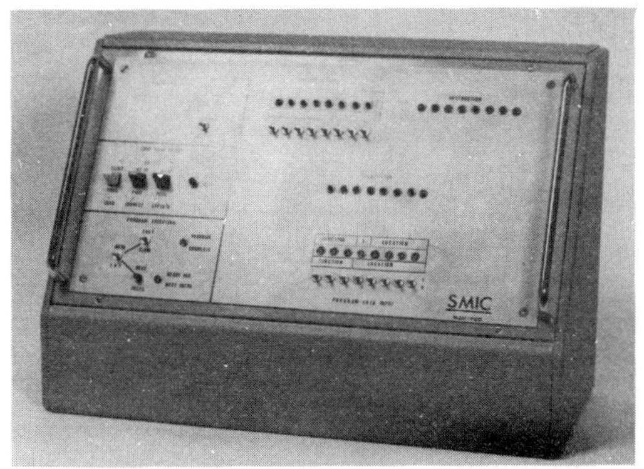

FIG. 2   External view of Super-M.I.C.

decoding it from the eight available and executing the equivalent microprocessor instruction(s) to update the accumulator, program counter instruction register and 'program complete' indicator as required.

Summary
S.M.I.C. has now been in laboratory use, for four years, in a series of experiments which include the use of M.I.C., an Intellec 8/80, an M6800 cross-assembler/ simulator package and a Data General Nova 2/10. The aid has been found to be

particularly useful for students with little experience of computer usage or knowledge of binary arithmetic. In addition, most of the students found S.M.I.C. to be a useful preliminary to the microprocessor lecture course recently introduced into their syllabus.

3   AUTOMATIC AUTOMOTIVE TRANSMISSION CONTROL

Control Requirements
For many years, the control of the automatic transmission used in the large commercial vehicles from a well-known British bus and truck manufacturer has been achieved with an actuator on the gear-box. The actuator is an electro-pneumatic system to which driver commands are relayed by a controller unit in such a way that the correct gear for optimum fuel economy and vehicle performance is engaged at all times. This controller unit was originally designed using electro-magnetic relays and potentiometers but, lately, it has been realised that this solution has become economically unattractive and embodies serious reliability problems even though the unit is easily maintained by the vehicle service personnel. Because of the inflexible nature of the electro-pneumatic system, the control which it provides is limited to the few principal operating parameters which significantly affect vehicle performance. Even though economies now dictate otherwise, electro-pneumatic systems would achieve unwarranted complexity if secondary control functions were to be introduced. Nevertheless, by departing from the accepted control methods and by introducing the microprocessor as the control element, it is feasible not only to replicate the present performance, but to enhance its flexibility within a scheme[5] which remains economically attractive to the vehicle manufacturer.

The required control function is well-defined since the presently-used electro-magnetic relay system has been thoroughly evaluated in the fleet of vehicles. For obvious reasons then, the main brief for the microprocessor system should be an acceptable direct replacement capable of manipulating the presently used signals. As shown in Fig. 3, this brief defines the requisite interface in terms of the following controls:

(i)   Driver commands — These are inputs to the controller from the driver cab; start, automatic, hold 3rd, hold 4th and reverse, each of which is derived from a 5-position switch in the form of a gear stick. A 'kick-down' facility is actuated by full depression of the accelerator pedal.
(ii)   Vehicle status — comprises controller inputs giving essential information on vehicle condition; road speed, air pressure and currently engaged gear.
(iii) Control outputs — These are the actuator signals; one for each of the gears (5 forward, one reverse), one to the throttle-dip valve to reduce the fuel supply during gear shifts in order to ensure a smooth change and a warning lamp to give visible indication of a malfunction.

Microprocessor Implementation
In proposing and developing a microprocessor solution for this application, the design philosophy has been to minimise the complexity of the hardware by rel-

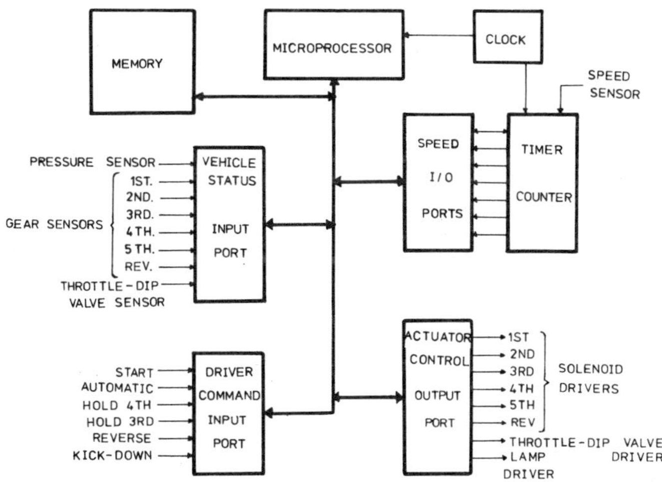

FIG. 3   Block diagram – microprocessor implementation of automatic transmission controller.

egating all the tasks to the software. Whilst a solution might be taken through hard-wired logic, it is possible to treat all the signals as inputs or outputs to a micro-processor and perform all the necessary computations and logic decisions within its software. The resulting system is thus made flexible since the control algorithms can be modified with relative ease. The required control is depicted in Fig. 4.

The supporting configuration, in the present prototype, uses only 12 integrated circuit packages in conjuction with one of the currently available 8-bit micro-processors. This compares favourably with the 50 or so elements (relays, potentio-

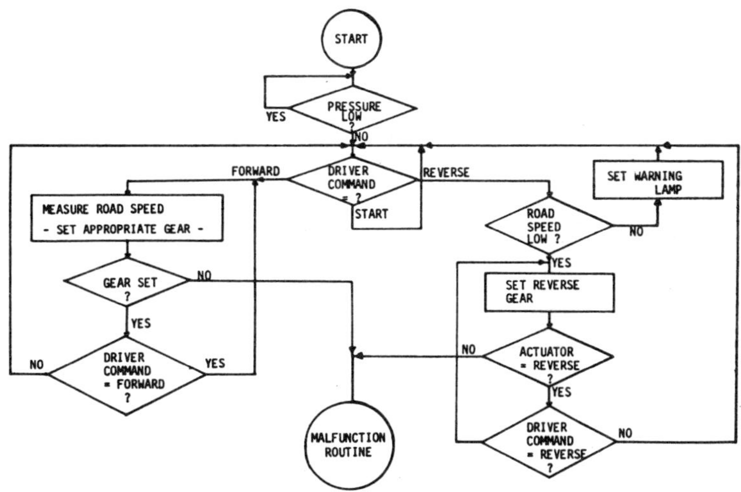

FIG. 4   Simplified flow-diagram of controller software.

meters, etc.) of the previously-used units and further reductions are now possible
with the availability of the newer single-chip microcomputers.

Summary

There are several benefits which accrue from this use of the microprocessor, of
which most are directly related to the versatility of the software packages. As an
example, it is expected that new variables may be handled by the controller to
take account of engine speed and to prevent the use of gears above 'second' if the
vehicle door is still open. Such an improvement in the relay system could not be
achieved without extensive modifications to the existing unit. Likewise, maintenance of the controller is also simplified despite the increased complexity of the
control functions. So that service may be continued by those with a mechanical
rather than electronic training, a complete self-testing facility has been developed as
a separate robust plug-on unit. It embodies a test-program and extra I/O channels
to perform exercises on the main controller. Malfunctions are converted into simple
codes which indicate, via a 7-segment display, the nature of the fault and the maintenance procedure required to rectify it. The previously daunting fault-finding tasks
are now a trivial and speedy exercise during vehicle maintenance.

4   COMPUTER-ASSISTED PATIENT MONITORING

Clinical Needs

The physiological balance of patients undergoing intensive or coronary care is usually
critical to the point at which some form of continuous monitoring becomes clinically
expedient. The rapid and often subtle changes which herald the onset of trauma
would pass undetected if the straightforward nursing routines which suffice in other
areas of medicine were not somehow augmented in the intensive-care situation.
Here, it is necessary to assist the clinical team with some form of 'intelligent' configuration which is capable of analysing, in real-time, the signals from several
physiological transducers connected to a small number of patients. Furthermore,
it is essential that the occurrences of abnormal activity must be communicated
promptly and precisely to the attendant personnel. Clearly, this clinical need can
best be served by the introduction of a minicomputer monitoring scheme to analyse
the transducer signals and provide output data to suitable display devices.

Monitoring Requirements

There is usually little consistency in the monitoring requirements for individual
patients, since each will manifest symptoms according to his present condition.
Nevertheless, temperature, blood pressure, pulse rate and certain respiratory
functions are often required for monitoring purposes and the appropriate transducer devices are widely available. Even less is there a consistent aim in the
clinical evaluation of the information conveyed by the electrical analogue outputs
from these devices. For most practical purposes, therefore, the monitoring configuration must be flexible and capable of executing algorithms for a wide range of
clinical activities and for a varying number of patients. To this end, a Patient

Monitoring System (P.M.S.) has been developed[6] which uses both a minicomputer
and a microprocessor acting as a 'front-end-processor' on the incoming physiological
data. The presence of the microprocessor in the system secures the required degrees
of flexibility.

P.M.S. configuration

Fig. 5 depicts the present P.M.S. configuration. It consists of (up to) six bed-units
each of which houses an A/D and D/A converter together with a small keyboard. A
visual display unit (V.D.U.) and special-purpose graphical display unit (G.D.U.) are
included for user-interaction and data-display respectively, and these complete the
eight-slave cluster of monitoring peripherals. Data communication within the
cluster is achieved on a single bidirectional digital highway such that all data
transactions between computer and slave peripherals are under the control of an
intelligent supervisor based on a microprocessor. The rôle of this supervisor is two-
fold.

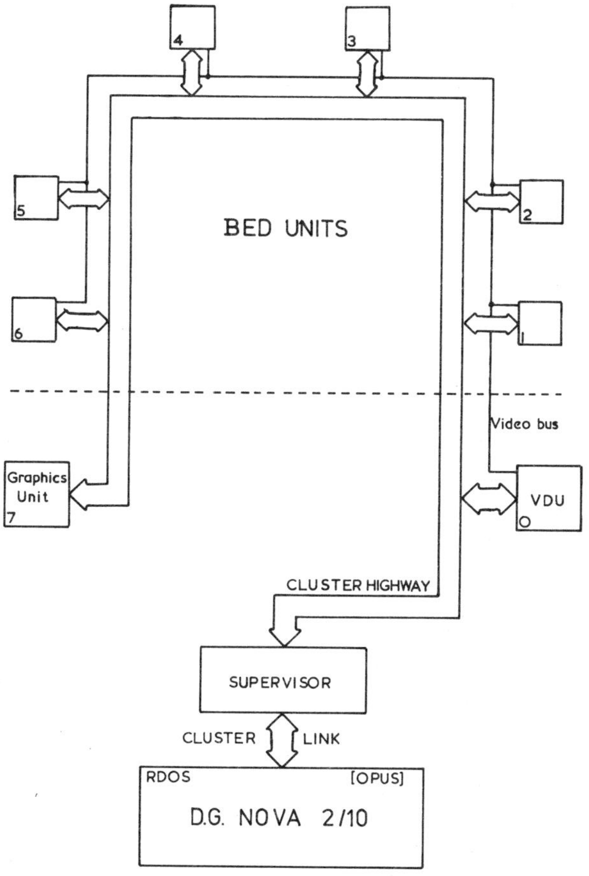

FIG. 5   *P.M.S. cluster configuration.*

Firstly, it is responsible for controlling the highway and servicing the slaves. The bed-units provide digitized sample data from their analogue transducer channels together with data from the keyboards and control panels which has to be routed to the main computer. Likewise, the V.D.U. and G.D.U. require data from the computer to be directed to them. Secondly, the supervisor is responsible for providing correctly-timed commands to each of the bed-units to initiate the A/D conversions on each of their six analogue input channels. As they stand, each of these channels is an uncommitted input port via which the clinical team may connect into the system any of the transducer systems at their disposal. The frequency responses of the physiological functions which may be monitored vary considerably and hence a dynamic allocation of sampling rates is required. Thus, instead of providing the bed-units with a hard-wired and fixed sampling cycle, the microprocessor embodies a timetable which it uses to initiate all the A/D conversions of the cluster. In turn, this timetable is updated by the executive monitoring software (known as OPUS) of the main computer as and when requirements change.

On receipt of a 'sample' command, the bed-units return a 16-bit word in which 12 bits encode the sample value and, the remaining 4 bits, the channel of origin. The highway is an 8-bit byte medium and so each word is structured as byte pairs suitable for pre-processing in an 8-bit microprocessor. Depending on its current program, the microprocessor may also be used to compare present sample values from a given channel with the previous samples or with previously determined upper and lower limits, and compress any data which is not required by the main software of OPUS. In the same way that OPUS is used to update the sampling time-table so also is it arranged to modify the microprocessor 'function-table' which determines the precise action of the latter's program.

Summary
It has been shown[6] that the philosophy of P.M.S. with its use of the microprocessor, limits, to a manageable level, the total volume of data which must be analysed in a typical sized intensive care unit. Not only does the microprocessor configuration simplify the hardware requirements of the six bed-units and so reduce their overall cost, but it also enables the execution of data-integrity checks which are essential in an application of this kind.

The first of these is a simple consequence of the timetable scheme which obviates the need for autonomous sampling mechanisms in the bed-units. The second is consequential on the versatility of microprocessors. At regular intervals, the supervisor intiates and receives, from the bed-units, status words which flag their main subsystem activities. The failure of power supplies or of simple check procedures provides immediate warning of errors in the system which can then be distinguished from true clinical episodes in the patients.

5 CONCLUSION

These three articles have presented a general review of microprocessor systems in a form which might be useful to those embarking on a teaching and research programme. Wherever possible the common features and distinguishing characteristics of the major product ranges have been presented to enable the reader to decide which features would be most suitable for his needs. It is expected that the three application examples cited in this paper will be subjected to an up-grading as the next generation of higher-speed, compact devices appear on the market. We therefore make no extravagant claims for the success of any of these projects except that each represents a departure from an existing philosophy made possible only by the advent of the microprocessor.

6   ACKNOWLEDGEMENTS

The authors wish to record their thanks to colleagues in the Microprocessor Engineering Unit and the Digital Processes Group, U.M.I.S.T. for their contributions to the extensive microprocessor facilities and, in particular, to J. Allwork and G. Dinéley for their cross-product software. The authors would also be pleased to establish contact with other users or potential users of microprocessors with a view to a liaison in this rapidly expanding field.

7   REFERENCES

[1]   Powner, E. T., Escuder, M. A. and Depledge, P. G. 'Introduction to Microprocessor Systems – Part 1' *Int. J. Elect. Enging Educ.*, **14**, No. 1, (1977). Reprinted here pp. 12–18.

[2]   Powner, E. T., Escuder, M. A. and Depledge, P. G. 'Introduction to Microprocessor Systems – Part 2' *Int. J. Elect. Enging Educ.*, **14**, No. 2, (1977). Reprinted here pp. 19–32.

[3]   Heath, F. J. and Grubb 'A Digital Computer for Sixth-Forms' *Int. J. Elect. Enging Educ.*, **3**, No. 3, (1965).

[4]   Depledge, P. G. 'Computer Operation Demonstrated by Microprocessor'. *M.Sc. Dissertation, U.M.I.S.T.*, (Oct., 1975).

[5]   Escuder, M. A. and Powner, E. T. 'Automatic Transmission Controller using a Microprocessor' – *Automobile Electronics IEE Conference Publication Number 141*, (1976).

[6]   Best, P. J., 'Digital Applications for Medical Analysis in Intensive-Care'. *Ph.D. Thesis, U.M.I.S.T.*, (June, 1976).

A REVIEW OF AVAILABLE MICROPROCESSORS

P. G. DEPLEDGE
Microprocessor Engineering Unit, Department of Electrical Engineering and Electronics, University of Manchester Institute of Science and Technology, England

INTRODUCTION

The purpose of this review is to update the table of available microprocessors included in the first of a series of papers entitled 'An introduction to microprocessors' which appeared in this journal[1] and to provide an indication of recent development trends in this field. The original table, which is now over two years old, does not reflect many of the conceptual developments that have occurred in the intervening period. The advances have primarily been due to the increase in circuit component density achieved in N-channel metal oxide semiconductor (NMOS) integrated circuits. The levels of NMOS integration have typically been doubling every year since the mid 1960's as shown in Fig. 1. This is likely to continue well into the 1980's. Over the past two years this has led to the general availability of 16,384 bit random access memory (RAM) chips, 65,536 bit read only memory (ROM) chips, 32,768 bit UV erasable electrically reprogrammable ROM's (UV-PROM) and a variety of microprocessor/microcomputer devices. The long-awaited 65,536 bit (64k) dynamic RAM will also become readily available this year.

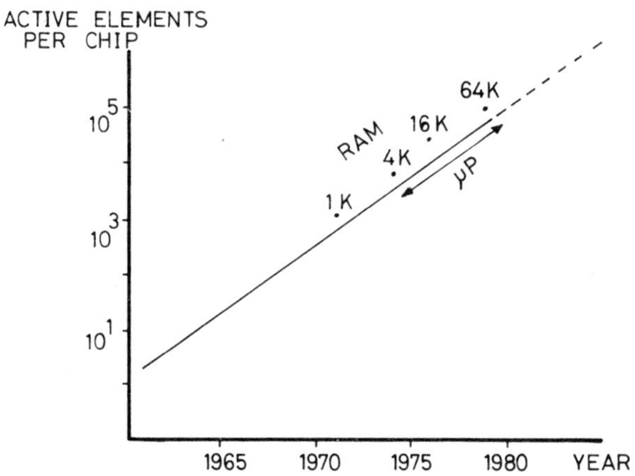

FIG. 1   Active elements/chip evolution (courtesy Motorola Inc.).

The increase in integration levels achieved has been used in three basic ways by the microprocessor manufacturers. First the 'second generation' single-chip microprocessors such as the 8-bit Intel 8080 and Motorola M6800 have been improved to make them simpler to use and to provide a more elegant systems architecture. Thus the Intel 8085, which provides a single power supply 8080-like processor and includes a system controller and clock generator, has been made available. This chip, when used in conjunction with an Intel 8155 and an Intel 8755 provides a three-chip system with the power of an 8080 and with 2k bytes of UV-PROM, 256 bytes of RAM, 38 parallel I/O lines, 1 serial I/O line and a programmable 14-bit counter timer. An equivalent 8080 based system would have required 10 chips and 3 power supplies two years ago. Similarly, Motorola have upgraded the M6800 to include 128 bytes of RAM and a clock generator in the new M6802 chip. A matching ROM — I/O chip, the MC6846 is available to provide a powerful two-chip system equivalent to the M6800, MC6871 clock generator, MC6810 RAM, MC6830 ROM, $\frac{1}{2}$ MC6820 PIA, and $\frac{1}{2}$ MC6840 timer.

A second method of taking advantage of the increased integration levels is to produce single-chip microcomputers. A single-chip microcomputer can be defined as a general-purpose processor that contains a microprocessor, pro-gram memory (ROM or UV-PROM), data memory (RAM), some I/O capa-bility and a clock oscillator on a single silicon chip. The number of single-chip microcomputers has mushroomed in the past years, due to the potentially large market for such devices. Typical applications would be in dedicated control applications, for example in domestic appliances and automobiles. Obviously the scales of production in such applications are very large and so this lucrative market has recently attracted much attention by the microcomputer manufacturers.

The final method of using the higher integration levels is to produce advan-ced single-chip microprocessors, frequently with sixteen bit wordlengths. Typical of these are the Texas 9900 and the more recent Intel 8086 and Zilog Z8000. Although at present the number of applications requiring the power of such processors is limited, many traditional minicomputer roles, for example in control systems, can now be achieved with cheaper microprocessors.

SINGLE-CHIP MICROCOMPUTERS
The spectrum of single-chip microcomputers in terms of processing power is shown in Fig. 2, with some common devices as examples. All the devices shown in this figure have been released during the past two years, indicating the vitality of this corner of the microprocessor market. To give some idea of the power of these low-end devices the basic characteristics of those shown will be described.

The Intel 8021 is an ultra-low-cost 8-bit microcomputer mounted in a 28 pin dual-in-line package. The device has very loose supply voltage tolerances (4.5 to 6.5 volts) and can use an external resistor as the timing component rather than a more expensive crystal. The microcomputer includes 1k bytes of mask

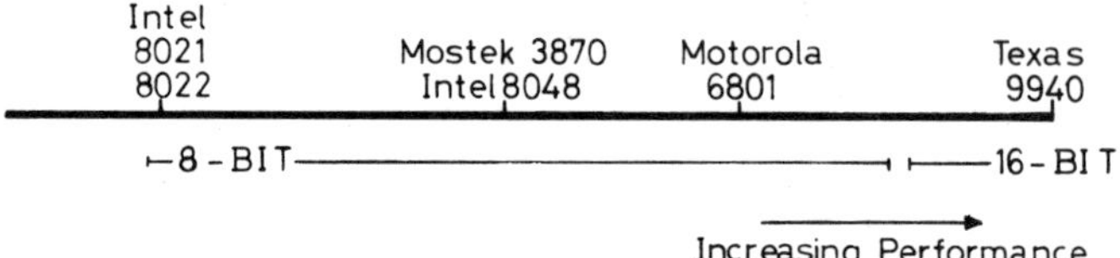

FIG. 2   Single-chip microcomputer spectrum.

programmable ROM, 64 bytes of RAM, an 8-bit programmable timer and
provides 21 I/O lines. A typical application for the 8021 would be in a micro-
wave oven, acting as a keyboard scanner, display driver and oven controller.
A very interesting partner to the 8021 is the Intel 8022. This NMOS device not
only includes all the facilities of the 8021 but includes a further 1k bytes of
ROM, a dual-channel analogue-to-digital converter, an 8-line analogue
comparator input, a zero crossing detector (useful when controlling thyristors
to ensure minimum R.F. interference), interrupt logic and a further 5 I/O lines.
The integration of the ADC onto an otherwise digital device brings the evolution of a complete system on a chip much closer. The 8022 is very well-suited
to applications where touch-pad keys are used, since the analogue comparator
inputs can be driven by low voltage touch switches and compared with a single
threshold voltage.

Further up the scale are the Mostek MK3870 and Intel 8048 devices. The
MK3870 includes 2k bytes of mask programmable ROM, 64 bytes of RAM, 34
I/O lines an 8-bit programmable timer and an internal clock. Furthermore, this
device is software compatible with the popular Fairchild F8 multi-chip system.
The basic Intel 8048 includes 1k bytes of mask programmable ROM, 64 bytes
of RAM (partially used as internal registers), 27 I/O lines, an 8-bit programmable timer and an internal clock. A UV-erasable PROM version, the 8748, is
available, as is an enlarged memory version, the 8049, with 2k bytes of ROM
and 128 bytes of RAM. The 8748 is particularly useful for development work
since it can easily be reprogrammed. An interesting member of the Intel 8048
family is the 8041/8741 Universal Peripheral Interface (UPI). This device is
intended to serve as an 'intelligent' peripheral controller to interface directly to
a master processor data bus. The UPI concept allows a system designer to fully
specify the control algorithm in the peripheral processor without relying on the
master, Fig. 3. Thus, devices like printer controllers and keyboard scanners can
be completely self-contained, relying only on the master processor for data
transfer. The 8741 is similar to the 8748, except that it includes a special
asynchronous bus interface register and a slightly modified instruction set. The
UPI uses the bus register to send or receive data without being synchronised to
the master processor. Intel have, in fact, used this device to produce several
8080/8085 bus compatible peripheral controllers.

Another interesting development in the single-chip microcomputer range is
the Motorola 6801. This device is based on the M6800 and includes 2k bytes of
ROM (Mask or UV-erasable), 128 bytes of RAM, 33 I/O lines, a 16-bit pro-

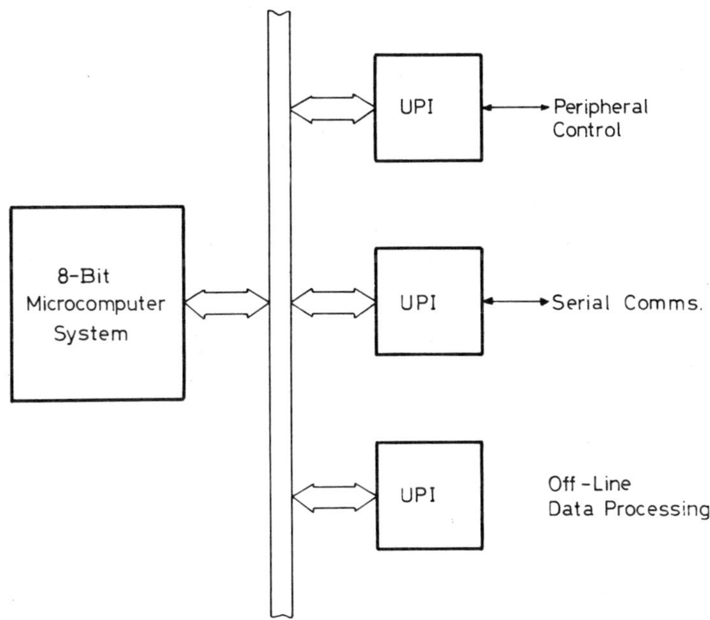

*FIG. 3   Multiple-processor system using universal peripheral devices
(INTEL UPI-41/8741).*

grammable timer, 1 asynchronous serial I/O port and a clock generator. The 6801 is object-code-compatible with the M6800 but includes additional 16-bit instructions and an 8-bit by 8-bit multiply command. Furthermore, many of the existing instructions now require less execution cycles. Finally, the first 16-bit single-chip microcomputer has recently been announced by Texas Instruments. Like the Motorola 6801 the new Texas device is based on an existing single-chip microprocessor. In this case the basis is the TMS9900 and the result single-chip microcomputer is the TMS9940. The 9940 includes 2k bytes of program memory (UV-erasable PROM or mask programmable ROM), 128 bytes of RAM and 16 I/O lines. A novel feature of the TMS9940 is that it includes facilities for a multiple processor system using an indivisible test-and-set register. This allows a number of TMS9940's to be connected on a common system bus and share resources.

Table 1 provides a comprehensive list of available single-chip microcomputers, detailing some of their main architectural features.

SINGLE-CHIP MICROPROCESSORS

The spectrum of single-chip microprocessors is shown in Fig. 4, with some common devices as examples. The devices at the lower end of the range, such as the 4-bit Intel 4040, although still widely used in existing designs are now being superceded by 8-bit single-chip microcomputers such as the Mostek 3870 and Intel 8048. Mid-range devices such as the Intel 8080 are being enhanced as

TABLE 1 *Single-chip microcomputers.*

MANUFACTURER	TYPE NUMBER	PROCESS TECHNOLOGY	WORD SIZE (INSTRUCTION/DATA)	MAXIMUM CLOCK FREQUENCY (MHz)/ ON-CHIP CLOCK?	SHORTEST INSTRUCTION TIME (μS)/NUMBER OF BASIC INSTRUCTIONS.	EXPANSION POSSIBLE?	INTERRUPTS?/ LEVELS.	RAM SIZE.	ROM/PROM SIZE.	I/O LINES.	COMMENTS.
AMI	S 2000	NMOS	8/4	1/Y	4/61	Y	N	64x4	1024x8	29	Can drive LED displays.
ESSEX INTERNATIONAL	SX-200	PMOS	8/4	0.4/Y	20/41	Y	Y/1	64x4	1024x8	16	Touch switch interface included.
GENERAL INSTRUMENTS	PIC-1650	NMOS	12/8	1.0/Y	4/31	Y	Y/1	32x8	512x8	32	ROM and I/O variations available (PIC 1655, PIC 1664).
MICROELECTRONICS	SBA	NMOS	8/1	0.8/Y	1.25/8	N	N	120x1	1024x8	31	Expandable variant available shortly. Boolean functions only.
	8021	NMOS	8/8	3/Y	10/68	Y	N	64x8	1024x8	21	Very cheap processor in 28 pin package.
	8022	NMOS	8/8	3/Y	10/68	N	N	64x8	2048x8	24	Features two channel A/D converter.
INTEL	8041	NMOS	8/8	6/Y	2.5/90	Y	Y/1	64x8	1024/8	18	Designed to be used as intelligent μP peripheral. 8741 is EPROM version.
	8048	NMOS	8/8	6/Y	2.5/96	Y	Y/1	64x8	1024/8	27	8748 is EPROM version. Two chip 8035/8755 version available. Note 1.
	8049	NMOS	8/8	11/Y	1.4/96	Y	Y/1	128x8	2048/8	27	Expanded 8748. Available without memory as 8039.
MOSTEK	3870	NMOS	8/8	4/Y	2/76	Y	Y/4	64x8	2048/8	32	Single chip version of Fairchild F8. MK 3872 has 2xmemory. See Note 2.
MOTOROLA	6801	NMOS	8/8-16	2/Y	1.25/99	Y	Y/3	128x8	2048/8	31	Includes all M 6800 instructions + multiply & divide.
NATIONAL	MM 5799	PMOS	8/4	0.4/Y	10/35	N	N	96x4	1536/8	23	LED drivers included.
SEMICONDUCTORS	MM 57140	PMOS	8/4	0.28/Y	16/35	N	N	55x4	630x8	24	LED and fluorescent drivers included.

Manufacturer	Type	Technology								Notes
NEC MICROCOMPUTERS	µPD 545	PMOS	8/4	0.44/N	10/58	N	Y/1	32x4	640x8	21	
	µPD 546	PMOS	8/4	0.44/N	10/80	N	Y/1	96x4	2000x8	35	42 pin package. Also known as UCOM-43.
	µPD 547	PMOS	8/4	0.44/N	10/58	N	Y/1	64x4	1000x8	35	42 pin package. Also known as UCOM-44.
	µPD 548	PMOS	10/4	0.2/N	10/72	Y	Y/2	96x4	1920x10	35	42 pin package. Also known as UCOM-42.
PANASONIC	MN 1400	NMOS	8/4	0.3/Y	10/75	N	Y/1	64x4	1028x8	30	
	MN 1402	NMOS	8/4	0.3/Y	10/57	N	Y/1	32x4	768x8	19	
ROCKWELL	MM 75	PMOS	8/4	0.1/Y	10/50	Y	Y/1	48x4	640x8	22	As MM 76 with reduced I/O.
	MM 76	PMOS	8/4	0.1/Y	10/50	Y	Y/1	48x4	640x8	31-39	Various versions available, with ADC, counter or display drivers.
	MM 77	PMOS	8/4	0.1/Y	10/50	Y	Y/1	96x4	1344x8	31	Has serial I/O channel.
	MM 78	PMOS	8/4	0.1/Y	10/50	Y	Y/1	128x4	2048x8	31	As MM 77 with more memory.
TEXAS INSTRUMENTS	TMS 1000	PMOS/ NMOS	8/4	0.4/Y	15/43	N	Y/1	64x4	1024x8	23/25	28 or 40 pin package. 35 V version available (1070/1270). Note 3.
	TMS 1022	PMOS	8/4	0.4/Y	15/43	N	Y/1	64x4	1024x8	N	Designed as a phase lock loop controller for citizen band radios.
	TMS 1100	PMOS/ NMOS	8/4	0.4/Y	15/40	N	Y/1	128x8	2048/8	23/28	Pin compatible with TMS 1000. 28 or 40 pin package.
	TMS 1121	PMOS	8/4	0.4/Y	15/42	N	Y/1	128x4	2048x8	N	Microwave oven controller.
	TMS 1330	PMOS	8/4	0.4/Y	15/42	N	Y/1	128x4	2048x8	31	
	TMS 9940	NMOS	16/16	5/Y	2/68	N	Y/4	128x8	2048x8	16	9940 E EPROM version. TMS 9900 compatible. Includes multi-processor interface.
WESTERN DIGITAL	CR 1872	PMOS	10/8	0.15/Y	6.25/37	N	Y/1	4x32	512x10	27	
ZILOG	Z 8	NMOS	8/8	4/Y	0.75/?	Y	Y/6	96x8	2048x8	32	Available spring 1979.

NOTES TO TABLE 1

Note 1   Official second sources: AMD, NEC and SIGNETICS. INTERSIL to produce CMOS version of 8748/8048.

    2   Official second sources: MOTOROLA, FAIRCHILD.

    3   MOTOROLA produce CMOS version.

TABLE 2 *Single-chip microprocessors (see notes at end of article).*

MANUFACTURER	TYPE NUMBER	PROCESS TECHNOLOGY	WORD SIZE (INSTRUCTION/DATA)	MAXIMUM CLOCK FREQUENCY (MHz)/ PHASES	SHORTEST INSTRUCTION TIME (μS)/NUMBER OF BASIC INSTRUCTIONS	ON-CHIP CLOCK?	INTERRUPTS?/ LEVELS	LANGUAGES SUPPORTED	COMMENTS
DATA GENERAL	MN 601 MICRO NOVA	NMOS	16/16	8.33/2	1.2/42	Y	Y/16	ASSEMBLER, BASIC, BUSINESS BASIC, FORTRAN	NOVA compatible instruction set.
FAIRCHILD	3850 (F8)	NMOS	8/8	2/1	2/76	Y	Y/1	ASSEMBLER	Minimum system comprises 3850 + program storage unit (3851, 3856 or 3857) Note 1.
	9440	I^2L	16/16	10/1	1.12/42	Y	Y/1	ASSEMBLER, BASIC, FORTRAN	NOVA 1200 compatible.
FERRANTI	F 100L	BIPOLAR (CDI)	16/16	8/1	0.94/29	N	Y/1	ASSEMBLER, CORAL 66	Has serial ALU. Full MIL temp range.
GENERAL INSTRUMENT MICROELECTRONICS	CP 1600	NMOS	10/16	5/2	1.6/87	N	Y/1	ASSEMBLER, 'SUPER ASSEMBLER'	CP 1610 similar with 2 MHz clock. Note 2.
	LP 8000	PMOS	8/8	0.8/2	5/48	N	Y/1	ASSEMBLER	Minimum 3 chip set, LP 8000, LP 6000 control memory and clock generator. Note 3.
INTEL	4004	PMOS	8/4	0.74/2	10.8/46	N	N	ASSEMBLER	Replaced by INTEL 4040. First 4-bit microprocessor.
	4040	PMOS	8/4	0.74/2	10.8/60	N	Y/1	ASSEMBLER	Functionally and electrically upward compatible with 4004.
	8008	PMOS	8/8	0.8/2	12.5/48	N	Y/1	ASSEMBLER, PL/M	A slower 0.5 MHz version also available. First 8-bit microprocessor.
	8035	NMOS	8/8	6/1	2.5/96	Y	Y/1	ASSEMBLER	8748/8048 equivalent without program memory. Note 4.
	8039	NMOS	8/8	11/1	1.3/96	Y	Y/1	ASSEMBLER	8049 equivalent without program memory.
	8080	NMOS	8/8	3/2	1.3/78	N	Y/1	ASSEMBLER, PL/M, BASIC, FORTRAN 77, CORAL 66	Available in several speed versions. Note 5.
	8085	NMOS	8/8	3/1	1.3/80	Y	Y/4	ASSEMBLER, PL/M, BASIC, FORTRAN 77	Software compatible upgrade of 8080. Note 6.
	8086	HMOS	16/16	5/1	0.4/134	N	Y/256	ASSEMBLER, PL/M-86, FORTRAN-86	Relatively advanced architecture. Address range 1 M byte. 24 addressing modes. 8 MHz version available shortly.
INTERSIL	6100	CMOS	12/12	4/1	2.5/81	Y	Y/1	ASSEMBLER, ALGOL, BASIC, FOCAL, DIBOL, FORTRAN	PDP-8 compatible. Note 7.
MOS TECHNOLOGY	650X	NMOS	8/8	4/1	0.5/56	Y	Y/1	ASSEMBLER, BASIC	40 pin device addresses 64 k bytes. Simpler 28 pin versions address 4 k or 8 k bytes. Note 8.
	651X	NMOS	8/8	4/2	0.5/56	N	Y/1	ASSEMBLER, BASIC	As 6500.

	6800	NMOS	8/8	2/2	1/89	N	Y/2	ASSEMBLER, BASIC, FORTRAN MPL	Available in several speed versions. Note 9.
MOTOROLA	6802	NMOS	8/8	1/1	2/89	Y	Y/2	ASSEMBLER, BASIC, FORTRAN MPL	M 6800 compatible. Includes 128 byte RAM on chip. Note 10.
	6809	NMOS	8/8-16	2/1	1/≈150	Y	Y/?	ASSEMBLER	Enhanced M 6800 instruction set. 3 chip minimum system. Available Spring 1979.
	14500B	CMOS	4/1	1/1	1/16	Y	N	-	Programmable logic controller. Requires external program counter.
	INS 8900	NMOS	16/16	2/1	8/45	N	Y/6	ASSEMBLER, SM/PL, BASIC	
NATIONAL	PACE	PMOS	16/16	2/2	8/45	N	Y/6	ASSEMBLER, SM/PL, BASIC	Superceded by INS 8900. Based on IMP-16.
	SC/MP	PMOS/ NMOS	8/8	4/1	5/46	Y	Y/1	ASSEMBLER, FORTRAN	PMOS version ½ speeds shown. Note 11.
NEC	μPD 541	PMOS	8/4	0.5/2	6.4/69	N	Y/8	ASSEMBLER	Designed to be used in cash registers.
PANAFCOM	MN 1610	NMOS	16/16	2/2	2/33	N	Y/3	ASSEMBLER	
RCA	CDP 1802	CMOS	8/8	6.4/1	2.5/91	Y	Y/1	ASSEMBLER, MICROFORTH, PL/M, BASIC	Supercedes RCA 1800 COSMAC. Note 12.
	CDP 1803	CMOS	8/8	6.4/1	2.5/91	Y	Y/1	ASSEMBLER, MICROFORTH, PL/M, BASIC	28 pin version of 1802.
	PPS-4	PMOS	8/4	0.2/2 0.4	5/50	N	Y/1	ASSEMBLER	Combination RAM/ROM/I/O chip to match. Note 13.
ROCKWELL	PPS-4/2	PMOS	8/4	0.2/2 0.4	5/50	Y	Y/1	ASSEMBLER	Similar to PPS-4. Note 13.
	PPS-8	PMOS	8/8	0.256/4	4/100	N	Y/3	ASSEMBLER	Combination RAM/ROM/I/O chip to match. PPS-8/2 available with clock on I/O chip. Note 14.
SCIENTIFIC MICROSYSTEMS	SMS 300	BIPOLAR	8/8	4/1	5/46	N	N	ASSEMBLER	
SIGNETICS	2650	NMOS	8/8	1.2/1	4.8/75	N	Y/1	ASSEMBLER. PLUS	Note 14.
	8X300	SCHOTTKY BIPOLAR	16/8	4/1	0.25/8	Y	Y	ASSEMBLER	
TEXAS	TMS/SBP 9900	NMOS/ I²L	16/16	4/4	2/69	N	Y/16	ASSEMBLER, PL/9900 FORTRAN, BASIC, PASCAL, CORAL 66	Uses 990 minicomputer instruction set. SBP 9900 is I²L. Note 15.
	TMS 9980	NMOS	16/16	2.5/1	4.8/69	Y	Y/4	ASSEMBLER, PL/9900, FORTRAN, BASIC, PASCAL, CORAL 66	Compatible with TMS 9900.
TOSHIBA	T 3190	PMOS/ NMOS	12/12	2.5/1	10/108	Y	Y/8	ASSEMBLER	
WESTERN DIGITAL	WD-16	NMOS	16/16	4/4	2.1/116	N	Y/16	ASSEMBLER	Multiple chip set. Similar to DEC PDP-11
ZILOG	Z-80	NMOS	8/8	4/1	1/158	N	Y/1	ASSEMBLER, PL/Z, FORTRAN, BASIC, COBOL	Instruction set superset of INTEL 8080. Note 16.
	Z-8000	NMOS	16/16	4/1	0.75/110+	N	Y/3	ASSEMBLER, PL/Z, FORTRAN, BASIC, COBOL	Available Spring 1979. Performance comparable to PDP 11/45 claimed. Note 17.

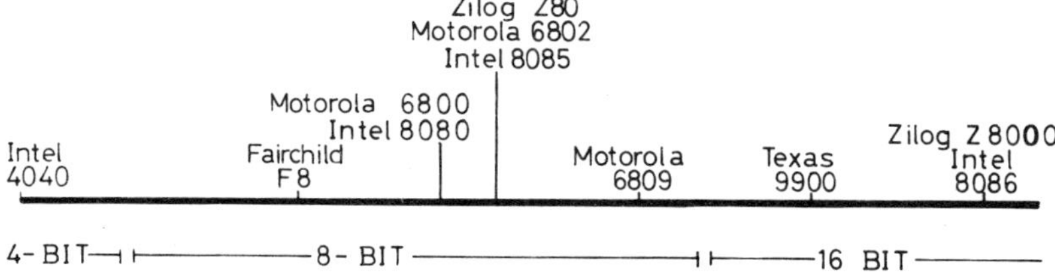

FIG. 4 Single-chip microprocessor spectrum.

described in the introduction, without necessarily increasing their computational power. Thus, most interesting developments in the classical single-chip microprocessor arena have been in the mid to high range of devices.

Motorola have announced the M6809, which is upwards compatible with the MC6800, but includes an extra index register, index/stack pointer register, a direct page register and allows 16-bit arithmetic. One of the main aims in developing the MC6809 was apparently to simplify code generation. Hence the instruction set, although compatible with its predecessors, has been extended, made more symmetric and, it is claimed, provides features to simplify compilation of structured high-level languages. The ability to write position-independent code (and hence also use standard program ROM's) is another result of this objective. Similarly, the provision of a direct page register, which allows quick access to any page in memory, simplifies the generation of software for multi-tasking operations. The MC6809 uses an on-chip 2MHz clock to give 1 μS instruction times. A minimum system configuration would require 3 chips.

Intel's contribution to this end of the spectrum is the 8086 16-bit device. This impressive device has both minicomputer-like features and performance. Intel's aim was to produce a symmetrical development of the 8080 capable of carrying out signed or unsigned 8 or 16-bit arithmetic (including multiply and divide), efficient string operations and enhanced bit manipulation. The software features of the 8086 include mechanisms for operations such as position-independent code, dynamic relocation and re-entrancy. The addressing range has also been extended to 1 megabyte. Typically, the current memory space would be divided into four areas, the program, data, stack and extra segments. Each segment is 65,536 bytes long and is accessed via the appropriate internal segment register. The ability to quickly change the current address space by modifying the segment register contents allows rapid context switching. Another interesting feature of the 8086 is its 6 byte instruction queue. This allows the memory to be kept busy by fetching words from the instruction stream, provided other systems elements are not using memory cycles. The execution unit can then extract bytes from the queue and execute them, thereby eliminating the instruction fetch time. The pipelining technique much enhances the processor performance. The standard 8086 requires an external 5MHz clock generator and an Intel 8282 system controller. A minimum (although impractical) system configuration would thus require 7 chips. The 8086 has execution speeds that are approximately 10 times that of the Intel 8080A and typically, an equivalent program would be 10–25% shorter. A direct competitor to the Intel 8086 is the Zilog Z-8000. The Z8000 is claimed to have a processing performance equivalent to a DEC PDP-11/34 minicomputer and features a 48 megabyte direct addressing range and 32-bit arithmetical operations. All this is achieved using NMOS technology and a relatively low 4MHz clock rate.

Table 2 provides a comprehensive list of available single-chip microprocessors detailing some of their architectural features.

CONCLUSIONS

The rate of component evolution in the microcomputer market is such that this review will undoubtedly be outdated at publication. However, this paper should give a good indication of the current 'state-of-the-art'. Due to rapid changes in pricing levels and structure, no mention of component cost has been included. It is sufficient to say that for the majority of low to medium volume applications the hardware costs are small in relation to software production costs.

REFERENCE

[1]   Powner, E. T., Escuder, M. A., Depledge, P. G., 'An Introduction to Microprocessors — Part 1', *I.J.E.E.E.*, **14**, No. 1, pp. 73–80, (Jan. 1977).

NOTES TO TABLE 2

Note 1   Second sourced by MOSTEK, MOTOROLA, SGS-ATES.
     2   Second sourced by EM & M, ITT.
     3   Second sourced by AEG, SGS-ATES.
     4   Second sourced by AMD, NEC, SIGNETICS.
     5   Second sourced by AMD, MITSIBUSHI, NATIONAL, NEC, SIEMENS, SIGNETICS, TEXAS.
     6   Second sourced by AMD, NEC, SIEMENS.
     7   Second sourced by HARRIS.
     8   Second sourced by ROCKWELL, SYNERTEK.
     9   Second sourced by AMI, FAIRCHILD, FUJITSU, HITACHI, SESCOSEM/THOMSON CSF.
    10   Second sourced by FAIRCHILD, HITACHI.
    11   Second sourced by ROCKWELL, SIGNETICS, WESTERN DIGITAL. (SC/MP II).
    12   Second sourced by HUGHES, SOLID STATE SCIENTIFIC.
    13   Second sourced by AEG.
    14   Second sourced by ADVANCED MEMORY SYSTEMS, NATIONAL.
    15   Second sourced by AMI.
    16   Second sourced by MOSTEK, NEC, SHARP.
    17   Second sourced by AMD.

It should be noted that not all of these second sources are by official mask exchanges.

THE ARCHITECTURE OF MICROCOMPUTER COMPONENTS

P. COOKE
School of Engineering, University of Sussex, England

BACKGROUND

Now that third and fourth generation microcomputers are in use, the arrangement of Fig. 1 may be regarded as showing the classical architecture. Regular interconnections in the form of a system bus is its most fundamental and distinctive feature. Typically the bus amounts to about 40 wires.

Almost continuous advances in manufacturing technology, coupled with design innovations, have led to a succession of microcomputer components of increasing sophistication and completeness. Table 1 presents the component types in order of emergence. Complete computers on a chip are usefully viewed in the way shown in Fig. 2.

Before discussing further the architectural features of contemporary and emergent microcomputer components it is necessary to consider the technological background that provides the driving force and rationale. Unifying concepts then become apparent.

A complete microcomputer system can be usefully viewed as:

(i)   a collection of small silicon chips; probably less than a thimblefull,
(ii) a collection of hardware-packages, sockets, printed-circuits, connectors, sockets etc. Their sole justification and purpose is to support and implement the interconnections between chips.

This analysis reveals the hardware costs as being interconnection dominated. In fact, were the manufacturing costs of the *actual* silicon chips to vanish, it would have little impact at the system level! However, the interconnection costs are well related to the chip-count, and almost proportional to the pin-count. In summary, the hardware costs of a complete microcomputer system tend to be proportional to the total system pin-count.

TABLE 1   *Microcomputer components of increasing completeness.*

1)	Fractional memory systems	(RAM & ROM e.g. M2102, 2708)
2)	Fragments of processing units	(bit-slice e.g. AMD 2900 series)
3)	Complete processing units	(microprocessors e.g. Motorola 6800)
4)	Programmable peripherals	(I/O input/output e.g. Zilog PIO)
5)	Single-chip computers	(including I/O e.g. Rockwell 6500/1)
6)	Single-chip computer systems	(computer + peripheral e.g. Intel 8022)

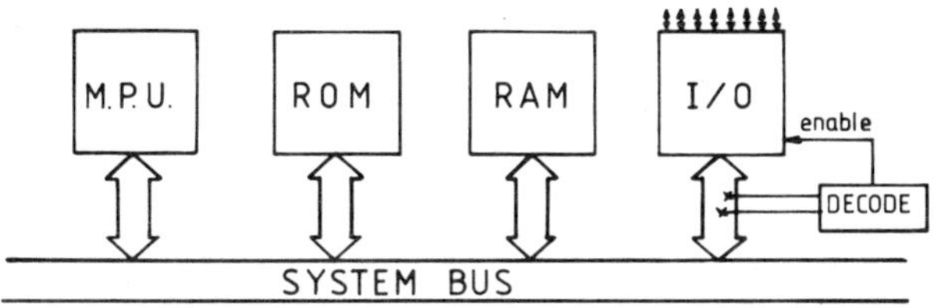

FIG. 1   *Classical architecture of a microcomputer.*

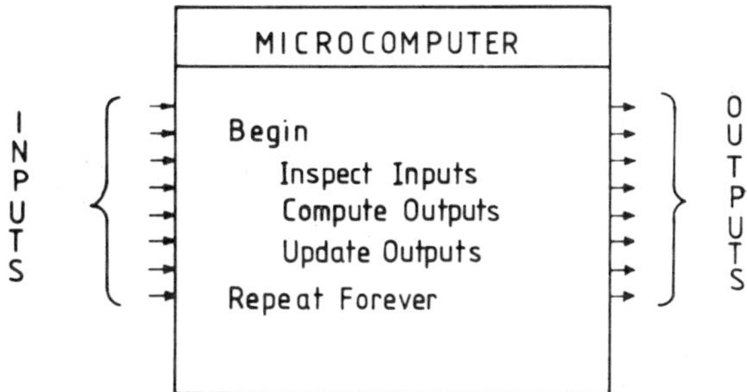

FIG. 2   *Generalised view of a microcomputer.*

DESIGN TRENDS

Continuing advances in manufacturing technology, offer increases in the circuit complexity achievable on a single chip. Turning this into an advantage at the system level requires that there be a reduction in the necessary pin-count. Alternatively stated, the semiconductor manufacturer seeks to maximise the useful functional complexity per pin-out. From this observation various related lines of development can be identified, viz:

(i) *Similar pin-out, but enhanced processing power*
Normally, a new class of microcomputer component represents the limit of achievable complexity. Subsequent progress in manufacturing technology then makes it possible to produce more powerful versions. For example, the Zilog Z80 is an enhanced version of the Intel 8080. Pin allocations are very similar, the new instruction set is a super-set of the earlier device, and the circuit complexity is almost double.

Since first introduced, all the classes of components identified in Table 1 have been produced in enhanced form. Memory improvements are perhaps the most striking example. Initially, in the late sixties, memory chips contained only tens of bits per chip. Now the 64K single chip memory is available; even bigger ones are promised.

(ii) *Encompass more within a chip, so reducing system pin-out*
Single chip computers provide the best example of this second line of develop-

ment. Referring to Fig. 1 it can be seen that to encompass the whole computer is to eliminate the inter-unit connections. This releases about 30 pins, sufficient for the totality of input-output wires in many applications. Savings in system pin-out are of course very substantial.

The first generations of single chip computers contain a very small RAM, of perhaps 128 bytes plus a masked ROM of about 2K bytes. Primarily these components are aimed at high-volume users of identical computers containing identical programs. For experimental or low-volume applications EPROM versions are sometimes available; but not cheaply.

Engineers wishing to use single-chip computers must be provided with special development tools. In a way these systems are a good example of how computers can be used to make possible the mass production of relatively low volumes of customised parts. Clearly, they are not well-suited to use in the teaching laboratory, although EPROM versions may have some merit.

(iii) *Time multiplexing*

Without time multiplexing, the microprocessor would not exist. Traditionally, the data-bus is used to transfer various sorts of information by dividing an instruction period into time-slots. Control and timing signals are used to define the significance of the message currently on the data-bus. Often information must be retained and used in later time-slots. This gives rise to latched de-multiplexors. The generalised form of this arrangement is given in Fig. 3.

Actual microcomputer components abound with examples. In Intel 8080 systems there is a requirement for additional control signals, and this is achieved via a so-called controller chip. A more elegant example is the way in which the 16 bit microprocessors transfer data over an 8 bit data bus. Two successive transfers at the hardware level appear to the programmer as a single transfer of 16 bits.

(iv) *Programability*

Programability infers waste, in the sense that not all of the hardware is in use all of the time. But such is the nature of all computing devices. In recent

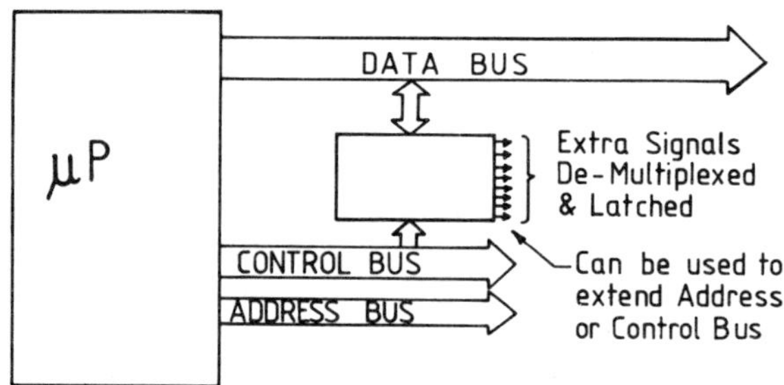

FIG. 3   De multiplexing from the data bus.

examples of programmable peripheral chips, it is more than likely that certain sections of the on-chip hardware will never be used. Nevertheless this strategy makes sense. The manufacturer addresses a large number of potential users. They get the advantage of a very sophisticated component, leading to reduced design time combined with a very low chip-count. A myriad of slightly different, but generally similar applications have been satisfied by a single type of component. Often the chip count for that class of function has been reduced by more than an order of magnitude. Compared to these advantages, the wastage of silicon area is not financially significant.

Two distinct lines of development have programability as their underlying theme, viz:

Static programability. Digital engineering abounds with examples where the voltage on one or more pins defines the function of another block of circuitry. Nevertheless the concept is useful at the chip level. Fig. 4 illustrates the principle.

An interesting practical variant is to — in effect — use more than two levels of quantisation. For example, the two normal binary logic levels can be supplemented by an exceptionally large, perhaps current-limited input, to define a third condition. Examples exist, not many, but the advent of on-chip analog to digital converters may change the situation.

Software programmed. Peripheral chips provide the interface between the external electronics and the microcomputer bus. Over and above the data bus — normally comprising 8 wires — very few of the address and control signals are needed. For instance, 16 input/output wires represent just two bytes of eight bits, needing only one address line, over and above chip-enable. This low usage of address-type inputs, releases pins for I/O. Usage of an additional address-type input permits data transfers to be of two classes; I/O or control.

In essence, the technique is that control words are internally latched and, after decoding, are used to determine the current operating mode. A single

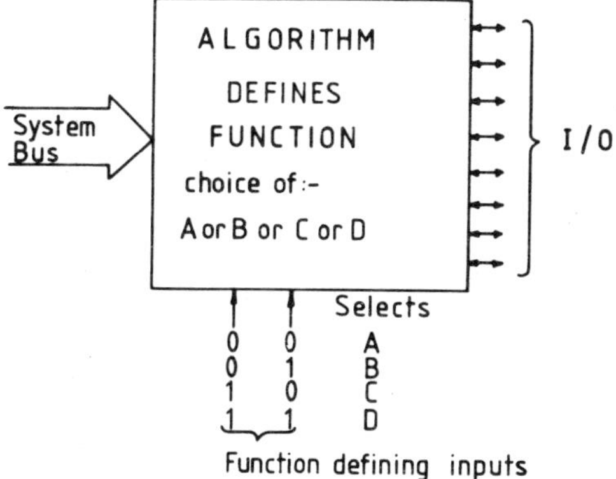

FIG. 4   Inputs define circuit function.

byte is sufficient to define one out of $2^8 = 256$ distinct operating modes. Moreover, there is no theoretical limit to the number of control bytes that can be sequentially sent. Fig. 5 shows the internal structure of an advanced programmable peripheral; it illustrates the use of the data bus to convey control and status bytes as well as data.

The alternative example of programability is when the peripheral chip is, in fact, a complete microcomputer in its own right. Technically, the distinguishing features of such a device is the inclusion of all the necessary safeguards to permit concurrent operation. Without being much aware of the difficulties inherent in implementing multi-processing systems, design engineers can achieve very complex multi-computer configurations.

Recently, semiconductor manufacturers have started to offer single-chip computers, already mask-programmed and arranged to act as dedicated peripherals. Chips to implement the IEEE 488 instrumentation bus transfer protocol have been realized in this way.

(v) *Internal duplication*

The final class of ways in which designers have improved the ratio of useful complexity to pin-out, is by internal duplication. For instance, even though a signal and its complement is required within several chips, it is better to have just one interconnecting wire. The complement is better generated by an invertor, on each chip. By this strategy a trivial increase in circuit complexity has 'released a pin'. More exotic examples are now common.

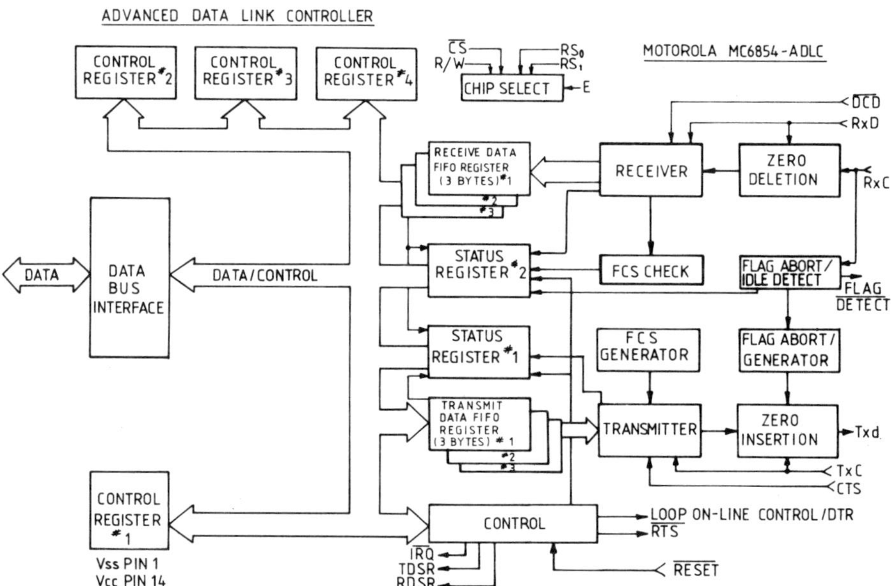

FIG. 5   Internal architecture of advanced programmable peripheral.

Normally, each of the major microcomputer components needs to be aware of the current time-slot, relative to a synchronizing marker. Rather than distribute on n wires the time markers T_1, $T_2 - T_n$, or even their coded equivalent, it is common practice to use a clock plus a synchronization signal. Then an internal state machine, duplicated to the necessary degree in each of the family chips, can deduce and make internally available, the required timing signals. More sophisticated examples include the transmission of status words during otherwise un-utilized time slots. Sometimes a chip will monitor the data bus, looking for a particular class of instruction; then the designers have, in effect, duplicated a fragment of the microprocessor's control unit.

BUS SYSTEMS

All microcomputers rely on a bus system. They can exist at several levels:

(i) *Internal:* both microprocessor units and programable peripheral chips have an internal bus. It enables inter-register transfers.

(ii) *Inter-unit:* this is the main bus and is shown in Fig. 1.

(iii) *Inter computer:* systems involving co-operating and concurrent processes can usefully have an additional bus to enable inter-computer transfers and shared data in a common area of store. The Intel Multibus is the most widely supported example of this class.

Besides the hardware and operating advantages of a bus system they make a vital contribution to comprehensibility. Byte serial transfers are easily visualized. Wiring patterns — in practice and on paper — are mainly regular and straightforward.

Within the system-bus are three groupings:

The data bus

In the typical system an 8 bit byte can be transferred in parallel. Words of two or more bytes can be sent in byte serial form. Furthermore, the data-bus will support transfers in either direction. The meaning and purpose of the data is determined by control signals.

The address bus

Binary coded addressing signals enable source and distinction to be selected by the microprocessor. Typically, there are 16 address signals, enabling an address field of $2^{16} \simeq 64K$ locations. This is often extended by various validating signals. Some microprocessors include memory, I/O, and single bit types; some are solely memory-mapped.

The control bus

Frequently-used signals that do not form part of the data and address are commonly collected together under the umbrella title of the control-bus. Besides timing signals, it mainly includes strobes and validating signals. These types indicate the purpose to which the address bus is to be put. Edge timings provide the datum from which critical times, such as access time, is to be measured.

Control signals are also used to indicate the timing, direction and significance of signals on the data-bus. Thus peripheral chips are able to synchronise with the microprocessor. By observing the data bus when the instructions are being fetched, the internal state of the microprocessor can be deduced. This sort of facility helps peripheral chips to appear very intelligent.

Using the various control signals in combination with the addressing facilities is *central* to the understanding, interconnection and design of micro-computer systems.

CONCLUDING REMARKS

Despite the continuing advances in microprocessor components, some sort of watershed has been reached. Referring to Table 1, it is easy to visualise that components of all types will appear in more powerful forms. It is clear that fragmentary computers will become less necessary, although the increasing dedication of the more complex chips presents new problems. However, it is far from clear that there is a natural progression beyond the last entry of Table 1.

Microcomputers which include on-chip analog digital converters are amongst the complete systems that are now available. More exotic combinations will doubtless follow. Some chips contain more than one processor, but functionally this may not be particularly apparent to the user.

Consequent on the availability of complete computer systems on a single chip, it is clear that the electronic engineer will design multiprocessor systems. With the aid of intelligent peripheral chips many are already doing so. Such design activity is several levels of complexity removed from the design and analysis of simple transistor circuits. This poses important questions for educationalists. How does one train young engineers to think at the necessary conceptual level? More worrying are questions such as, 'how relevant and important is the traditional and electrically based syllabus?'

CHOOSING THE MICROPROCESSOR FOR THE JOB

ROGER C. WATERFALL
Department of Electrical Engineering and Electronics, University of Manchester Institute of Science and Technology, England

INTRODUCTION

It might appear at first sight that all the facts necessary to make a choice of microprocessor are contained in their specifications. However, the data books are often very long-winded and very tedious to read. The different manufacturers present their data in different formats and performance criteria are specified under various conditions.

Sometimes, in the manufacturer's literature, case studies are presented and bench-mark programs listed, comparing the facilities and speed of operation of a few microprocessors. However, these comparisons are inevitably chosen to show one product in the best possible light. Fortunately, in many applications, the precise capabilities of the microprocessor are not the most important considerations. Often, any eight bit (or sixteen or four bit) microprocessor will provide a working solution to the problem.

GENERAL CONSIDERATIONS

The first question that needs raising is whether the particular microprocessor is in full-scale production and freely available. There have been occasions where the customer gains the impression that this is so, only to find, once he is committed to a design and places a firm order, that delivery is promised for six months in the future. It must be said that most circuits do come through, more or less, as promised, but, by their nature, sales staff tend to be optimistic with their forecasts of prices and delivery.

One of the better situations is where the buyer can select from several independent manufacturers of the identical article. Unfortunately, not many microprocessors are second-sourced and this can have serious consequences. For example, the whole production facility of a particular micro-circuit may be situated in a single factory. If this plant were to suffer a catastrophic fire, as has happened, then production would be interrupted for several months. Many micro-circuits are produced 'off-shore' where labour is cheap. Although this has not (to my knowledge) happened, the possibility of a military coup, with consequential damage and disruption, should be taken into account.

Even without such dramatic factors as detailed above, a single manufacturer of a particular item may decide that his production equipment might be more profitable applied to some other component, and so either stop production

completely or raise the price to an uneconomic level. In any case, the manufacturer can choose a price that is popular with him, and not one that reflects the
true worth of the package.

For the new user, the need for good technical back-up is paramount. It can
be surprising to discover that the U.K.-based microprocessor technical 'team'
of a large semi-conductor manufacturer consists of one man and a secretary. By
the time this team has toured the country, visiting exhibitions and giving
seminars, very little time is left for the grass-roots user. Sometimes the experience of such technical advisers is limited to their reading, augmented by a
one week intensive course at the manufacturer's headquarters, in the United
States. Experience is gained slowly, often only through feed-back from customers. The answers to most problems concerned with applying microprocessors are contained in the data books and applications manuals, but, unaided,
it can take a very long time to find them. The man of experience can sort out
many difficulties in a few minutes.

One should, of course, discover if the manufacturer really wants to sell to
you. It might appear obvious that he does, and yet there are several cases
where the manufacturer is only really interested in very large-volume orders, or
in high-specification, high unit-cost military sales. No matter how keen your
local representative appears, if company policy is to concentrate on other
markets, then you may find that your order receives a low priority and the
price and delivery may be less than satisfactory.

A careful study of the peripheral chips that are compatible with the microprocessor can be very rewarding. For example, perhaps one has a problem
involving the coding of a serial data stream using feed-back shift-registers. If
one manufacturer produces such an encryption unit in a single package, as one
of a microprocessor family, then that family must be considered very seriously.
A microprocessor, be it ever-so-elegant in concept and fast in operation, is not
much use if it needs a large number of small-scale integrated circuits to interface to the outside world.

Lastly, the supply voltages and power consumption must be considered. In
some applications, the microprocessor will be added onto existing equipment.
In this case, it would be convenient to utilise the existing power supplies. The
cost of an additional supply may well be as much as the cost of the microprocessor itself. In certain areas battery operation may be necessary, in which case
the overall consumption and number of supplies must be minimized.

On the following pages, three case studies of projects undertaken by the
Digital Processes Group at U.M.I.S.T. are discussed, pointing out the factors
that led to the choice of particular microprocessors.

CASE STUDIES

Case 1. Programming-aid for a numerically-controlled drilling machine
One of the machine-tools in the Electrical Engineering workshop is a
numerically-controlled drill designed for drilling printed-circuit boards. The

drill is controlled by specifying the XY position of each hole to be drilled, on a punched-paper tape. This tape is prepared off-line on a teletype and then fed into a tape-reader in the NC machine control unit. Many of the holes required in printed circuits are part of fixed, repeated patterns, for example, the 14 lead dual-in-line pattern shown in Fig. 1.

The control tape to specify this pattern of holes would give a teletype print-out as listed below; assuming the first hole to be 3 inches (X) and 5.5 inches (Y) from the origin.

1	X 03 Y 055
2	Y 056
3	Y 057
.	
.	
.	
7	Y 061
8	X 033 Y061
.	
.	
14	Y 055.

This method of specifying holes is very tedious and prone to errors. A student project was set up to design a stand-alone piece of equipment that would simplify this tape-preparation procedure[1]. The equipment was to be capable of interpreting a range of mnemonic instructions. For example, to drill dual-in-line patterns, the instruction is:

$$\text{DIL/3, 5.5, 14, 90.}$$

mnemonic. $\longrightarrow$
X & Y of 1st hole
no. of pins   angle to X axis. $(0° \text{ or } 90°)$

A feasibility study revealed that, of the microprocessors available for which we had hardware and software back-up, either the Intel 8080 or the Motorola 6800 would perform adequately. The deciding factor was that Motorola had available an evaluation kit closely matching our requirements and containing

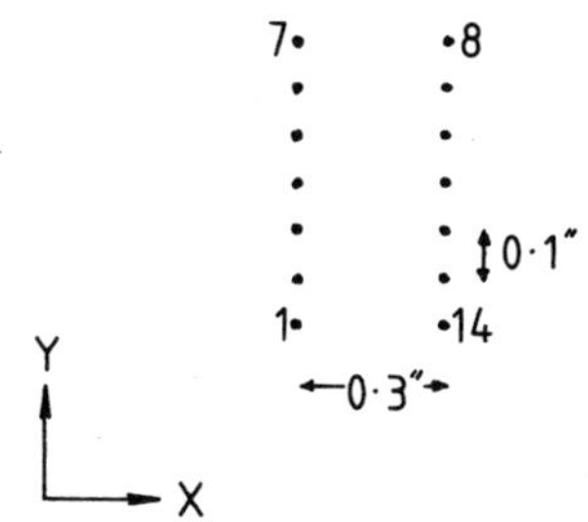

FIG. 1 *14 hole dual-in-line pattern.*

complete documentation, a printed-circuit board and all components (except EPROM), at a reasonable cost. This meant that the student, who was working on a short time-scale, did not need to bother designing a printed-circuit board, or interfacing to a teletype. He was able to concentrate on the software problem and the more mundane difficulties of putting the unit into a box. The resulting equipment is very simple and useful. The box itself has a mains lead, a socket for the serial data and control lines from the teletype and a start button.

Apart from pressing the start button of the microprocessor control unit, it is controlled via the teletype keyboard. A schematic is shown in Fig. 2. Besides translating the DIL mnemonic into the list of XY holes shown above, the equipment has many other facilities, for example if the instruction had been

DIL/3, 5.5, 40, 90

the microprocessor, detecting a 40 pin pattern, would automatically space the two rows of holes by 0.6 inch. The equipment allows inputs to be in metric or Imperial measure and automatically converts metric input to the fixed format in inches for the object tape. The equipment checks that holes are not specified outside the drilling table and checks for syntax errors in the input. Macro's for special patterns can be developed and stored either in RAM or off-line on paper-tape.

Many microprocessors would be capable of doing this job, but the M6800 was the most suitable because we had the hardware and software backing and the low-cost evaluation kit was very well-suited to the job.

Case 2. Foot gauge for children's feet
One of the major manufacturers of children's footwear expressed an interest in a semi-automatic foot gauge[2]. The design was conceived to have manually-operated slides pushed up to the toe and up to the sides of the foot being measured. The electronics had to convert the movement of the three slides into a size and fit. The sizes run from 6 to $13\frac{1}{2}$ for juniors and then 1 to 10 in seniors, and are on a straightforward linear scale. The fittings, however, have a range

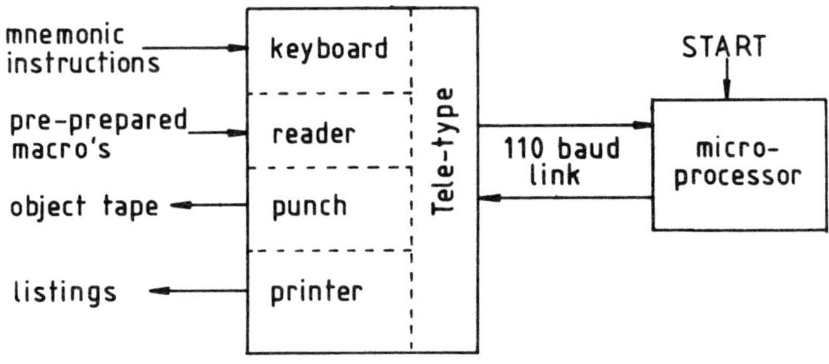

FIG. 2   NC machine programming aid.

for each size, and the increment between fits changes from the junior to senior range (Fig. 3).

The electronics was also required to compare two sets of readings, one from the left foot, one from the right, and find the longest length and widest width. From these results a suitable pair size was to be calculated, and displayed.

If the design had been adopted, there was a potential market for several hundred units. This meant that the system cost played an important part in the choice of microprocessor. At that time, 1975, the Intel 4040 appeared to be a reasonable choice of microprocessor, although we had no hardware development aids for this family and only an untried software simulator. An important factor was the amount of memory needed. Although some ROM was necessary, both to store the program and the look-up table for calculating the fit, the only RAM requirement was to remember the length and width of the first foot whilst measuring the second. The 4040 has 24 internal 8-bit registers. By careful programming it was possible to pack the complete program and the look-up table for the fit into one 256 byte ROM and to do without RAM altogether.

The programmable input/output chip in the 4040 family is also very convenient in that it has just sufficient ports for the job. The total integrated circuit list, for the prototype circuit is shown in Fig. 4.

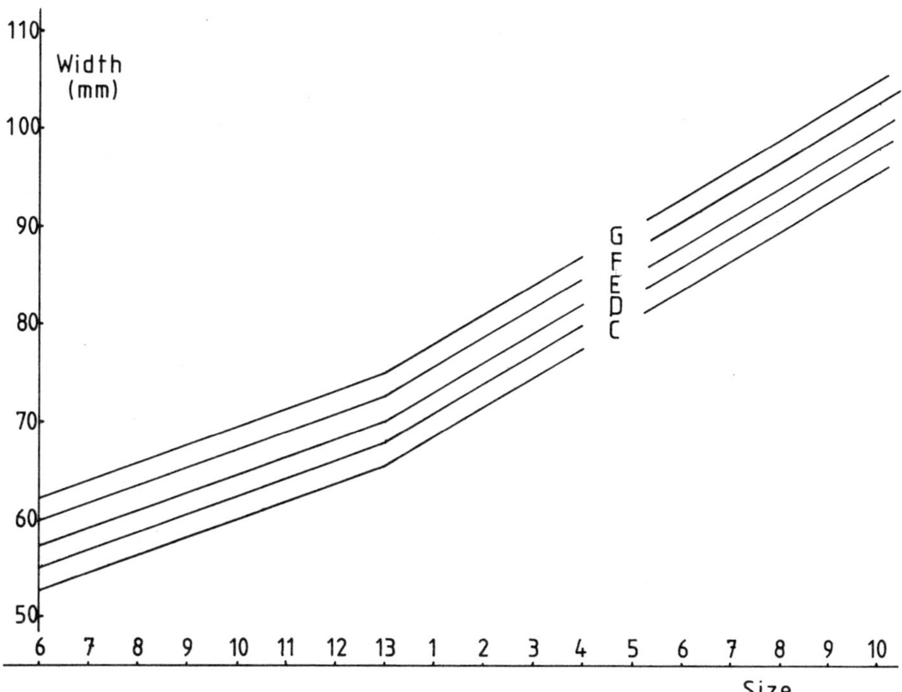

FIG. 3   Size/fit relationship for children's shoes.

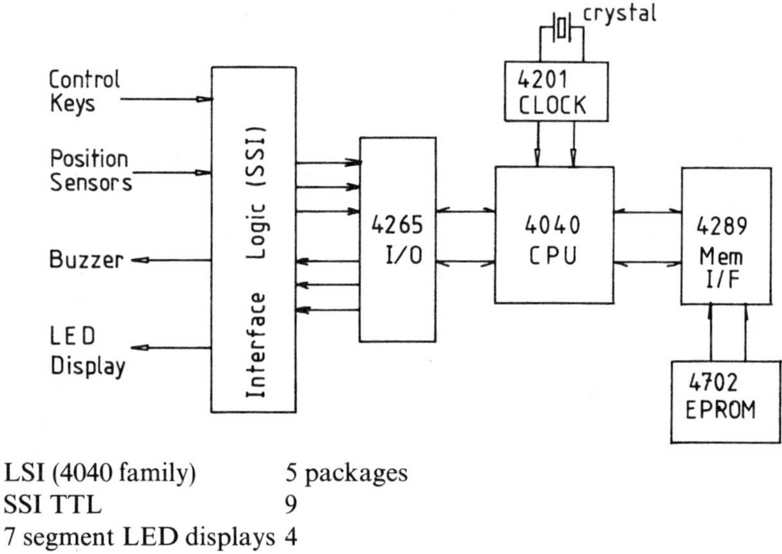

LSI (4040 family)   5 packages
SSI TTL   9
7 segment LED displays 4

FIG. 4   Schematic for foot gauge electronics.

The LSI components would be reduced to four if mask-programmed **ROM** were used, as would be the case in a production run. This would replace both the 24 pin **EPROM** and 40 pin memory-interface chip with a single 16 pin package.

Although no hardware aids were available, other than an **EPROM** programmer, because of the small program and simple circuitry, it was possible to de-bug the design (and discover a few errors in the previously untried simulator) using a two-trace oscilloscope. For more complex designs, more sophisticated de-bugging aids would have been necessary.

Because of the sizeable potential volume requirement in a unit where the electronics are a large portion of the basic cost, in this application it was important to utilise a low-cost microprocessor family.

Case 3. Printer interface to mass-spectrometer
The output from a mass-spectrometer is in the form of an intensity and a ratio. These readings are available for both a known reference and the sample under investigation. A whole series of results is taken for each sample. This output has to be arithmetically manipulated to give the figures required by the operator, i.e. the mean reference ratio, the enrichment and the standard deviation. To obtain the required results, the basic data was printed out, and then the operator keyed them into a programmable desk-calculator. The calculator performed the required arithmetic and printed out the results. It seemed an obvious improvement to insert a microprocessor between the mass-spectrometer and the printer, thus enabling the results to be printed out directly.

Most of the 8 bit microprocessors available would be capable of performing this job, particularly as the output from the mass-spectrometer is at a rate of about one word per second.

The predicted market for this particular unit is about ten per year and the cost of the mass-spectrometer of the order of £10k.

It was decided to use the TI 9900 16 bit microprocessor for this job. This is a fast and powerful microprocessor, with a component price to match. However, the overriding consideration was that another group in the company had decided to use the 9900 series as a real-time controller. Hence, they had the development equipment for this microprocessor. The company did not possess any other microprocessor equipment or experience.

Although the facilities of the 9900 were greatly in excess of the requirements, and the component cost perhaps £300 against £100 per unit, the extra cost of £200 (or £2000 p.a. for 10 units) can be safely neglected when compared with the cost of buying a new development system and the inherent delay until the design engineers gained the necessary experience.

CONCLUSIONS

Microprocessors are changing rapidly in nearly all respects. If the cases discussed here were to be evaluated now, then quite different solutions might be proposed. However, most of the observations and comments made would still be valid.

Obviously, a microprocessor chosen for a specific role must be capable of fulfilling that role, but very often the choice of microprocessor is fixed, not by the specification of the micro-electronics, but by other factors.

In simplistic terms the choice can often be made by answering the following three questions.

(i)   Of which microprocessors do you have experience?

(ii) What hardware and software development tools do you have?

(iii) Will a microprocessor satisfying questions (i) and (ii) do the job?

If yes — choose it.

If no — choose the most suitable one available and buy or rent the aids.

REFERENCES

[1]   Chan, T. F., *M.Sc. Dissertation, U.M.I.S.T.*, (1977).
[2]   Provisional patent no. 30248/76, Clarks Ltd.

THE USE OF PROGRAMMABLE POCKET CALCULATORS IN ENGINEERING INTRODUCTORY COURSES

M. BIONDI, V. MIDORO† and D. PESCETTI**
**Istituto di Scienze Fisiche, Università di Genova, Italy*
†*Laboratorio per le Tecnologie Didattiche, C.N.R., Genova, Italy*

INTRODUCTION

An optional short course, on the use of programmable pocket calculators in solving physics problems, has been included for the past two years in the physics curriculum for mechanical and chemical engineering students of the University of Genoa.

Our motivating philosophy is that the knowledge of the unique conceptual advantages and problems of the computer (or of the programmable calculators) should be acquired early in the engineering curriculum if the computer is to become a fundamental part of the engineer's problem-solving repertory. The computer can add a new dimension to the nature and content of the curriculum through its influence on the topics and their mode of presentation. In order to remain relevant to future needs, basic undergraduate courses must be appropriately modified to reflect the new points of view associated with computer applications; numerical analysis must be integrated into course work, and students should receive programming instruction at an early stage in their education. Programmable pocket calculators can make easier this achievement.

During the course, students are trained to use a programmable pocket calculator mainly to generate solutions for nonlinear differential equations. In fact, the behavior of many physical processes, particularly those in systems undergoing time-dependent changes, can be described by ordinary differential equations. Thus, methods of solution for these equations are of great importance to engineering students. Only a very few equations that arise from actual physical systems are simple enough to allow an analytical solution. There exist, in general, no methods capable of yielding an analytical solution of a nonlinear differential equation. The solutions of these equations can usually be generated numerically. The study of nonlinear physical systems can be therefore particularly motivating for the use of programmable calculators, which provide a speedy and cheap means for performing the iterative calculations of the numerical solution algorithm. Frequently, essentially new phenomena occur in nonlinear systems which cannot, in principle, occur in linear systems.

The principal aim of the study of the selected nonlinear systems, is to focus attention on those features of the problems in which nonlinearity results in distinctive new phenomena, and not only to improve the accuracy obtainable by linearization.

COURSE STRUCTURE

The course is organized into seven lessons of three hours each. Each lesson consists of a theoretical and a practical session. During the first half-hour the tutor illustrates the differential equation that describes some physical phenomena and the numerical method used to generate the solution. In the last two and a half hours, first the students, alone or in a small group, write the program to find numerical solution of the differential equation, then they input the written program and make it run several times to plot solution curves.

The students use programmable calculators Hewlett Packard HP 25 (parenthesis free notation) that were especially purchased by our Institute for this purpose. During the period of the course the students are allowed to keep the calculators at home (one calculator to every two students).

The short course is aimed at students in mechanical and chemical engineering in their second year, as an optional part of the course of 'Physics II' (Electromagnetism and Thermodynamics). It comes after one year of courses in classical mechanics, in mathematics and in chemistry. It is addressed to students with no prior knowledge of calculators, programmable or nonprogrammable. The mathematical prerequisites are some familiarity with elementary differential calculus.

The final examination consists in the numerical solution of an ordinary differential equation. The students who follow the short course are rewarded by an increase in their marks in Physics II.

To date about 80 students, divided into four groups, participated (about one fourth of the enrolled students).

CONTENTS OF THE COURSE

The contents of the short course are summarized in Table 1. We have always used the same iterative method for solving the differential equations: a proper combination of the 'middle point' and 'trapezoidal' approximations.[1,2]. The truncation error at each step in this method is of the order of h^3, h being the integration step.

Other methods are mentioned but not used during the course, because either they converge too slowly (such as Euler's method) or they require too much memory (such as Runge-Kutta's method)[1].

One of our students owned a HP 29, and solved all the equations in Table 1 also by the fourth-order Runge-Kutta algorithm (truncation error at each step of the order of h^5). That has been useful to us to verify the accuracy of our results.

Examples (a)–(d) of Table 1 (with different values for the parameters, a and b and the initial conditions) have been included to familiarize the students with the numerical algorithm. The students were requested to compare the approximate numerical solutions with the analytical solutions.

The numerical solution of equation (g) of Table 1 (Van der Pol's equation) is shown in Fig. 1. Its agreement with the solution reported by Hayashi,[3] is quite good (apart from a sign error in Hayashi's solution). The periodic steady-state behavior is a nonlinear phenomenon.

TABLE 1

DIFFERENTIAL EQUATION	INITIAL CONDITIONS	EXAMPLES OF PHYSICAL SYSTEMS	ITERATIVE PROCEDURES	INITIALIZATION
a) $\dfrac{dy}{dx} = -y$	$x=0,\; y=1$	RC series circuit, motion in a viscous medium	$y_n = \dfrac{2-h}{2+h}\, y_{n-1}$	
b) $\dfrac{d^2y}{dx^2} = -y$ $p = \dfrac{dy}{dx}$	$x=0,\; y=y_0,\; p=p_0$	LC series circuit, armonic oscillator	$y_n = y_{n-1} + h\, p_{n-\frac{1}{2}}$ $p_{n+\frac{1}{2}} = p_{n-\frac{1}{2}} - h y_n$	$p_{\frac{1}{2}} = p_0 - (h/2)\, y_0$
c) $\dfrac{d^2y}{dx^2} + a\dfrac{dy}{dx} + by = 0$	$x=0,\; y=y_0$ $\dfrac{dy}{dx} = p_0$	Forced oscillations in RLC series circuits and in linear mechanical systems	$y_n = y_{n-1} + h\, p_{n-\frac{1}{2}}$ $p_{n+\frac{1}{2}} = \dfrac{1}{2+ha}\left[(2-ha)p_{n-\frac{1}{2}} + \right.$ $\left. -\, 2hby_n\right]$	$p_{\frac{1}{2}} = \dfrac{1}{4+ha}\left[(4-ha)p_0 + \right.$ $\left. -\, 2hby_0\right]$
d) $\dfrac{d^2y}{dx^2} + a\dfrac{dy}{dx} + by = c\sin\omega x$	$x=0,$ $y=y_0\,;\; \dfrac{dy}{dx} = p_0$	Forced oscillations in RLC series circuits and in linear mechanical systems	$y_n = y_{n-1} + h\, p_{n-\frac{1}{2}}$ $p_{n+\frac{1}{2}} = \dfrac{1}{2+ha}\left\{(2-ha)p_{n-\frac{1}{2}} + \right.$ $\left. +\, 2h\left[c\sin(n\omega h) - by_n\right]\right\}$	$p_{\frac{1}{2}} = \dfrac{1}{4+ha}\left[(4-ha)y_0 + \right.$ $\left. -\, 2hby_0\right]$
e) $\dfrac{d^2y}{dx^2} = -\sin y$	$x=0,\; y=y_0$ $\dfrac{dy}{dx} = p_0$	Pendulum	$y_n = y_{n-1} + h\, p_{n-\frac{1}{2}}$ $p_{n+\frac{1}{2}} = p_{n-\frac{1}{2}} - h\sin y_n$	$p_{\frac{1}{2}} = p_0 - \dfrac{h}{2}\sin y_0$

Equation	Initial conditions	Description	Recurrence	Starting value
f) $\dfrac{d^2y}{dx^2} + y + \mu\, y^3 = 0$	$x=0,\ y=y_0$ $p=p_0$	Nonlinear oscillator	$y_n = y_{n-1} + h\, p_{n-\frac{1}{2}}$ $p_{n+\frac{1}{2}} = p_{n-\frac{1}{2}} - h(y_n + \mu\, y_n^3)$	$p_{\frac{1}{2}} = p_0 - \dfrac{h}{2}(y_0 + \mu\, y_0^3)$
g) $y'' - \mu(1-y^2)y' + y = 0$ (Van der Pol's equations particular case: $\mu=1$)	$x=0$ $y=0,\ p=0.05$	Oscillations in nonlinear electrical circuits	$y_n = y_{n-1} + h\, p_{n-\frac{1}{2}}$ $p_{n+\frac{1}{2}} = \left\{\left[2+h\mu(1-y_n^2)\right]p_{n-\frac{1}{2}} + \right.$ $\left. - 2hy_n\right\} / \left[2-h\mu(1-y_n^2)\right]$	$p_{\frac{1}{2}} = \left\{\left[4+h\mu(1-y_0^2)\right]p_0 + \right.$ $\left. - 2hy_0\right\} / \left[4-h\mu(1-y_0^2)\right]$
h) Duffing's equation $y'' + 0.20\, y' + |y|y =$ $\doteq 1.50 \cos 2x + 0.50$	$x=o$ $y=0,\ p=0$	Forced oscillations in nonlinear electrical circuit	$y_n = y_{n-1} + h\, p_{n-\frac{1}{2}}$ $p_{n+\frac{1}{2}} = \dfrac{1}{2+0.2h}\left\{(2-0.2h)p_{n-\frac{1}{2}} + \right.$ $\left. + h\left[3\cos(2nh) + 1 - 2|y_n|y_n\right]\right\}$	$p_{\frac{1}{2}} = \dfrac{2-0.1h}{2+0.1h}\, p_0 + \dfrac{h}{4+0.2h} \cdot$ $\cdot\left[3\cos h + 1 - 2|y_0|y_0\right]$
i) $y'' + a\, y' + \sin y - b = 0$ particular case: 1) $a=0.41;\ b=0.4$	$x=0$ $y=y_0,\ p=p_0$	Driven damped pendulum, motion of a synchronous induction motor, Josephson weak link	$y_n = y_{n-1} + h\, p_{n-\frac{1}{2}}$ $p_{n+\frac{1}{2}} = \dfrac{1}{2+ha}\left[(2-ha)p_{n-\frac{1}{2}} + \right.$ $\left. + 2hb - 2h\sin y_n\right]$	$p_{\frac{1}{2}} = \dfrac{1}{2+ha/2}\left[(2-ha/2)p_0 + \right.$ $\left. + hb - h\sin y_0\right]$
l) $\dfrac{d^2x}{dt^2} = -\dfrac{x}{r^3}$ $\dfrac{d^2y}{dt} = -\dfrac{y}{r^3}$ $r = (x^2 + y^2)^{\frac{1}{2}}$	$t=o$ $x=0.500$ $y=0.000$ $\dfrac{dx}{dt}=0$ $\dfrac{dy}{dt}=1.6300$	Motion in a gravitational field (Kepler's problem)	$x_n = x_{n-1} + h\, x'_{n-\frac{1}{2}}$ $y_n = y_{n-1} + h\, y'_{n-\frac{1}{2}}$ $x'_{n+\frac{1}{2}} = x'_{n-\frac{1}{2}} - h\, x_n/r^3_{n+1}$ $y'_{n+\frac{1}{2}} = y_{n-\frac{1}{2}} - h\, y_n/r^3_{n+1}$	$x_0 = 0.500\quad y_0 = 0.00$ $x'_{\frac{1}{2}} = -\dfrac{h}{2}\, x_0/r^3_0$ $y'_{\frac{1}{2}} = 1.6300 - \dfrac{h}{2}\, y_0/r^3_0 = 1.6300$

Program listings (N = number of loops)

a)
$$R_0 \quad h; \quad R_1 \quad y_0, y_n; \quad R_2 \quad N; \quad R_3 \quad N.$$

2; RCL 0; −; 2; RCL 0; +; +; STO 4; RCL 4; STO X 1; 1;

STO − 2; RCL 2; g x=0; GTO 17; GTO 09; RCL 3; STO 2; RCL 1;

R/S; GTO 09 .

b)
$$R_0 \quad h; \quad R_1 \quad y_0, y_n; \quad R_2 \quad P_0, P_{n-1/2}; \quad R_3 \quad N; \quad R_4 \quad N .$$

RCL 1; RCL 0; X; 2; +; STO − 2; RCL 0; RCL 2; X; STO + 1;

RCL 0; RCL 1; X; STO − 2; 1; STO − 3; RCL 3; g x=0; GTO 21;

GTO 07; RCL 4; STO 3; RCL 1; R/S; RCL 2; R/S; GTO 07 .

c)
$$R_0 \quad h/2; \quad R_1 \quad y_0, y_n; \quad R_2 \quad P_0, P_{n-1/2}; \quad R_3 \quad a; \quad R_4 \quad b; \quad R_6 \quad -1; \quad R_7 \quad N .$$

RCL 0; RCL 3; X; STO 5; CHS; 2; +; RCL 2; X; 2; RCL 0; X;

RCL 4; X; RCL 1; X; −; RCL 5; 2; +; +; STO 2; RCL 6; g x<0 ;

GTO 27; GTO 31; 2; STO X 0; RCL 7; STO 6; RCL 0; RCL 2; X; STO + 1;

1; STO − 7; RCL 7; g x=0; GTO 41; GTO 01; RCL 6; STO 7; RCL 1; R/S;

RCL 2 .

d)
$$R_0 \quad h; \quad R_1 \quad y_0, y_n; \quad R_2 \quad P_{1/2}, P_{n+1/2}; \quad R_3 \quad \omega h, n\omega h; \quad R_4 \quad \omega h; \quad R_5 \quad a;$$
$$R_6 \quad b; \quad R_7 \quad N .$$

RCL 2; RCL 0; X; STO + 1; g RAD; RCL 3; f sin; c; X; RCL 1;

RCL 6; X; −; 2; X; RCL 0; X; 2; RCL 0; RCL 5; X; −;

RCL 2; X; +; RCL 0; RCL 5; X; 2; +; +; STO 2; RCL 4;

STO + 3; 1; STO − 7; g x≠0; GTO 01; RCL 1; R/S; RCL 2.

e)
$$R_0 \quad h; \quad R_1 \quad y_o, y_n; \quad R_2 \quad P_0, P_{n-1/2}; \quad R_3 \quad N; \quad R_4 \quad N .$$

g RAD; RCL 1; f sin; RCL 0; X; 2; +; STO − 2; RCL 0;

RCL 2; X; STO + 1; RCL 1; f sin; RCL 0; X; STO − 2; 1;

STO − 3; RCL 3; g x=0; GTO 24; GTO 9; RCL 4; STO 3; RCL 1;

R/S; RCL 2; R/S; GTO 09 .

f) R_0 h/2; R_1 y_0,y_n; R_2 $P_0,P_{n-1/2}$; R_3 μ; R_4 -1; R_5 N .

RCL 1; g x^2; RCL 1; X; RCL 3; X; RCL 1; +; RCL 0; X;
STO $-$ 2; RCL 4; g x$<$0; GTO 16; GTO 20; 2; STO X 0; RCL 5;
STO 4; RCL 2; RCL 0; X; STO + 1; 1; STO $-$ 5; RCL 5; g x=0;
GTO 30; GTO 01; RCL 4; STO 5; RCL 1 .

g) R_0 h/2; R_1 y_0,y_n; R_2 $P_0,P_{n-1/2}$; R_3 μ; R_4 -1; R_5 N .

RCL 0; RCL 3; X; 1; RCL 1; g x^2; $-$; X; STO 6; 2; +;
RCL 2; X; RCL 0; RCL 1; X; 2; X; $-$; 2; RCL 6; $-$; $\div$;
STO 2; RCL 4; g x$<$0; GTO 29; GTO 33; 2; STO X 0; RCL 5;
STO 4; RCL 0; RCL 2; X; STO + 1; 1; STO $-$ 5; RCL 5; g x=0;
GTO 43; GTO 01; RCL 4; STO 5; RCL 1.

h) R_0 h; R_1 y_0,y_n; R_2 $P_{1/2},P_{n+1/2}$; R_3 2h,2nh; R_4 1,50; R_5 0,20;
R_6 (2+0,2h); R_7 N.

RCL 0; RCL 2; X; STO + 1; g RAD; RCL 3; f cos; 3; X; 1; +;
RCL 1; RCL 1; ABS; X; 2; X; $-$; RCL 0; X; 2; RCL 0; RCL 5; X;
$-$; RCL 2; X; +; RCL 6; $\div$; STO 2; RCL 0; 2; X; STO + 3; 1;
STO $-$ 7; RCL 7; g x=0; GTO 41; GTO 01; RCL 1; R/S; RCL 2.

i) R_0 h/2; R_1 y_0,y_n; R_2 $P_0,P_{n-1/2}$; R_3 a; R_4 b; R_5 -1; R_6 N.

g RAD; 2; RCL 0; RCL 3; X; STO 7; $-$; RCL 2; X; RCL 4;
RCL 1; f sin; $-$; 2; X; RCL 0; X; +; RCL 7; 2; +; $\div$; STO 2;
RCL 5; g x$<$0; GTO 28; GTO 32; 2; STO X 0; RCL 6; STO 5;
RCL 0; RCL 2; X; STO + 1; 1; STO $-$ 6; RCL 6; g x=0; GTO 42;
GTO 01; RCL 5; STO 6; RCL 1; R/S; RCL 2.

R_0 h/2; R_1 x_0,x_n; R_2 y_0,y_n; R_3 $x_0,x_{n-1/2}$; R_4 $y_0,y_{n-1/2}$; R_5 1, GM;
R_6 N; R_7 -1.

l) RCL 5; RCL 1; X; RCL 0; X; RCL 5; RCL 2; X; RCL 0; X;
RCL 1; g x^2; RCL 2; g x^2; +; f $\sqrt{x}$; 3; f y^x; $\div$; STO $-$ 4;
R $\downarrow$; f LAST x; $\div$; STO $-$ 3; RCL 7; g x$<$0; GTO 29; GTO 33;
2; STO X 0; RCL 6; STO 7; RCL 0; RCL 3; X; STO + 1; RCL 0;
RCL 4; X; STO + 2; 1; STO $-$ 6; RCL 6; g x=0; GTO 47; GTO 01;
RCL 7; STO 6; RCL 1.

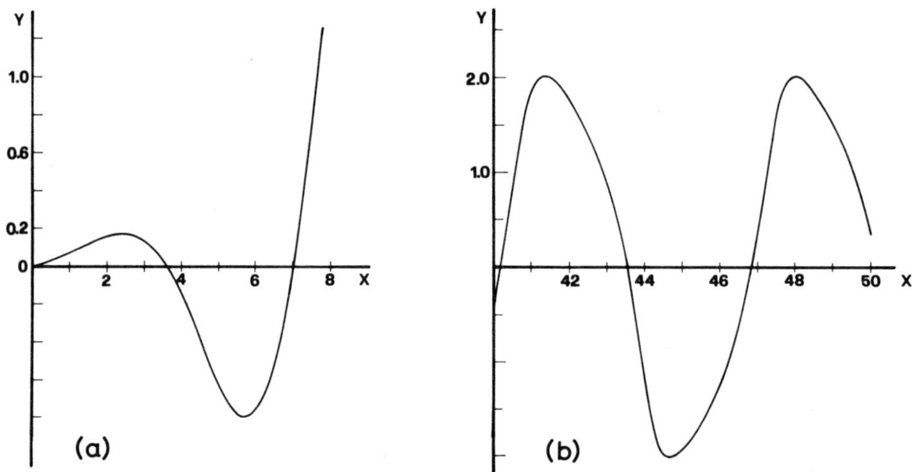

*FIG. 1   Diagram indicating the numerical solution of Van der Pol's equation.
(a) transient state, (b) steady state.*

The numerical solution of equation (h) of Table 1 (Duffing's equation) is shown in Fig. 2. Our results agree with those reported by Hayashi[4]. The occurrence of the $\frac{1}{2}$-harmonic oscillation is a nonlinear phenomenon. A discussion of example (1) can be found in reference 2.

Equation (i) of Table 1 describes the behaviour of many physical systems, for example: the compound pendulum[5], the synchronous induction motor[6] and the Josephson weak link[7].

This equation has no general analytical solution. The numerical solution shows that the steady-state behaviour depends on the initial conditions (nonlinear phenomenon).

The method has its own internal check of accuracy, since the step length h can be shortened to check whether this produces any significant change in the results.

CONCLUSIONS

The free access of the students from large first-year lecture classes to the facilities of 'Computer Centres', equipped with high speed computers, does not appear easily workable, and is not actually done in our university.

Programmable pocket calculators are still too expensive to be owned by all students. However, what appears to be now possible is to organize a 'Calculator Centre', on the model of the libraries, for lending the calculators (for use at the Centre or at home). The budget difficulties are not too severe. We are working in such a direction in our university.

Judging from the interest which the students maintained throughout the

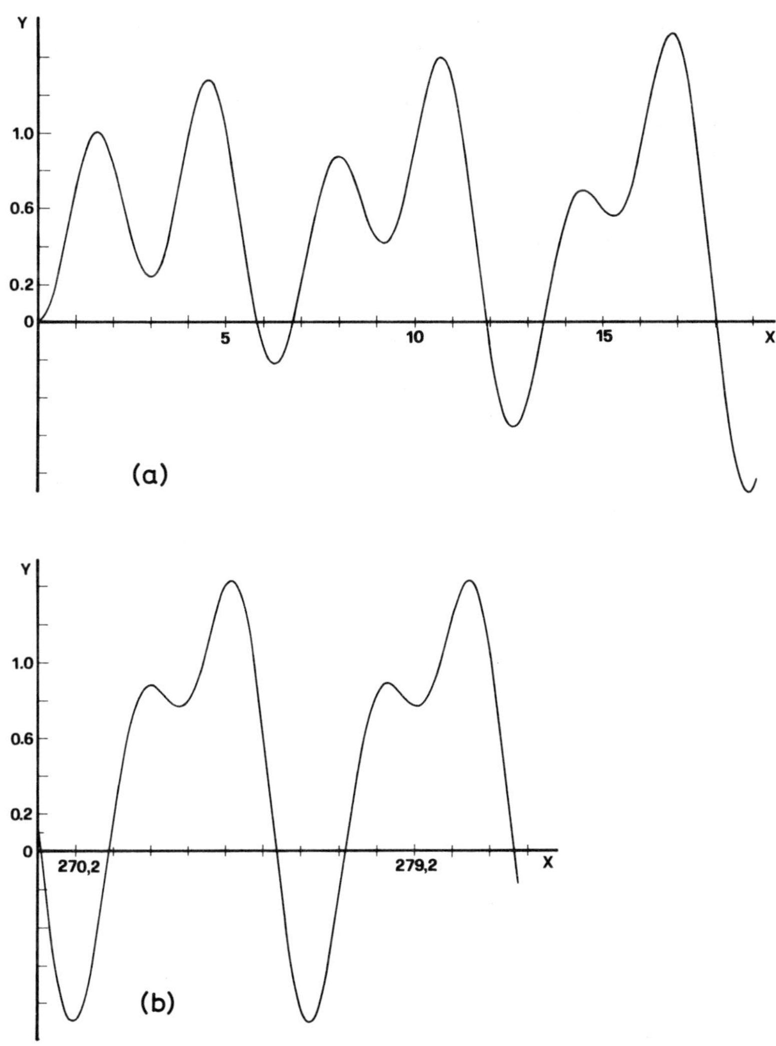

FIG. 2   *Diagram indicating the numerical solution of Duffing's equation.*
(a) transient state, (b) steady state.

short course, and from the quality of their reports during final examinations, we believe that the course presented meets a demand for numerical work closely related to the study of significant physical systems. The students appeared to grasp not only the basic concepts of numerical analysis and programming, but also an idea of the general capabilities and limitations of the computer.

ACKNOWLEDGEMENT
The authors wish to express their gratitude to Professor Arrigo L. Frisiani for

his extremely valuable recommendations. M. Biondi and D. Pescetti are indebted to the C.N.R. for financial support throughout the contract no. 78.00967.

REFERENCES

[1]   Example reference for numerical analysis: Conte, S. D., de Boor, C., *Elementary Numerical Analysis*, McGraw-Hill, (1972).

[2]   Feynman, R. P., Leighton, R. B., Sands, M., *The Feynman Lectures on Physics*, Vol. I, Chapter IX, Addison Wesley, (1963).

[3]   Hayashi, C., *Nonlinear Oscillations in Physical Systems*, p. 64, McGraw-Hill, (1964).

[4]   Ref. 6, p. 67.

[5]   Pedersen, N. F. and Hoffmann Soerensen, O., *Am. J. Phys.*, **45**, 994, (1977).

[6]   Alexandrovit, A. and Rootenberg, J., *Int. J. Elect. Engng. Educ.*, **7**, 313, (1969).

[7]   Falco, Charles M., *Am. J. Phys.*, **44**, 733, (1976).

A LABORATORY EXPERIMENT ON MICROPROCESSORS

S. J. CAHILL
School of Electrical and Electronic Engineering, Ulster Polytechnic, Northern Ireland

1 INTRODUCTION

In order to keep digital system education abreast of recent developments in programmed logic, it is necessary to extend the traditional random logic course to include the microprocessor (MPU). One approach to this additional component is to treat the MPU as a natural extension of random logic.

The design of MPU-based equipment involves an appreciation of both hardware and software concepts. Hardware design problems are solved in much the same way as random logic; viz. conceptually on paper, and with breadboarding techniques being used in the development and debugging stages. Software design involves the conceptual phase, which is implemented by algorithms and listings.

The software may be tested and debugged by entering and running the program in a software development system. Such prototyping systems are often general purpose microcomputers, with integral special-purpose software aiding in user program manipulation and debugging. Such development systems are the software equivalent of the breadboard.

Where the microprocessor-based design is being used to replace random logic circuitry, the hardware engineer must have some appreciation of software at the machine language level, in addition to the normal hardware techniques. It is for this category of students that this laboratory has been designed.

2 THE PHILOSOPHY OF THE EXPERIMENTAL APPROACH

A range of excellent development aids exist for MPU development[1]. Where large groups of students are being catered for, cost considerations restrict these to the single-board evaluation kits. Unfortunately these kits suffer from a lack of hardware flexibility, in that the architecture of the system cannot readily be altered by the student. Additionally LSI is often used for the efficient implementation of the support circuitry. However, for teaching purposes, a less sophisticated support system is preferable to demonstrate and reinforce the principles involved.

A better solution to the teaching problem is the use of a bus-orientated breadboard as the basis of a student-constructed microcomputer. Simple modules or single integrated circuits may be preassembled onto plug-in printed-circuit boards, inserted into the breadboard, as shown in Fig. 1. These

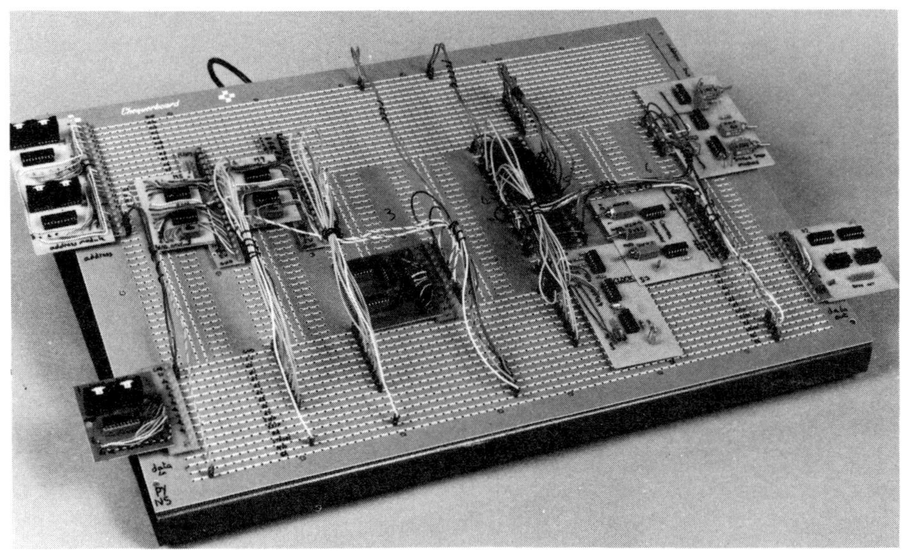

FIG. 1   The completed microcomputer.

modules are patched into the two 16-way buses, to the desired configuration. The breadboard is a standard unit manufactured by Fairhurst Instruments Ltd, Dean Court, Woodford Road, Wilmslow SK9 2LT, Cheshire.

The modules are manufactured by our own technician staff. In keeping with the philosophy of treating the microprocessor as just another integrated circuit, and not something 'magic', only standard TTL devices are used for all the supporting logic. This emphasises that the microprocessor may be treated as a normal device.

The microprocessor chosen for this experiment is the 6800. This device is eminently suitable for MPU experimentation because of its simple and uncluttered internal architecture, and the lack of multiplexing of the pins [2,3]. Machine programming in hexadecimal is straightforward [4,5,6]; and it is readily possible (and desirable) for the student to hand-assemble his programs, without requiring additional software support. However, because of the inherent flexibility of the technique, any microprocessor may be used in a similar manner.

3   THE EXPERIMENTAL CONTEXT

The laboratory experiment described in this paper has been used to illustrate the hardware aspects of MPU design for the school's final year higher technician courses (Higher National Diploma and A3 Higher National supplementary certificate). The course comprises a single two-hour lecture for each of 30 weeks. The subject matter ranges from conventional gate and counter design, through MSI and LSI, terminating in ten lectures on microprocessors. The supporting series of laboratory experiments mirror the lecture material, covering combinational and sequential circuits, accumulator adders, RAM and PROM memories and three-state bus driving. These are two-hour experiments, and are undertaken at fortnightly intervals.

The microprocessor element involves a total of eight hours, although some of the support modules (for example memory) have been introduced in earlier experiments.

4   THE MICROCOMPUTER CONFIGURATION

The aim of the laboratory experiment is to construct a simple prototyping system, whereby the machine language program may be entered (in hexadecimal) into the memory, with the microprocessor halted (direct memory access — DMA). When running, the microcomputer is to execute the program, after being initialised to the starting address. This is prestored in the two highest memory locations — the 6800 reset vector.

Fig. 2 shows the block schematic of the experiment microcomputer. This has been designed around the following specification:

(i)   An 8-bit microcomputer based on the 6800 MPU.
(ii)   A 256-byte RAM at memory locations 0000 to 00FF, to be used for data storage and the stack.
(iii) A 256-byte ROM at memory locations C000 to C0FF, to be used for program storage and reset/interrupt vector storage. This is simulated by RAM to facilitate alterations during program debugging.
(iv)   An output port at address 4000 displaying a hexadecimal byte; with the latched data being externally available.
(v)   An 8-bit hexadecimal coded data-input port, addressed at location 4000.
(vi)   A 16-bit hexadecimal-coded address port, which is to provide the address during DMA.
(vii) User controls for HALT; RESET; R/W; LOAD; SINGLE STEP; and READ ONLY (the latter preventing accidental overwriting of the program RAM during the program execution).

The memory map for the specified microcomputer is shown in Fig. 3.

Lack of space precludes a detailed analysis of the component modules, but a brief description is given below. However, the author will gladly supply on request both the digital laboratory notes used by the students, and also the printed-circuit layouts.

4.1   *Control interface module*

Under normal running conditions this module generates $STROBE = VMA \cdot \phi_2$, and the MPU directly controls the R/W line. Under DMA the user provides these signals, using the LOAD and R/W switches respectively. This change-over is accomplished by using the BUS AVAILABLE (BA) status output to switch over from the MPU generated signals to the user's control switches. BA goes high when the MPU is halted. In addition the module provides buffering, and holds the RESET switch.

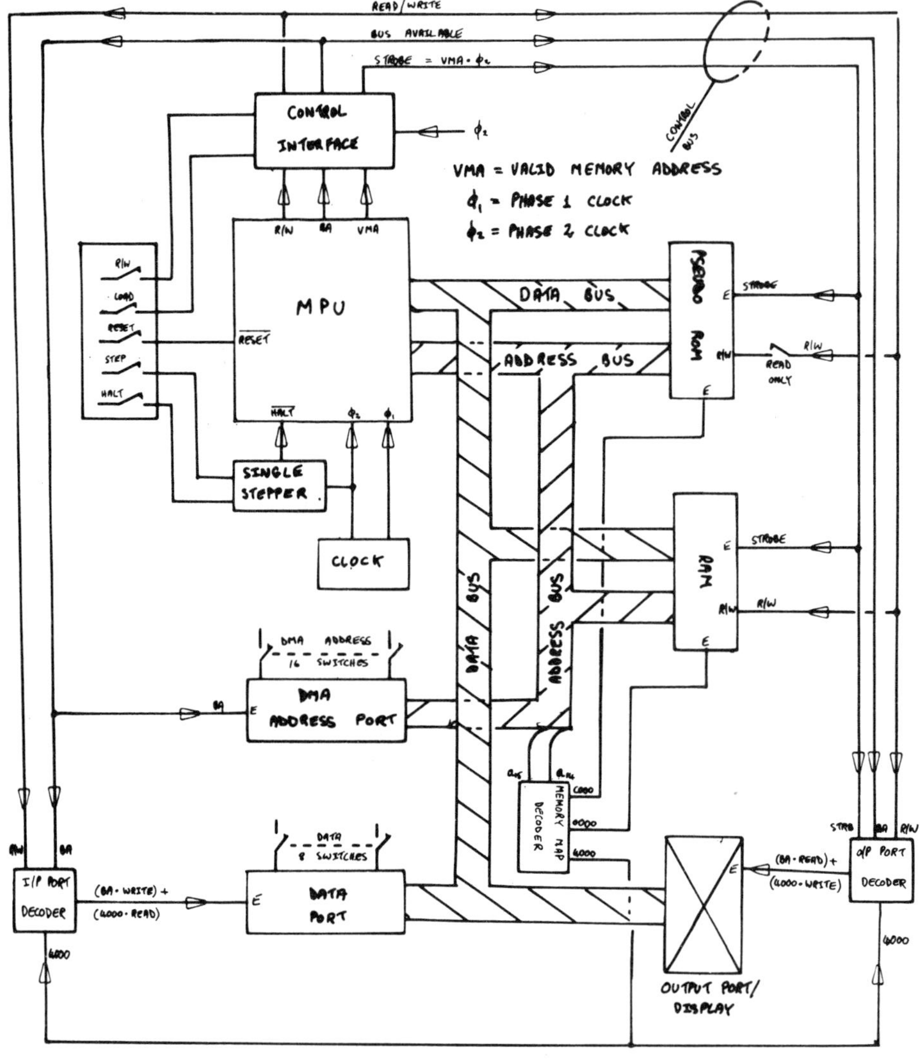

FIG. 2   Block schematic of laboratory microcomputer.

4.2   Clock module

The 6800 MPU requires a 2-phase non-overlapping clock. This is generated using a D latch (S1B, C & D) as a phase splitter, driven by a square-wave oscillator, S1A. High-current open-collector gates are used to give the full 5 ± 0.3V clock levels. Pull-up and damping resistors give transition times of less than 50 ns into a 160 pF load, as required by the 6800 MPU[2]. Standard TTL clock signals $\phi 1$, $\phi 2$, are provided as timing for the other modules. The component values shown in Fig. 5 give a nominal clock frequency of 200 kHz.

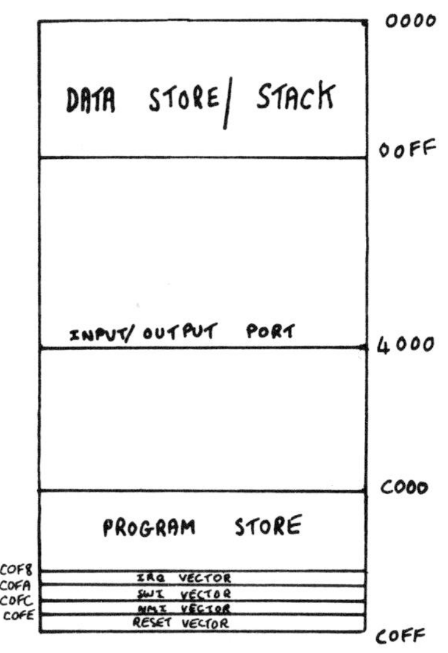

FIG. 3   Memory map.

4.3   *Single-step module*

This module provides the following facilities:

(i)   A debounced switch to activate the $\overline{\text{NMI}}$ interrupt.

(ii) A GO/HALT switch synchronised by ϕ_2 (F2A) to halt the MPU at the correct part of the cycle.

(iii) A single step facility which brings $\overline{\text{HALT}}$ high for one clock period each time the STEP switch is activated. The timing for this is provided by the three-state ($00 \rightarrow 10 \rightarrow 11$) dead-end counter F1. State 10 is decoded by NIC, and passed on to NID if the GO/HALT switch is at HALT.

4.4   *Input module*

This comprises a dual hexadecimal thumbwheel switch (EECO model 2A-21-50-34G, available from Waycom Ltd, Wokingham Road, Brackness, Berkshire RGR IND, England), buffered from the bus by an octal three-state driver. Either the National DM81LS95 or Texas SN74LS244 devices are suitable. As can be seen from the left-hand side of Fig. 1, three modules are used. One for the data bus, and two for the 16-bit address bus.

4.5   *Output module*

A dual-digit display is provided by using two Texas TIL 311 (or RS components RS586-734) hexadecimal latches/decoders/displays. Two 4-bit 74LS75 latches are used prior to the displays, to provide latched data for external purposes.

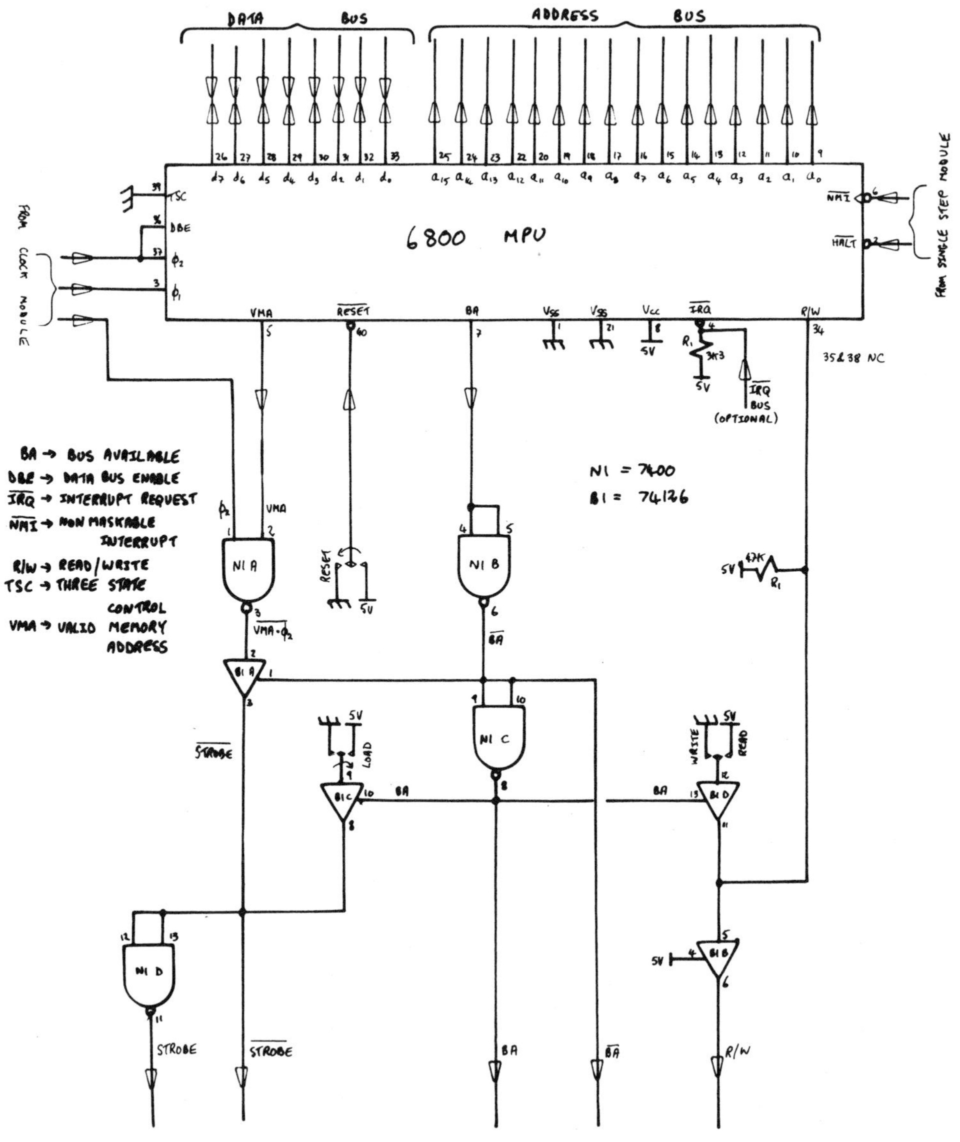

FIG. 4   Control interface and MPU.

4.6   *Memory module*

Two 256 × 4 bit 2112 RAM's are used in parallel to provide a 256-byte memory module. A switch in the R/W line allows the program store to be used in a READ-ONLY mode, once the program has been loaded. Both data and program stores use identical modules.

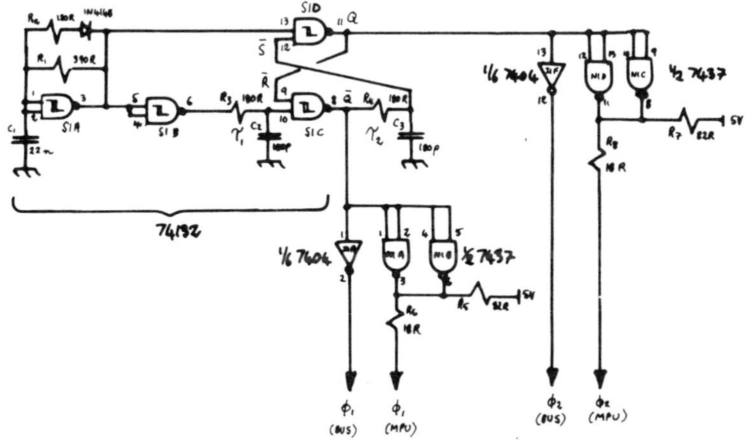

FIG. 5   Clock module.

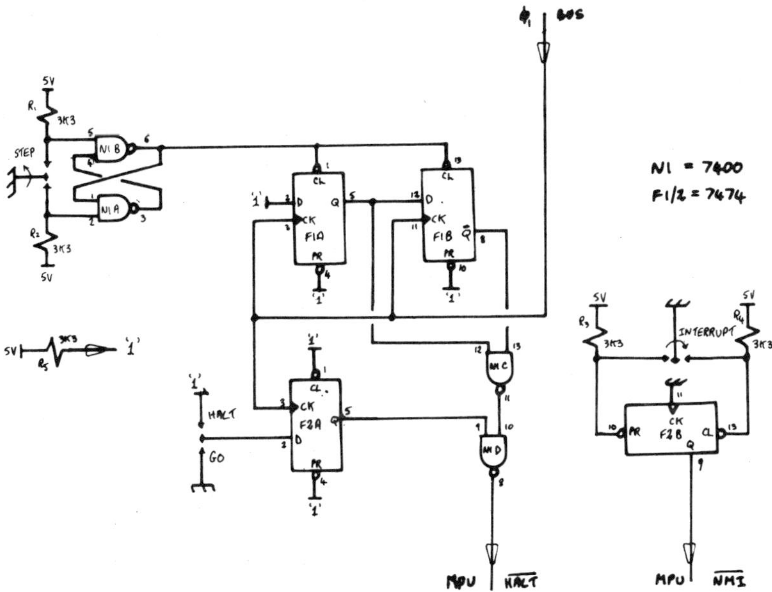

FIG. 6   Single step module.

4.7   *Memory map module*

This module decodes the address bus to:

(i)   Enable RAM when $a_{15}a_{14} = 00$ (0000 to 00FF)

(ii)   Enable RAM/ROM when $a_{15}a_{14} = 11$ (C000 to C0FF)

(iii)   Enable input when $a_{15}a_{14} = 01$ (4000) and R/W = high (READ), or when halted (BA = 1) and R/W = low (WRITE data into memory from input).

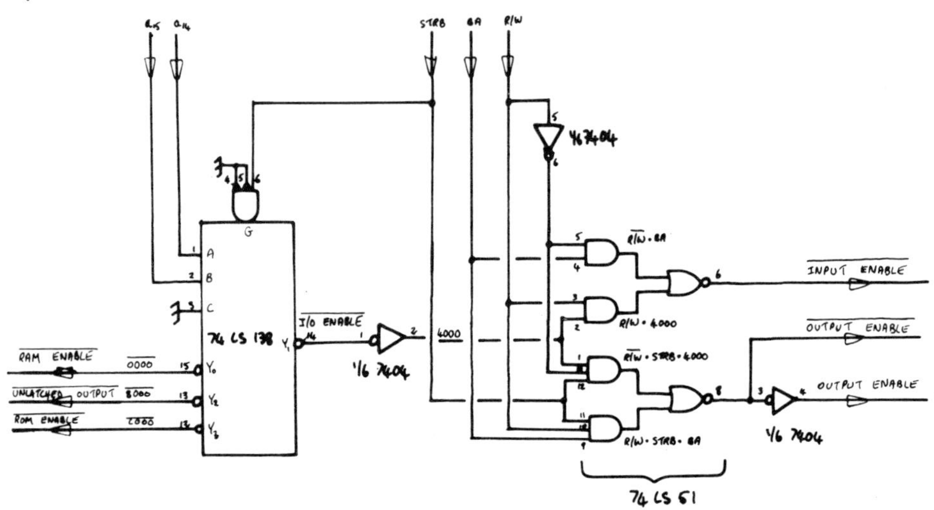

FIG. 7   Memory map module.

(iv) Enable output when $a_{15}a_{14} = 01$ (4000) and R/W = low (WRITE), or when halted and R/W = high (READ data from memory to output). Strobing is necessary for the output.

5 EXPERIMENTAL PROCEDURE

Each module is tested by the student on a 'stand alone' basis before patching into the breadboard. Once the complete microcomputer has been constructed, the overall operation must be established by loading and running a commissioning program; a simple example of which is listed below:

Step	Label	Location	Mnemonic	Data	Commentary
10	START	C000/1/2	(LDA A)$_E$ 4000	B6-40-00	Input data → A
20		C003/4	(ADD A)$_I$ 06	8B-06	Add six
30		C005/6/7	(STA A)$_E$ 4000	B7-40-00	Display answer at readout
40		C008/9	BRA START	20-F6	Go back to START
		C0FE/F	RESET VECTOR	C0-00	Program starts at C000

After loading the program, the microprocessor is vectored to the starting address when the RESET switch is pulsed.

Because of the program loop, all waveforms will be repetitive. For example, step 10 produces a pulse at the data-input module enable, followed at the output enable by a pulse resulting from step 30. This repetitive nature of the program allows waveforms to be monitored at all the component modules, which will quickly uncover any source of malfunction.

With the system running correctly, it is instructive to compare the generated waveforms (such as memory enables), against those given in the appropriate data sheets.

The hardware capabilities of the basic MPU system may be easily extended by the addition of alternative modules. For example, replacing the output module by a peripheral interface adaptor (PIA) will enable the student to familiarise himself with the software and hardware aspects of this device.

Some software development at machine level can be undertaken by the student. For example, the development of a simple moniter on PROM to enable the use of more sophisticated peripheral equipment, such as a keyboard. Use of the WAIT FOR INTERRUPT (WAI) instruction as a program break-point may be used to illustrate the concepts of the interrupt and stack. A simple interrupt routine may be written which displays the contents of the MPU registers, dumped into the stack by the WAI instruction.

Where this approach to MPU experimentation is being used for higher-level classes, such as for BSc students, emphasis may be directed towards design, rather than analysis. A typical design exercise is the provision of a serial output suitable for a teletypewriter (TTY). This will involve the provision of an asynchronous communication interface adaptor (ACIA), a TTL to 20 mA loop convertor, and suitable software development for the ACIA. Another possibility is to set the students the task of designing a microcomputer using a different MPU, such as the 8080. The class may be conveniently divided into groups for this exercise, each group designing one module.

6   CONCLUSION

Student reaction to the approach to MPU experimentation presented in this paper has been enthusiastic. The microprocessor is seen to be a logical development of the advent of LSI in random logic. As a consequence of this, the student is happy to accept the use of the commercial development system used by themselves during tutorial sessions, to verify the solutions to software examples (the Motorola ADS system with a large screen moniter).

7   REFERENCES

[1]   Best, P. J. et al., 'Introduction to Microprocessor Systems — Part 3', *Int. J. Elect. Enging. Educ.*, **14**, no. 3, pp. 269–279, (1977).

[2]   *M6800 Application Manual*, Motorola Semiconductor Products Inc, (1975).

[3]   Mazur, T. 'Put together a Complete Microcomputer', *Electronic Design*, **26**, no. 15, pp. 66–77, (July 19, 1976).

[4]   *M6800 Programming Manual*, Motorola Semiconductor Products Inc, (1975).

[5]   Steger, J. P., 'Introduction to Microprocessor Programming', *Electronic Engineering*, **47**, pp. 43–47, (October, 1975).

[6]   Leventhal, L., 'Put Microprocessor Software to Work', *Electronic Design*, **26**, no. 16, pp. 55–64, (Aug. 2, 1976).

A FLEXIBLE DEVELOPMENT SYSTEM FOR MICROPROGRAMMABLE MICROPROCESSORS

K. R. DIMOND and J. A. KING
The Electronics Laboratories, University of Kent at Canterbury, England

1 INTRODUCTION

It is now some years since microprocessors were made available to the electronics industry. The first microprocessors were born out of compromise, compromise between the conflicting constraints of the semi conductor manufacturer, the most important of these being cost, size of device, speed of operation and power dissipation. The devices which were incorporated into one integrated circuit had limited word length and speed of operation and had restricted input-output capacity, the speed of operation being determined principally by the technology employed, namely MOS.

An alternative approach was adopted by some semiconductor manufacturers and this was to employ a bipolar technology which would give much better operating speeds. This approach meant that a complete processor could not be fabricated in one integrated circuit, but would have to be made up of several integrated circuits connected together. This approach gives rise to increased cost of production, larger printed circuit board area, and cost of interconnection, but it does provide a bonus in terms of flexibility, for it is possible to tailor the processor to the precise application, and not have to 'bend' an unsuitable structure into the appropriate form for a particular application. This flexibility in configuration comes from the ability to be able to microprogram these processors. The technique of internal control of a computer will be discussed in greater detail in a later section.

One problem with a microprocessor is the way in which a programmer communicates with the device. With a minicomputer, low-level communication can take place by means of the switches on the control-panel. With the microprocessor, there is no control panel. An important development in microcomputer systems was the introduction of prototype development aids. Nowadays, most of the 8 and 16 bit single chip machines have a support chip which enables a teletype to take on the rôle of the front-panel, namely starting program execution at a specified point and inspecting registers etc. In addition, most have facilities for loading previously assembled programs into the memory and to a greater or lesser extent facilities for program diagnosis, i.e. setting of addresses which, when encountered, cause a return to a monitor program (break-points). From these first rudimentary systems, development systems have progressed dramatically. Systems are now available which have floppy-disc storage and allow programs to be assembled without using cross-facilities; they also enable the operation of processor, memory and peripherals to be monitored in detail.

For the multi-chip microprogrammed microprocessors the situation is very different; there are few design aids and prototyping units available. Those units which are available are dedicated to a particular range of microprocessors and cannot be used with devices of another manufacturer. The aim of this paper is to describe how a flexible prototyping unit may be constructed using a host minicomputer, for use with a range of microprogrammed microprocessors.

2 MICROPROGRAMMED-MICROPROCESSORS

Any current microprocessor is made up of a series of registers which hold the operands etc., together with an arithmetic-logic unit to combine selected register contents using appropriate operations. All machine instructions require for their execution a number of register-transfers and/or arithmetic-logic operations. For example, in any machine instruction the value of the program counter has to be updated; if the instruction is not a jump or branch instruction, then the updated value will just be the previous value incremented. For branch or jump instructions the value will be that specified in the other fields of the instruction.

Consider the situation in Fig. 1. Here there is a simple processor made up of 3 registers and an Arithmetic Logic Unit (ALU). The contents of the registers may be interchanged by putting the contents on the appropriate bus (A or B). Similarly the result of the arithmetic-logic operation can be fed back to the registers by the bus C. For this structure to realise useful operation, a set of control signals is required which selects which of the registers is to drive the input bus of the ALU, which of its repertoire of instructions the ALU is to perform, and where the result of this operation is to go.

The classic way of generating these control signals would be to build a sequential machine which would take the operation code, and clock signals and generate the appropriate control signals. Wilkes[1] considered this problem of control of computers and realised that the control signals could be thought of as being generated by a low-level program, the micro-program.

A simple microprogrammed controller has the structure shown in Fig. 2. Here we see that the control signals are stored in a table. The state of the control signal is stored for every step in the execution of the machine instruction. In addition, there is part of the table which determines the next set of control signals to be produced. Each of the rows of the table is called a micro-instruction, and each column of the control field is called a micro-operation, i.e., it controls one basic entity.

The sequential operation of this controller is as follows. Initially the register is set to a value which has been derived in some way from the machine code of the processor. This value then addresses a certain row of the table; as this row is addressed, the appropriate control signals are then generated. In addition, the next address field is applied to the inputs of the register so that the next

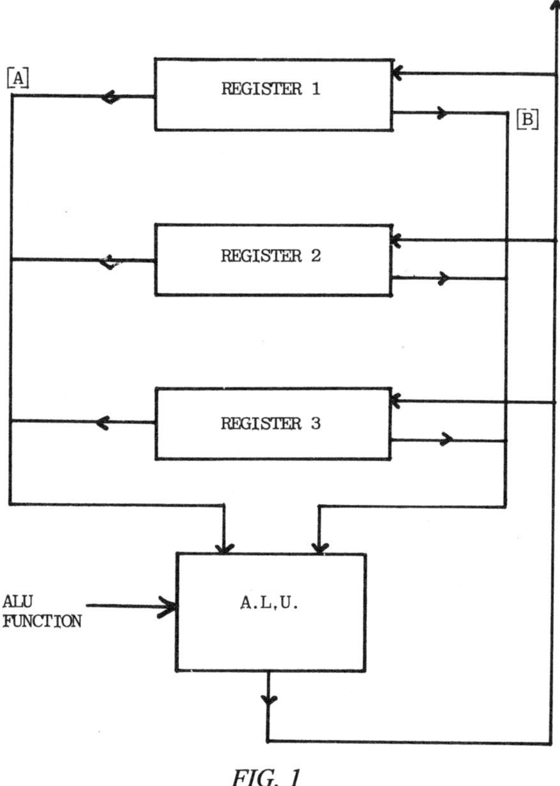

FIG. 1

microinstruction in the sequence is identified. This basic approach can be extended by modifying the address of the next microinstruction by some conditional information, which then means that the flow of microprogram control is dependent on conditions inside or outside the processor.

It will readily be appreciated that microprogramming is an extremely flexible way of controlling the operation of a processor. The table of next addresses and microoperations enables a variety of different instruction sets and control structures to be achieved using the same basic machine.

Current microprogrammed microprocessors have an overall structure as shown in Fig. 3. Here it will be seen that the processor consists of three main units. The RALU carries out the same function as in our illustrative example above. The microprogram memory is the implementation of the table representing the microinstructions. The microprogram sequencer needs a little more description. This unit provides more sophisticated control facilities for microprogram execution. In all minicomputers there are structures which allow for unconditional and conditional branching and for incorporating subroutines into the program. These facilities are included because programmers find them essential if efficient programs are to be written. Exactly the same is true of the microprogram. There must be facilities for branching and subroutining etc. All

Next address field
control field
D
E
C
O
D
E
R
0
1
2
Register
To control transfers
between registers
To control
ALU
function

FIG. 2

To Control Peripherals
Microprogram
address
Microprogram
Control
Unit
MCU
Microprogram
Memory
Register and
Arithmetic
Logic
Unit
RALU
Microprogram
branch address
arithmetic conditions
Machine Instruction
Operations Code.
Data Input/Output
to R.A.L.U.

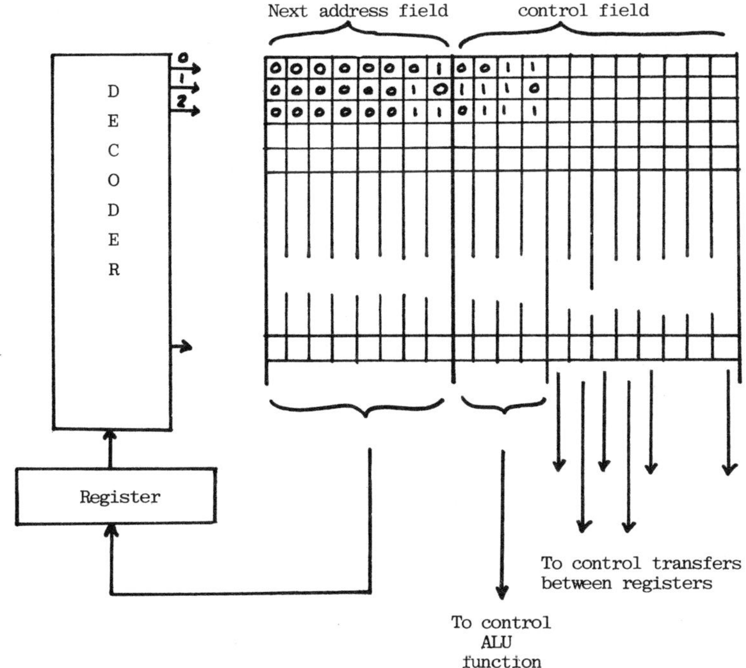

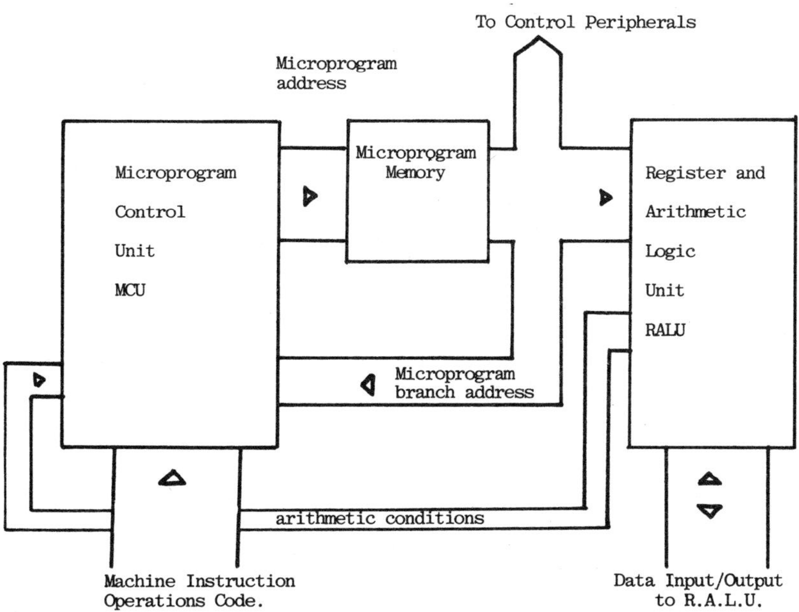

FIG. 3

these structures require only a minor modification to the overall microprogram structure and are incorporated in the MCU.

At the present time it is not possible to incorporate all the logic for an MCU or an RALU into a single integrated circuit. In fact, if this were the case, flexibility in design would be severely limited. Hence these devices are partitioned. They are partitioned in a modular fashion so that, by combining a suitable number of devices in parallel, a unit of the required width may be built up. This approach has been almost universally described as the bit-slice approach. In this way the appropriate length of register in the RALU can be constructed by connecting together the appropriate number of slices. For the MCU it will be seen that this has to operate on data fields to produce the appropriate microprogram address. Thus an MCU of appropriate addressing capability i.e. microprogram address width can be made up by connecting the requisite number of 'MCU' slices together. The earliest components were based on a two-bit width of 'slice', i.e. each slice had register elements two-bits wide and of course an arithmetic unit of equivalent size. Nowadays these devices have a width of four bits making for much more compact realisations.

3 STRUCTURE OF THE PROTOTYPING UNIT

There are two separate parts to the design of any digital system, one is familiarisation with the basic components, the other is the development of the system with all the attendant hardware, firmware and software. With microprogrammed microprocessors, the basic components are quite complicated. They all have a large number of internal storage elements and hence they have a great many internal states. It therefore takes quite some considerable time to investigate their behaviour fully. The simplest way to carry out this investigation is to connect switches to all the inputs of the device and to connect indicator lamps to the outputs, but this is a very cumbersome system to use. The main problem is that to examine the contents of several registers, many different switch patterns have to be entered; a mistake in any one of these may change the state of the component, and hence require all the instructions to be supplied again.

What is required is a simple means of exciting the inputs and finding out what changes they invoke, but for this to be done in a controlled environment, one which helps the user. The most flexible way of controlling this testing environment is by generating the inputs and reading the outputs of the device using a general-purpose computer. This can be provided with facilities which enable a whole series of commands to be issued once a simple command has been input.

The second stage of development is when the components are themselves connected together and the firmware and software are being developed. During the early stages of this phase the design is likely to have a very flexible structure. Any prototyping system must have a great deal of flexibility if it is to be of real use. Again, the use of a general-purpose computer in the overall system allows a great deal of flexibility.

The overall structure of the prototyping system is described in Fig 4. The
host computer is a PDP 11/40 with RT-11 operating system. One 16-bit
parallel interface provides communication between the microprocessor components and the host machine. It will be seen that the output and input of the
interface are connected to multiplexors. These allow up to 16 different inputs
and 16 different outputs to be connected to the interface. Selection of the input
and outputs is done by 4 bits in the interface control and status registers. To
allow communications with the microprocessor components, all their functional inputs are connected to output ports and their outputs are connected to
input ports. Whilst most of the designs which have been carried out so far have
been for 16 bit machines, there are a large number of input and output ports so
it would be quite easy to develop systems with a much wider word-length. The
interconnection of these inputs and outputs is carried out by programmed
instructions within the host machine. It is this method of interconnection which
provides the overall flexibility.

4   SOFTWARE CONFIGURATION

There are two approaches which might be used to develop the software for this
system. One is to develop a very flexible suite of programs which will allow the
user to use all the facilities at his disposal in a variety of different configurations. This provides the software system designer with severe problems, since
it is difficult to know initially how a unit may be used at a later stage, and it is
difficult to predict the sort of components that manufacturers will provide in
the future.

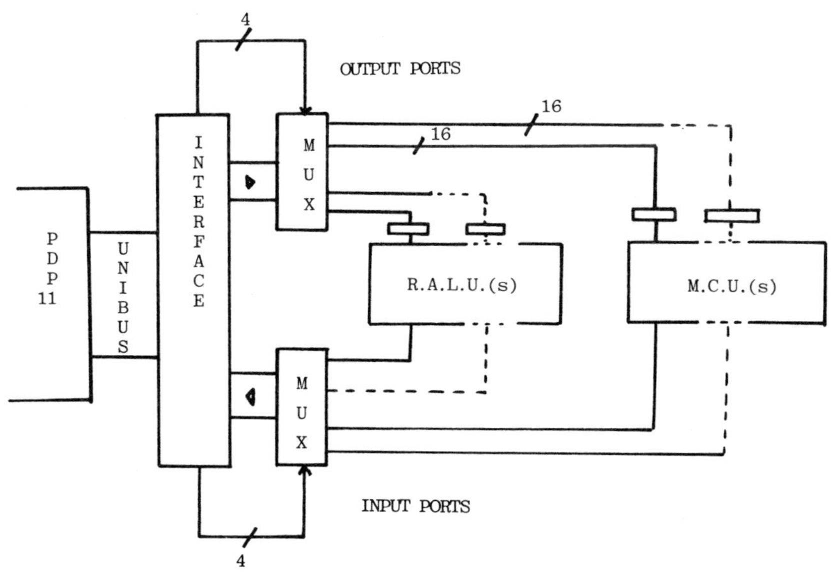

FIG. 4

In view of these difficulties, this approach was not adopted; instead, extreme flexibility was provided by incorporating a software interface to the hardware of the development system within an existing high-level language. By choosing this method, the user may manipulate data and input and output it to the hardware, using the high-level language program, which he himself has written. He can therefore make the program as lavish or simple as he chooses. In considering the language to use, uppermost in our thoughts was that there should be good interaction, and ease of program modification. Thus it was decided to incorporate a set of special assembly language subroutines, for communication with the hardware, into the BASIC language on the PDP-11. When the user wishes to communicate with the interface, and thence to the microprocessor components, he simply evokes the appropriate subroutines using the 'CALL' command.

The choice of BASIC does have one disadvantage, and that is the question of speed of operation. The BASIC implementation is by means of an interpreter, and hence will inevitably run slower than a compiled code. It is felt that this is a small sacrifice to pay for the widespread knowledge of BASIC and the ease of program development.

Whilst the detailed arrangements of the software drivers are installation-dependent, it is possible to describe how the software for driving the interface was subdivided into subroutines. There are two subroutines for inputting data to the computer and two for outputting from the computer. These are referenced as follows:

'ICNT' — sets the port selection bits for the input interface control and status register.

e.g. 10 CALL 'ICNT' ('0001') will take its string argument '0001' and set the selection bits on status register to '0001' (Port 1).

'IBUF' — reads a 16 bit data word from interface into its argument.

'OCNT' — sets the port selection bits for the output interface control and status register.

'OBUF' — outputs its string argument to the interface as a 16 bit data word.

These four 'CALL' statements can be used to carry out communications with the interface unit and hence the microprocessor components.

5 FAMILIARISATION WITH MICROPROCESSOR COMPONENTS
It has already been said that in order that a designer may become familiar with a microprocessor component, he must have facilities to enable him to exercise the device. If this is done with a manual system then mistakes in inputs can propagate themselves and obscure the true operation of the device. When a host computer becomes part of the exercising unit then the situation becomes much more controlled. If the host computer can be programmed in a simple highly interactive language then the complete system may be tailored to a

particular designer's needs. The switches and indicator lamps are replaced by a visual display unit. This provides a much more convenient method of determining the operation of the unit.

To elaborate on this point, consider how a designer might become familiar with a RALU chip. In the description of the basic components of a microprogrammed microprocessor, it was seen that the operation of this unit was controlled by an instruction bus. The repertoire of instructions which the RALU will carry out will include AND, OR, ADD, SUBTRACT, these operations being carried out on selected registers in the device. Now it would be quite possible to specify which operation is to be performed by inputting to the VDU and thence to the RALU the binary quantity which causes this operation to be performed. But it is quite likely that, during a sequence of several operations, errors can be made. The accuracy of inputting commands can be improved quite dramatically by representing the binary operation by mnemonics. When a mnemonic is entered, most probably as a string variable, the BASIC program handling the communication between the VDU and the RALU can translate this string into its equivalent binary form. As an example of more complicated operations, there will be occasions when a sequence of instructions are used repeatedly. Rather than inputting these instructions singly, it would also be quite possible for the communication program to invoke this sequence of instructions when a user-defined pseudo-instruction is entered. This is an example of a simple macro facility.

6   MICROPROGRAM DEVELOPMENT

Once the designer has become familiar with the basic microprocessor components, the next phase in system design is to develop the structure of the processor and the microprogram. There are several approaches which may be adopted. The most straightforward is the construction of a 'bread-board'; this is a set of microprocessor and associated integrated circuits connected together in a form which can be reasonably easily modified. A second approach is to purchase a prototyping unit, if there is one available. A third method is to simulate the whole unit on some larger computer.

The first approach, employing a bread-board, is quite common, but has the disadvantage that changes in bus structure etc. are reasonably time-consuming to make. The second alternative, that of purchasing a prototype unit, has the disadvantage that it will be unlikely to be compatible with any other different microprocessor. The third approach, that of simulation, gives the utmost flexibility, as all facilities etc. can be changed under software control. The problems occur when the microprocessor action has to be simulated, as it is difficult to identify all possible modes of operation from the manufacturers' data sheets.

The approach which we have adopted for a prototype unit overcomes most of the above disadvantages. There seems little point in simulating a microprocessor when it already exists. When flexibility of connection is needed then it is sensible to do this by means of software. In a teaching environment, it is

important to be able to use the same basic facilities for a range of microprocessors. The structure of the system is given in block form in Fig. 5. This should
be looked at in conjunction with Fig. 3. Here it will be seen that the main
components of the microprocessor, the RALU and MCU are connected to the
host computer by the multiplexed interface. The simple input-output subroutines, which have been described, allow communication with the microprocessor components to the interface. In order to connect these units together,
all that is required is a few statements in BASIC, to take the output from one
unit and relay it to the input of another unit.

The microprogram memory does not exist as a separate unit at this stage in
the design. Instead an area of the main memory of the host machine is dedicated to this function. This allows microinstructions to be changed very
easily, using a variety of high-level editing techniques. It will be seen from the
diagram that the MCU device generates the microinstruction address. As soon
as the current address is valid, it is read in to the host processor. Here there is a

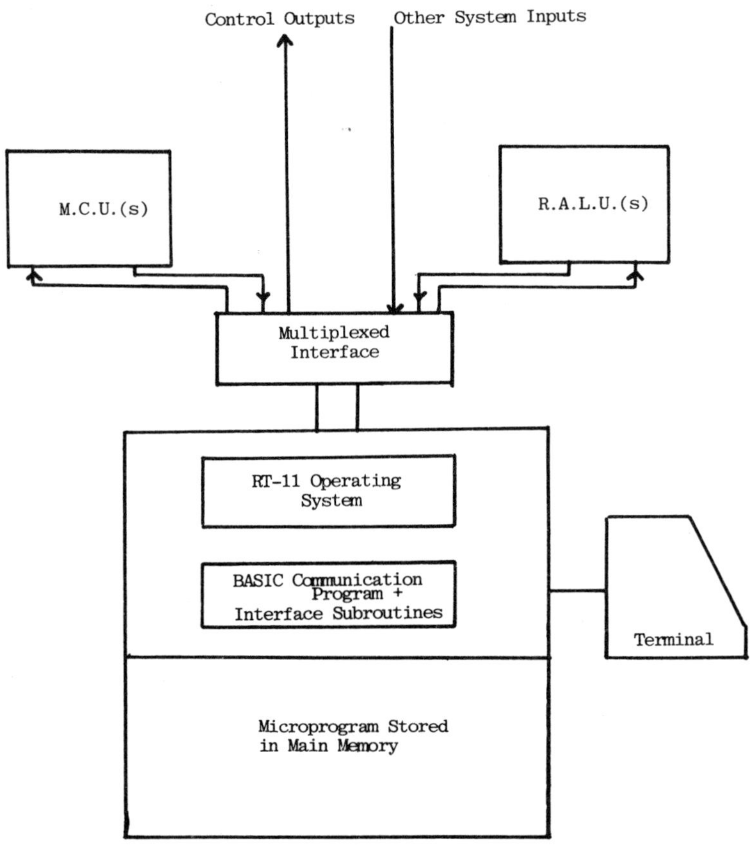

FIG. 5

mapping routine which takes the microinstruction address and then maps this to the real address of this microinstruction in memory. This is accessed and the microinstruction is passed back to the appropriate inputs of the RALU etc. Additional control fields can either be output to the visual display unit or could be output to a spare output port on the interface. Once the microinstruction has been accessed then the rest of the microinstruction execution can continue. In its simplest form, the microinstruction memory could consist of a 'string array' in BASIC and hence the mapping routine is very simple. For more complicated and larger microprograms this microprogram memory could be stored in memory in a suitable format and accessed by an assembly language subroutine.

It will now be apparent that the prototype system will execute micro-instructions quite slowly. The approach does, however, have one very significant advantage, and that is that as every stage of microinstruction execution requires the host computer to carry out an action, in the course of this action the host computer can allow the user to determine the state of the microprocessor. In this way the microprogram may be executed a single microinstruction at a time and the action of each microinstruction on the microprocessor can be ascertained before the next is executed.

As the program for interconnecting the units and accessing microinstructions is written in BASIC then it is possible for the user to modify the degree of interaction required, depending on the state of development of the micro-program. Thus modules of microprogram which have been well-tested can be executed with no extra user interaction, whilst untested modules would be tested with a great deal of interaction.

The slow speed of execution is likely to prove a problem only during the final stages of development. This will be when the microprogram logic has been proved, and it is important to test out interactions of the microprocessor with the peripheral equipment. For this final stage, it is necessary to build a separate microprogram store employing high speed RAM. For this phase the prototype unit is of use in loading the RAM when power is first applied to the system.

7 CONCLUSION

This article has described a flexible microprogrammed microprocessor development system which has been developed at the University of Kent. The techniques employed are very flexible and can be used with any micro-programmed microprocessor or any reasonably large microcomputer acting as host. The facet of the project which has proved most useful is the incorporation of special driver routines in the language BASIC. This has made the software development extremely easy and provided almost limitless flexibility.

8 REFERENCE

[1]   Wilkes, M. V. 'The best way to design an automatic calculating machine', *Manchester University Computer Inaugural Conference Proceedings*, p. 16, (1951).

A BASIS FOR LABORATORY WORK WITH BIT-SLICE MICROPROGRAMMABLE MICROPROCESSORS

A. C. DAVIES and D. IBRAHIM
Department of Electrical and Electronic Engineering, The City University,
London

INTRODUCTION

The fixed-instruction-set single-chip MOS microprocessors (such as the 8080 &
6800) are now commonplace in electrical engineering and in computer science
departments of universities and polytechnics, and provision of undergraduate
lecture courses and laboratory work on such microprocessors and their
applications is increasing rapidly.

Although such general-purpose microprocessors have almost unlimited
applications and the importance of their impact on electronic system design
can hardly be over-emphasized, nevertheless there are some application areas
where higher speed, longer wordlengths or other special requirements make the
bipolar bit-slice microprogrammable microprocessors (such as the Intel 3000,
AMD 2900, and Fairchild 9400) attractive. Also, working with microprogrammable microprocessors seems likely to provide a better understanding of the
internal operation of programmed machines, and therefore is of importance
from an educational point of view. The overwhelming majority of microprocessor users have no opportunity to influence the design of microprocessor chips
(their creativity is limited to the ways in which they utilize them for applications) whereas the microprogrammable devices permit the user to experiment
with different instruction sets and, within limits, to try out different
architectures.

There appears, therefore, to be a strong case for extending educational
activities associated with microprocessors to include bit-slice devices.

OBSTACLES TO USING BIT-SLICE MICROPROCESSORS

There are some rather obvious reasons why few electrical engineering or computer science departments have so far embarked on work with bit-slice processors.

The cost reason.   The individual components are more expensive, and likely to
remain so because they are necessarily a multi-package solution to a restricted
range of engineering problems (in marked contrast to the vast market which
confronts the single-chip general-purpose microcomputer, as a result of which
commercial pressures cause the spectacular price reductions that are so
common as to be almost taken for granted).

Self-contained single board MOS microcomputers with a simple monitor-debug program in ROM and a teletype interface can be purchased for around £150. These provide an inexpensive way of starting microprocessor work, and usually have sufficient facilities for them to be incorporated into prototype equipment for real applications.

Although some manufacturers of bit-slice processors provide single-board 'learning kits' for a comparable price, these have only a primitive interface (toggle-switches and light-emitting diodes), and are in no sense complete microcomputers. They are intended only to provide some familiarity with microprogramming and with the features of the particular bit-slice chip family. To construct a complete microcomputer from bit-slice components is a far more expensive task.

The concept reason.   When the Intel 8008 was first introduced, unfamiliarity with the concepts involved was one of the major obstacles to engineers wishing to use the device. Given facilities now widely available, the novice need only learn the essentials of the assembly language of a particular general-purpose microprocessor, and he can then quite quickly proceed to using a simple micro-processor development system and continue until he has working software for at least straightforward applications. This can be achieved prior to understand-ing the hardware-details (interconnections, timing, bus control signals, etc.). He need never know much about the internal operations of the microprocessor (in fact, the manufacturer often does not divulge the details of this anyway).

In contrast, a much more thorough understanding of hardware details is needed in order to even begin to use bit-slice processors, and the selection of an instruction set and its implementation in microinstructions is a complex procedure, for which there are no readily-available software tools. The novice must progress through all these stages and construct, or have constructed, a substantial piece of hardware before he has even the beginnings of a usable microcomputer. The software tools (assemblers, simulators, monitor-debug routines, etc.) which the user of a general-purpose microprocessor takes for granted are not available to him, and he is in a rather worse position than someone who writes 8080 software in hexadecimal machine code!

SOLUTIONS

Just as the user of a general purpose microprocessor can better understand the significance of the hardware details after he has written some successful software, and thus has understood what the hardware is for, it seems likely that if the user of a bit-slice processor could more easily experiment with the relationships between instructions and microinstructions, and with details of microprogram execution, he would subsequently be better able to compre-hend the hardware, and make a critical judgement of alternative architectures.

The learning kits provided by manufacturers are intended for exactly this purpose, but their primitive user-interface and limited facilities are an impedi-ment to easy learning.

At the City University, a 'learning kit' for the AMD 2900[1] has been used as a laboratory experiment for final year engineering undergraduates taking computer engineering. Each group has typically spent two 3-hour laboratory periods working with it, the objective being to give them some practical experience of using microprogramming concepts.

Limitations that have become apparent include the time taken in loading the microprogram via toggle switches, and recording and understanding the behaviour by observation of a row of light-emitting diodes while single-stepping through the microprogram.

To overcome these limitations, and to provide for further development of the experimental work, a controller using an F8 microprocessor has been developed to simplify and extend the use of the learning kit. The toggle switches have been removed, and replaced by connections to the I/O ports of the F8, and the signals which activate the light-emitting diodes are also taken to these I/O ports. All the manual operations are thus replaced by control signals from the F8, which also stores the outputs for subsequent tabulation and study.

The F8 system is built up from a single-board evaluation kit comprising CPU, 1K byte RAM, four 8 bit bidirectional input/output ports (one of which is used for the teletype/VDU interface) and 1K byte of ROM containing a monitor-debug program (DDT1)[2].

The control program (AMD2900 MONITOR) is stored in a 2708 1K byte EPROM, and utilizes various subroutines (such as teletype input and output routines) available in the F8 Monitor (DDT1). The basic essentials of the AMD2900 Monitor could be provided by a program of about 256 bytes, but the extra space available in the 2708 has been used to store helpful messages to guide the user during operation and to provide extra facilities. As a result, the AMD2900 Monitor almost completely fills the 2708.

After switching the power on, a 'reset' button enables the system to be put into F8 Monitor command-mode, from which the command E1000 (= execute program with start address 1000) initiates operation in the 2900 Monitor command-mode.

The memory map of the system is shown in Fig. 1. The RAM is used for storing the microprogram (prior to loading into the AMD2900) and for storing the results of an execution-run on the AMD2900. Additionally, the last 80 bytes (designated RAM save area) are used by the F8 Monitor in connection with its breakpoint routine, but this is not relevant to the operation of the 2900 Monitor[3].

THE AMD2900 LEARNING KIT

The AMD2900 kit incorporates one 2901 four-bit bipolar microprocessor, one 2909 microprogram sequencer, the microprogram memory (in RAM), and some other registers and multiplexers. The 2901 microprocessor contains the arithmetic and logic unit (ALU), 16 scratch-pad registers and a 4-bit extension (Q) register.

The microprogram memory consists of 16 words of 32 bits, each word being

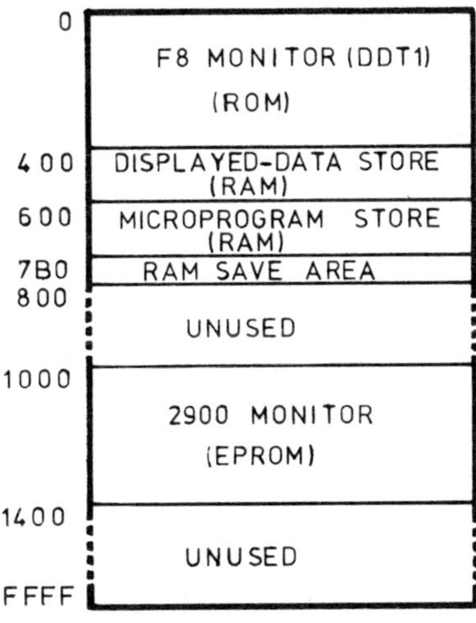

FIG. 1   F8 Memory map.

divided into eight 4-bit fields, defined as follows:

Field	Significance
7	Branch address
6	Next instruction control
5	ALU destination and MUX1
4	ALU source and MUX0
3	ALU function and carry-input bit
2	A register address select of 2901
1	B register address select of 2901
0	D (Direct data input of 2901)

MUX0 and MUX1 are single bits which control shift and rotate microoperations in the 2901. The 16-word register file of the 2901 has two ports A and B, providing a two-address instruction capability.

During execution of a microprogram one of eight alternative groups of four bits may be monitored

Display Code	
0	Microprogram sequencer output
1	2901 output
2	Flags (carry-out, overflow, sign, zero)
3	Miscellaneous (parity, generate, propagate, test condition)
4	Status register (holds states of flags)
5	2901 shift
6	2907 bus (inverted 2901 output)
7	2907 receiver (equal to 2901 output)

The 'next instruction control' field in each word is decoded in a PROM which provides for various conditional branch and subroutine-call micro-instructions. Fig. 2 shows the principal system components.

A more complete explanation and further details are given in the handbook supplied with the kit[1].

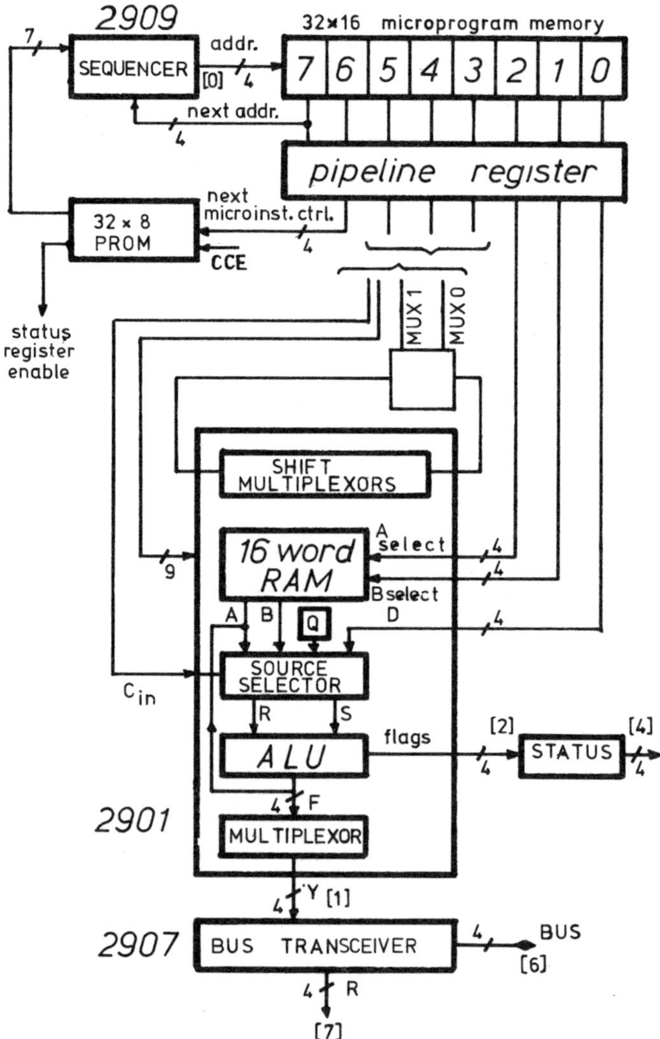

FIG. 2   *Principal AMD2900 kit components. Digits in square parentheses correspond to display code.*

CONNECTING THE F8 AND 2900

The four eight-bit I/O ports of the F8 are allocated as follows:

Port 0 4 bits used for clock, memory-load, run-mode and load-mode
4 bits used for data display light-emitting diodes
Port 1 4 bits used for microprogram memory address
4 bits used for microprogram memory data
Port 4 3 bits used for RAM and multiplexer selection
Port 5 3 bits used for teletype/VDU interface (Asynchronous, 20 mA loop, 110/300 baud)

These connections are illustrated in Fig. 3.

In load-mode, a pulse from the memory-load bit of port 0 causes the memory data to be loaded (address and data both being provided at port 1 and the field being provided at port 4). In run-mode, a pulse from the clock bit of port 0 single-steps the 2901, and the data displayed on the light-emitting diodes (as selected by the display code at port 4) is transferred via port 0 into the RAM of the F8.

STRUCTURE OF THE 2900 MONITOR

The basic structure of the 2900 monitor program is conventional, as indicated by the following code. More details are illustrated in Fig. 4.

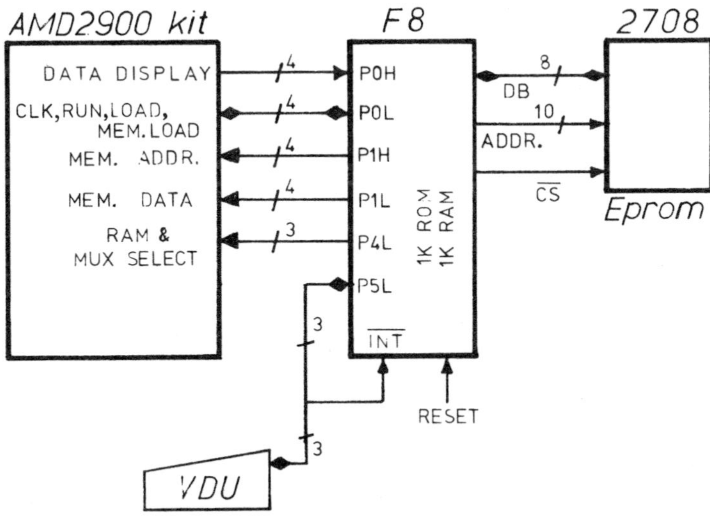

FIG. 3   F8 and AMD2900 interconnections (DB = data bus; ADDR = address; P0, P1, P4, P5 = 8-bit I/O ports; H = most significant half-byte; L = least significant half-byte).

```
decode and implement command

Loop:   print '$'
        read  command letter
        if(command-letter = 'E') do execution routine
        if(command-letter = 'M') do memory-display routine
        if(command-letter = 'T') do tabulation of previous execution
        if(command-letter = 'H') print list of available commands
        if(command-letter = 'Q') return to F8 monitor
        if(command-letter = 'S') set fast load and execute mode
        if(command-letter = 'F') set slow load and execute mode
        if(command-letter = 'L') load microprogram from F8 RAM
        if(command-letter = 'N') do microprogram-entry routine
        if(unrecognised command) print '?'
        goto loop


execution routine

read N,D
if(1<N<255) then print 'EXECUTING'
                  execute N microinstructions in display mode D
                  print 'FINISHED'
             else if(N=C) then dowhile (system not reset) print 'EXECUTING'
                                                           execute continuously in
                                                           display mode D

                                 endwhile
                                 return to F8 monitor
                             else print 'N TOO LARGE'
                  endif
endif
goto loop

memory display routine
read N
F8RAMpointer:= 600+8N
print N
        F8RAMpointer - value
        microprogram word with address N
goto loop
```

FIG. 4   Outline of 2900 Monitor program.

print 'heading'
perform print '$'
       read 'command'
       decode and implement command
until (command = quit)
goto F8 monitor

The F8 monitor has dump and load commands which enable the microprogram
to be saved on paper tape. Each microprogram word is stored as eight sequential
bytes starting with field 7. The most significant half of each byte holds the
address (0 to F) and the least-significant half specifies the contents of the 4-bit
field. Thus, if microprogram address 6 were required to hold the 32 bit word
FF338040 this would be stored in the F8 RAM as 6F,6F,63,63,68,60,64,60. The
field sequence within any word must be adhered to, but the words themselves

102

may be stored in any sequence. The last field of the last word is followed by FF which acts as a terminator for the load routine in the 2900 monitor.

Execution of the 2900 monitor is initiated from the F8 monitor, to which the user may return by typing a Q (= quit) command.

To prompt the user to enter a command, the F8 monitor types a period '.' and the 2900 monitor types a currency symbol '$', so that it is easy to distinguish which one is executing. An 'H' (= help) command provides the user with a list of all available commands.

The microprogram in the F8 RAM is loaded into the 2900 system by the 'L' (= load) command, after which execution of any number of microinstructions (from 1 to 255) can be specified. The execute command takes the form E N,D where the first (N) parameter specifies the number of microinstructions to be executed. If $N = C$, execution continues indefinitely until the system-reset button is operated. The group of four bits to be monitored during execution is selected by the second (D) parameter of the E command and is displayed on light-emitting diodes during execution and simultaneously stored in the F8 RAM for subsequent tabulation (using the 'T' command) to facilitate understanding of the preceding execution-run.

Hexadecimal notation is used throughout for addresses and data (except when specifying the number of execution steps, which is entered as a decimal number).

Fast and slow modes of loading and execution are provided by 'F' and 'S' commands. The default mode is slow, the rate being approximately one microinstruction per second, so that the user can observe the behaviour on the light-emitting diode display (and could also use a logic-probe to monitor other signals in the system).

In the fast mode, loading and execution are speeded up by a factor of 256, and on the time-scale of user-interaction are effectively instantaneous.

EXAMPLE

Fig. 5 shows the results of loading and executing a simple microprogram which carries out a repeated rotational left shift of the data in register 0 of the 2901.

The required microprogram has only three words, as follows:

Word 0   X 2 3 7 3 X 0 2
Word 1   X 2 7 B 3 X 0 X
Word 2   1 1 7 B 3 X 0 X

Here, X denotes a 'don't care' half-byte, for which 0 was used in the example.

For clarification, everything typed by the user has been underlined in Fig. 5.

The microprogram was entered into the memory of the F8 system by the 'N' command and was displayed by the 'M' command, one word at a time. For each microinstruction word, its start address in the F8 RAM is also printed (600, 608 and 610 in the example), because the user may need this information when dumping the microprogram on paper tape. After loading by the 'L' command, execution in display mode 1 was selected, and therefore after execution the data displayed by the 'T' command shows the sequence of

```
.E 1000

THE CITY UNIVERSITY AMD2900 MONITOR V2
TYPE H FOR HELP
$ H
COMMANDS:
L     LOAD MICROPROGRAM
E N,D EXECUTE N MICROINSTRUCTIONS IN DISPLAY MODE D
        N=C FOR CONTINUOUS RUN. D=0 TO 7
N     NEW MICROPROGRAM
M N   PRINT CONTENTS OF ADDRESS N   N=0 TO F
T     PRINT RESULT OF RUN
H     ASK FOR HELP
$     DELETE COMMAND AND RESTART
Q     JUMP TO F8 MONITOR
S     SET SLOW MODE
F     SET FAST MODE

$ N
00:  0 2 3 7 3 0 0 2 +
01:  0 2 7 B 3 0 0 0 +
02:  1 1 7 B 3 0 0 0 *
$ M 0 0600 0 2 3 7 3 0 0 2
$ M 1 0608 0 2 7 B 3 0 0 0
$ M 2 0610 1 1 7 B 3 0 0 0
$ F
$ L
LOADED

$ E 25,1
EXECUTING.
 FINISHED
$ T
2 4 8 1 2 4 8 1 2 4 8 1 2 4 8 1 2 4 8 1 2 4 8 1 2
$ E 257   N TOO LARGE
$ Z?
$ Q
.T 600,618
0600   00 02 03 07 03 00 00 02   10 12 17 1B 13 10 10 10
0610   21 21 27 2B 23 20 20 20   FF
.
```

FIG. 5   *Example run of 2900 Monitor program.*

AMD2901 outputs which occurred:
    0010
    0100
    1000
    0001
    0010 etc.

A delay occurs between the 'EXECUTING' and 'FINISHED' messages,
dependent on the number of microinstructions being executed and on the
execution mode (fast or slow).

After leaving the AMD2900 monitor by means of the 'Q' command, the 'T'
command of the F8 Monitor was used to display the microprogram as it is
stored in the F8 RAM.

CONCLUSIONS

The system described improves the user-interface with the AMD2900 learning
kit, by providing it with a simple software monitor. Microprograms may be
saved and re-loaded from paper tape, and results from executing a microprogram can be printed for subsequent study.

It may seem that to use a microprocessor system to control a relatively
simple learning-kit can hardly be justifiable economically. However, the F8
system (apart from the 2708 EPROM) is connected via two edge-connectors to
the remainder, and may be unplugged for use elsewhere when not required with
the AMD 2900. The only hardware involved permanently with the AMD 2900
learning kit is an aluminium box, wiring, sockets, and the 2708. Even the 2708
could be unplugged, erased, and re-used for other applications.

FURTHER DEVELOPMENTS

Another program (within the F8 system) could be developed to facilitate the
preparation of the microprogram (e.g. using mnemonics to set up the microcode). Alternatively, since the microprogram can be loaded into the RAM of
the F8 system from paper tape, a microassembler running on another computer could be developed to produce the load tapes.

ACKNOWLEDGEMENTS

One of the authors (D. I.) wishes to thank the Science Research Council for
financial support.

REFERENCES

[1]   *Am2900 Evaluation and Learning Kit Instruction Manual*, Advanced Micro Devices Inc.,
       Sunnyvale, California, (1976).

[2]   *F8 Evaluation Kit*, Application Note, Mostek Corporation, Carrollton, Texas, (1975).

[3]   Davies, A. C. and Ibrahim, D., 'An interactive controller for the AMD2900 learning kit',
       I.E.E. Colloquium on 'Teaching laboratories for microprocessors', Savoy Place, London,
       (January 1979).

MICROPROGRAMMING AND MICROPROCESSORS: INVESTIGATION OF DEVELOPMENT SYSTEMS

RAY GIBSON
Department of Electrical and Electronic Engineering, University of Western Australia

INTRODUCTION

The design of logic systems using microprogramming techniques is assuming greater popularity as the number of supporting devices continues to increase and their associated cost decreases. The relatively low cost of PROM and PLA's, the many different bit-slice processor chip sets available and the more abundant supporting documentation for these chip sets are among factors contributing to their more widespread usage.

Although bit-slice microprocessors are noted for their versatility and very high speed of operation, these same features present serious problems to the designer when he is attempting to implement a system based on such processors. The following discussion outlines some of these difficulties and describes solutions taken by the author to overcome them.

MICROPROGRAMMED SYSTEMS

A brief outline of a microprogrammed system will now be presented, more detailed information can be obtained from the excellent reference[1], and associated topics in references[2, 3, 4].

The two essential elements of a microprogrammed system are shown in Fig. 1; they are the control store (microprogram memory), and the sequencer.

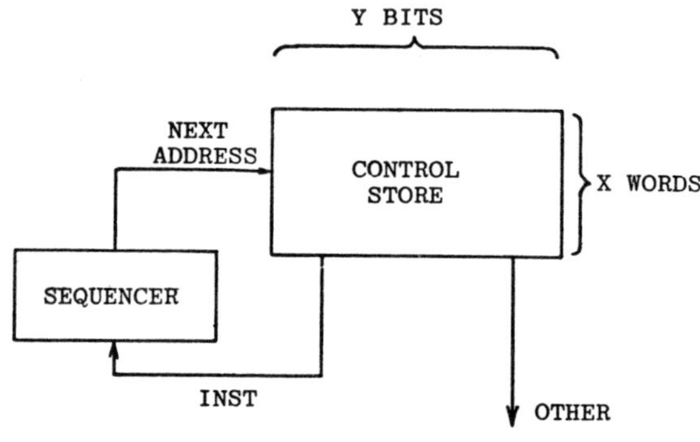

FIG. 1

The control store consists of an x-word by y-bit memory, each of the x words containing y bits which are grouped into various fields to control some particular activity within the system.

The sequencer is that section of a microprogrammed system responsible for controlling program flow through the control store. Essentially the sequencer determines the next address in the control store from which a microword is read to affect the next system state. Often several fields, such as polarity control, condition multiplexer controls, branch address, etc., are dedicated to the sequencer to enable complex 'next instruction' decision making. Although the arrangement in Fig. 1 may be sufficient to produce the required degree of control for a particular application, a much more powerful system can be produced by the addition of bit-slice processing elements. Fig. 2 shows such an arrangement with four 4-bit slice processing elements cascaded to provide a 16-bit data processing capability. Such a system is very powerful, capable of high speed (typically 200 ns per instruction), and can be configured to produce almost any form of control by combining microword bits with central processor bits.

As shown in Fig. 2, status signals (available from CPE) can be included in the sequencer inputs to allow the usage of instructions which are conditional on the results of the processor, e.g. JUMP IF ZERO.

DEVELOPMENT PROCESS

The development process for a microprogrammed bit-slice-based system follows a fairly predictable pattern. The steps associated with this process are outlined below, using the design and construction of a peripheral (e.g. DISK) interface for a computer as an example.

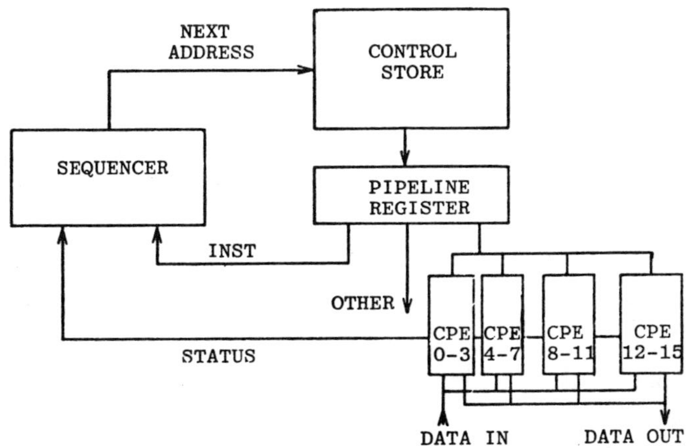

FIG. 2

(a) Preliminary investigation (Speed constraints favour the use of a bit-slice microprocessor).
(b) Construction of block diagram.
(c) Specification of bit slice chip set to be used (e.g. 2900 series).
(d) Specification of microword width (e.g. 40 bits).
(e) Specification of microword format.
(f) Writing the microcode (a microprogram).
(g) Assembling the microcode.
(h) Debugging the microprogram.
(i) Loading microcode into ROM.
(j) Layout and production of printed circuit board.
(k) Testing of completed interface.

Steps c, d and e are interrelated, and changes in any one step may require revision of all three.

Step c is perhaps the most difficult initially, as this requires detailed knowledge of at least one bit-slice microprocessor family. Items g, h and k require some supporting hardware and software before a microprogrammed system can be produced efficiently.

DEVELOPMENT SYSTEMS

Currently there are few bit slice development systems available, with only one (SYSTEM 29, ADVANCED MICRO DEVICES), offering complete support and others offering partial support.

The critical requirement of a system capable of supporting real time development projects is that it must have the ability to operate at a speed greater than or equal to that of the project under development. Such a requirement implies that the development system itself should be based on a bit-slice microprocessor, and variations in development systems of this type lie in the means of controlling and interacting with this processor.

The basic function of the development system is to provide a means of debugging the microcode. The simplest way of achieving this is to provide a writable control store, so that microcode may be loaded into memory, executed, modified, executed etc., until an error-free program results.

Desirable features of such a development system are now listed:

(i) It should provide a means of readily modifying a microword.
(ii) It should provide a means of varying the instruction timing, including single stepping, so that the various parameters of the system under development can be monitored.
(iii) It should allow the setting of a breakpoint, so that program execution can be conditionally halted and an examination of the state of the system be made.
(iv) The system should have the capability of supporting either pipelined or non-pipelined architecture and furthermore, in the case of pipelined architecture, should offer the means of inserting the pipeline register in either the Data or Address lines of the control store.

(v)   The development system should ideally support a number of different bit-slice families. (This is important, as some bit-slice families are better suited to particular applications).This feature also implies that facilities be provided to allow changing the format (field definition) of the microword.

One approach to producing a development system satisfying the above requirements is shown in Fig. 3. This system is essentially a bit-slice microprocessor, controlled by a conventional microprocessor system. This approach has two possible disadvantages, one being in the complicated nature of the interface (which must be capable of generating control store addresses and large data words, along with the many control signals required), the other being evident when the development system is produced in an environment with existing computing facilities, leading to duplication of many costly items (DISK DRIVES, TERMINALS etc.).

The approach taken by the author was to construct a development system which was essentially manually operated, while making extensive use of the existing facilities of a host minicomputer. This system will now be considered from both hardware and software aspects.

HARDWARE

The development system is shown in Fig. 4. A writable control store of
1K × 48 bits of high speed RAM (35 ns ACCESS TIME) was constructed on two identical printed circuit boards, each containing 1K × 24 bits; provision was made for additional memory up to a total of 4K × 48 bits.

The decision to use a 48 bit microword was based on previous experience and was thought to be adequate for applications likely to be encountered (development of computer interfaces).

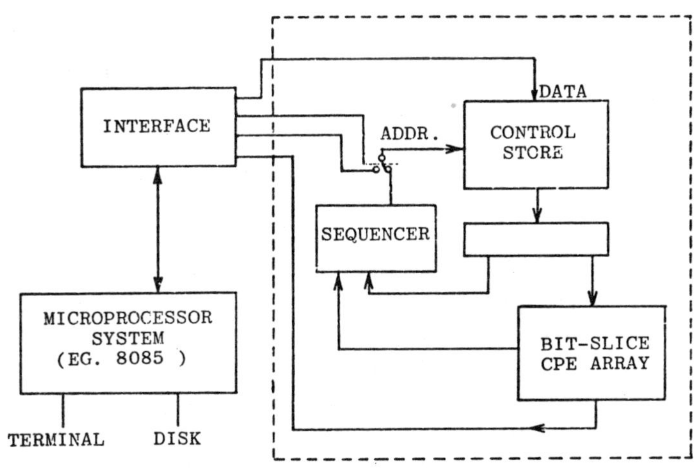

FIG. 3

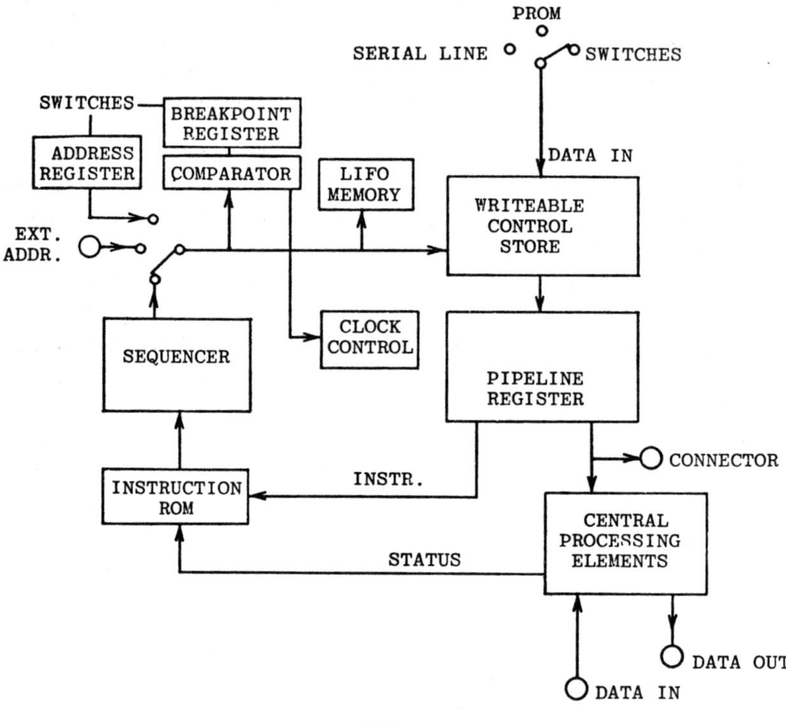

FIG. 4

The writable control store can be loaded in one of the three following ways:

(i)   Manually, via a set of Data and Address switches; provision is made to load either isolated memory locations or a contiguous block of memory using an autoincrement address feature.

(ii) By means of a serial line connected to a standard RS 232 terminal port on the host computer.

(iii) From a removable PCB containing EPROM, previously loaded via a PROM programmer attached to the host computer. This feature is valuable in situations where the serial line mentioned in (ii) above is unavailable.

The breakpoint register shown in Fig. 4 is loaded via switches, and continuously compares its contents with the contents of the address bus, causing the processor clock to halt when a match occurs.

As each instruction is executed, the address of that instruction is stored in a LIFO memory so that, upon reaching a breakpoint, it is possible to examine the past history of the program up to a maximum of 256 instructions.

After the memory has been loaded, the system is switched to the 'RUN' mode, causing the clock to start and thereby commence execution of the program at one of 8 manually selected rates (including single step).

The instruction ROM shown in Fig. 4, is a removable PROM, allowing simple modification of the development system instruction set. The ROM (32×8) accepts as inputs 4 bits from the instruction field in the microword and 1 bit from the CPE to produce a set of 8 control signals for the sequencer.

Both the memory address bus and memory data output (MICROWORD) are available at external connectors to enable testing of the completed printed circuit board. This is accomplished by cabling the external data and address connectors to the PROM sockets on the PCB, thus substituting the writable control store for PROM.

Data paths associated with the central processor elements are also available at two external connectors (one for input and the other for output), to simplify connection to the processor during development. Upon obtaining a satisfactory solution in terms of an error-free program, it merely remains to produce a printed circuit board containing all circuitry external to the development system as well as CPE, sequencer chips and ROM, equivalent to the development system.

The presentation of the development system was arranged in such a way that the state (or condition) of the processor was visible at all times. This was achieved by using a very large 'front panel' type construction, with the system drawn in block diagram form, and all switches, connectors and LEDS (light emitting diodes) inserted at the appropriate points. Ribbon cable was used for most of the behind-panel wiring, keeping all signal lines as short as possible to achieve the highest possible operating speed. Patch-boards were inserted at various points to allow for changing format etc. and sections which are chip-set dependent (CPE and sequences), were contained on single wire-wrappable boards to allow a simple means of supporting different bit-slice chip sets. All significant signal lines were monitored using LED's totalling approximately 200.

SOFTWARE

Software support for the development system centred around a PDP-11 minicomputer; the two major supporting programs being a micro assembler and a PROM programming utility.

The writing of the microassembler was a relatively simple task and was arranged in such a way that the user defines the fields comprising the microword, inputs the microprogram (using symbolic addresses) and receives as output a disk file suitable for down-line loading to the development system or as input to the PROM programming utility to program the necessary PROMS.

The PROM programming utility is the supporting program for a PROM programmer capable of programming fusible link (extremely important) and UV erasable PROMS. Input to this utility is in the form of a single disk file which is segmented by the program according to the number and configuration of the PROMS to be programmed.

Software simulation of the system being developed may be possible, but is rather difficult because of the large number of bits contained in each word, and is generally inadequate where real-time projects are concerned.

CONCLUSION

The system, described above, has been used with great success by the author, both as a teaching aid and as a production development system. It has provided a valuable insight into the application of bit-slice microprocessors and microprogram development, with all of its features being very necessary at some stage of the development.

Initially hand coding and manual entry of programs into the system were used but as programs increased in size, the effort expended in writing a micro assembler was well worthwhile.

The significant characteristic of this system is that it allows the program under development to run at a speed comparable to that at which it will run in its final form.

REFERENCES

[1]   *The Microprogramming Handbook*, *AM-PUB029*, Advanced Micro Devices, 901 Thompson Place, Sunnyvale, California, U.S.A.
[2]   Adams, W. T. and Smith, S. M., 'How bit slice families compare', *Electronics*, (August 1978).
[3]   Hedges, T. M., 'Replacing hardwired logic with microcode', *Electronics*, (Nov. 1978).
[4]   Katzan, H. *Microprogramming Primer*, McGraw-Hill, (1977).

AN ALTERNATIVE APPROACH TO THE DEVELOPMENT OF MICROPROCESSOR SOFTWARE — A HARDWARE/SOFTWARE SIMULATOR

M. G. RODD and G. T. GRAY
Department of Electrical Engineering, University of Cape Town, South Africa

INTRODUCTION

The systems engineer embarking on designs which are to include microprocessors, faces three major hurdles. Firstly, there is the complexity of the essential
knowledge to be rapidly assimilated if he is to understand fully (and hence use
efficiently) the microprocessor system he chooses. Secondly, there is the
subsequent development of software; few engineers have been taught to
programme at relatively low levels, so this stage is not as easy as it might
seem[1]. Thirdly, there is the vital area of 'debugging' the software, not only in
terms of whether the instructions are correct and in the right sequence, but also
the overall verification of the programme in its working environment, i.e. in its
interaction with the external world.

The vast majority of microcomputer applications are dedicated systems,
involving the bare essentials required for the job, with programmes committed
finally to Read Only Memory. This implies that no provisions for programme
verification will be made (i.e. no normal peripheral devices, front panels, etc.) It
may be argued that the answer is to produce an initial system, similar to the
final product, but having the necessary facilities to provide for software verification. This is acceptable only if the final product is to be marketed in vast
quantities. If a variety of different systems is to be developed, however, and the
versatility of the microcomputer is to be fully explored, the situation changes,
and another solution must be sought. A similar situation will arise if the precise
specifications of the final system cannot be drawn up at the early design stage,
and if modification seems likely during the development and commissioning
stages.

The obvious solution lies in the use of a microprocessor development system,
which will typically comprise a microprocessor system with sufficient memory
to enable the use of a small operating system, assemblers and debug routines,
etc., together with the associated peripherals such as VDU's, teletypes, floppy
discs, etc.[2]. Such a system is further enhanced by the use of in-circuit emulation
structures, which permit very close contact between the destination system and
the development system (Ref. 2). There are certain drawbacks to this approach.
Most microprocessor development systems are aimed at a specific
manufacturer's family of processors, and upgrading the system to meet the

requirements of a new processor can be expensive. The situation is, admittedly, slightly eased by the introduction of microprocessor development systems which can be used for the development of a range of different target micropro- cessor systems. The idea here is that one purchases the basic development system, together with appropriate peripherals, software etc., and then inserts a 'personality card' which is used to emulate the desired target microprocessor. The software is organized such that the input language remains the same for all possible target microprocessors, but the system is internally adapted to pro- duce the appropriate machine instructions for the desired processor.[3]

Another approach which has been widely adopted, lies in the use of simu- lation techniques. Most microprocessor users have available existing mini- or mainframe computer systems, and much interest has been shown in the use of these facilities to meet the new demand. Any acceptable system must consist of the simulation not only of the machine instruction set of the particular micro- processor under consideration, but also of its related hardware, including peripherals, i.e. of the complete system.

CLASSICAL APPROACH TO SIMULATION

The classical method of simulating a system will involve three stages. Firstly, the system must be 'IDENTIFIED', that is, a thorough knowledge must be developed of the various components of the system and their interaction. Secondly, a 'MODEL' of the system must be built, based on the knowledge obtained in the first stage. This may be a computerised model (digital, analogue or hybrid), or a miniature replica. Thirdly, the model must undergo a 'VERIFICATION' stage, to establish the fidelity of the simulation. This will, of course, typically involve modifications to the model.

If these stages are applied to microprocessor simulation, a lengthy and expensive exercise lies ahead. The particular microprocessor to be used must be carefully examined in minutest detail. This certainly involves more than just a careful reading of the manufacturer's specifications, which are notorious for their inaccuracies and 'small print'. In practice, it will undoubtedly lead to the building-up of a minimal real system, with the resulting delay. Once the weird and wonderful behaviour of the microprocessor is fully understood, a simu- lation programme to perform similarly may be written, typically in a high-level language. This programme will, naturally, be comprehensive and lengthy, and will require to be run on a reasonably large computer system. The simulation may then be verified by detailed comparison with the actual microprocessor created earlier. The simulation is then available for use. If the microprocessor used is changed, the whole procedure must, of course, be repeated!

It must be noted here that such programmes are available from certain manufacturers for their microprocessors or, in many cases, from time-sharing service facilities. These are, however, generally costly, and will not necessarily meet the requirements of the desired hardware configuration. Also, in many cases, the available simulation programmes are written for specific host computers, and will require modification if they are to be run on a different machine, even though the ultimate input language remains unchanged. Typically such programmes themselves are written in a suitable high-level language, which, theoretically, should allow easy transportation to machines other than those for which they were developed. However, in practice, the situation is not so ideal, and anyone who has had to perform such an exercise will know only too well the pitfalls that arise.

A HARDWARE/SOFTWARE SIMULATION

An alternative technique for the simulation of microprocessors has been developed by the authors. This technique covers the three steps in simulation mentioned above, and may be described as a hardware/software simulation. The method involves the direct interfacing of a microprocessor and a minicomputer. All input, output and control lines of the microprocessor are interfaced to the minicomputer, which in turn controls and monitors the microprocessor's performance. The concept is extended further. Using Direct Memory Access techniques, the microprocessor shares the minicomputer's memory, thus permitting complete monitoring of the status and contents of the microprocessor memory, and reducing capital costs. Peripherals for the microprocessor may be provided in two ways. The microprocessor may communicate, via the minicomputer, with the latter's own peripherals. Secondly, any peripherals required by the microprocessor which are not available on the minicomputer, may be simulated by suitable minicomputer programmes.

The great virtue of this technique lies in the complete validity of the model, for the model is the microprocessor itself. The steps involved in producing such a linked system are relatively simple. Firstly, the input/output structure of the microprocessor and the minicomputer must be fully understood, and an interface developed. A small quantity of computer software must be written to control and monitor the microprocessor and to simulate the peripherals required. In practice, this simulation system has proved possible to implement within a relatively short period.

A change of microprocessor does not present any major problem, involving simply a redesign of part of the interface and, possibly, some software changes. This certainly ensures a shorter turn-around time when compared with the classical simulation approach. Accepting that both methods will require the presence of an established computer system, the method of simulation proposed in this paper is quite obviously the less costly.

The rest of the paper describes a hardware/software simulation system, based on the above concept, and specifically developed to simulate an Intel 8080 microprocessor, the host minicomputer being a Varian 620.

OUTLINE OF A HARDWARE/SOFTWARE SIMULATION SYSTEM

(a) *Hardware interface:*
The hardware interface between the microprocessor and the minicomputer must make provision for four basic operations:

(i) Direct memory access between the minicomputer's memory and the microprocessor. This provides a memory for the microprocessor.

(ii) Control signals. These permit the minicomputer to control and monitor the microprocessor.

(iii) Input/Output data channels. These enable the microprocessor to send data to, and receive data from, the minicomputer.

(iv) Interrupt control. The microprocessor used in the system described here, has interrupt capabilities. It is also capable of raising an interrupt on the host machine when it requires attention.

The hardware interface may conveniently be broken into two sections, as indicated in Fig. 1, and termed here the Varian Interface and the 8080 Interface.

At the start of each machine cycle of the 8080, the 'sync' pulse is used to strobe the status information on to its data bus and the 8080 interface holds this information. The Varian interface can sense, under programme control, each of these status bits, and so the minicomputer can determine the condition and requirements of the 8080.

Note: Appendix 1 gives a brief description of the input/output structure of the minicomputer and the microprocessor under consideration in this paper. Signals referred to in the descriptions which follow are described in this appendix.

(b) *Software interfacing:*

As mentioned previously, a certain amount of software is necessary to control

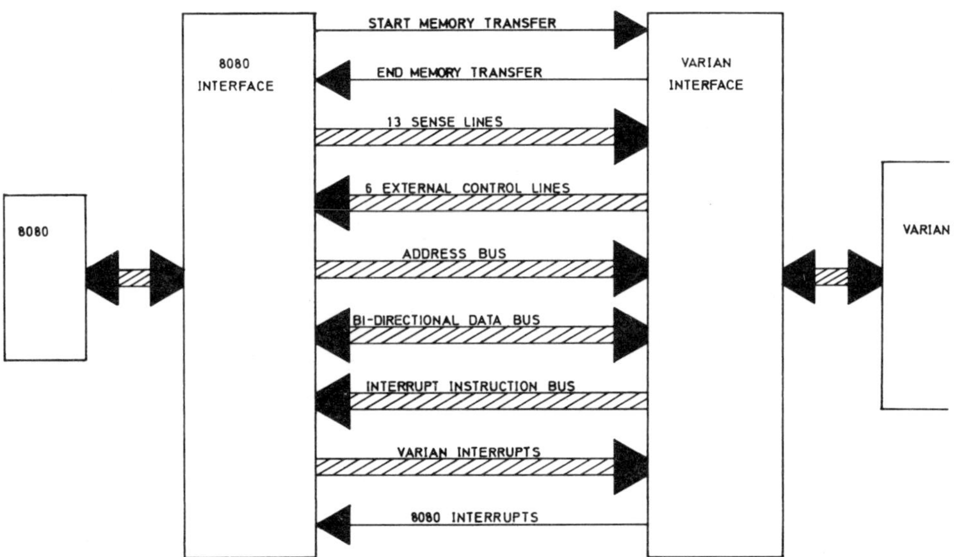

FIG. 1   *Interconnections between the 8080 and the Varian interfaces.*

and monitor the microprocessor. The software will consist of the following sections:

(i)   Memory management.
(ii) 'Front Panel' facilities. The normal front panel facilities would be to stop and start the computer. With the versatility available in the system under discussion, however, far more features may be included.
(iii) Peripheral simulation.
(iv) Interrupt handling.

SYSTEM OPERATION

(a) *Memory management.*   As mentioned previously, the minicomputer memory is shared by the microprocessor. This is achieved by using Direct Memory Access techniques. (It is worth noting that the shared-memory concept means lower cost as well as providing direct control and monitoring). DMA techniques are used rather than normal 'input/output under programme control' so as to permit faster microprocessor memory access times, and to lessen software requirements for the minicomputer.

DMA is initiated by the microprocessor, generating a request for memory access via the 8080 interface. The Varian interface responds by generating the necessary signals, causing the Varian to initiate a DMA cycle. Until the cycle is completed, the 8080 is held in a 'WAIT' state, controlled by the 'READY' line.

(b) *Front panel facilities.*   A programme, linked to the Varian's standard 'DEBUG' programme, controls the hardware interface so as to provide a variety of valuable functions. Features are as follows:

(i)   *Programme control.*   An 8080 programme may be 'stepped' through, Instruction-by-Instruction or Byte-by-Byte. (The 8080 instruction set is composed of single-, double- or triple-byte instructions). The byte-by-byte stepping is implemented by means of an external control signal from the Varian, which starts the 8080's instruction cycle and then stops the cycle at the end of the memory access demand. When the cycle is stopped, the data on both the address lines and the data lines may be input to the Varian and displayed on its console. Stepping-through instruction-by-instruction is obtained by monitoring the 8080's status information, one bit of which indicates the start of a new instruction sequence.

(ii) *Interrupt control.*   The Varian may initiate an interrupt to the 8080, using the Varian interface to transfer an interrupt signal to the 8080 interrupt channel.

(iii) *Data modification.*   When stepping through an 8080 programme, the Varian may, under operator control, alter the contents of the data bus to the microprocessor.

(iv) *Trapping.*   Under programme control, an 8080 'HALT' instruction may be inserted into a programme being executed. This allows the operator effectively to 'trap-through' a programme and display (by means of a series

of input/output instructions inserted into the 8080's instruction sequence)
the contents of registers within the 8080. An additional trapping mechanism
is available whereby the Varian can monitor the incoming address bus, and
cause programme execution to cease when a specified address is requested.

(c) *Peripheral simulation.*   One of the basic concepts embodied in this form of
simulator is the simulation of microprocessor peripherals. The minicomputer
must therefore have a set of programmes which respond in a similar fashion to
the required peripheral. These programmes are accessed as follows: When the
8080 executes an input/output instruction, the 8080 interface generates an I/O
request signal to the Varian interface, which in turn generates an interrupt to
the Varian. At the same time, the 8080 is held in a 'WAIT' state. The Varian
inputs, via the Varian interface, the specified device address. This address then
determines the appropriate peripheral simulation routine, which will take over
control of the hardware interface, as and when necessary.

If the 8080 input/output system is itself interrupt-orientated, the Varian will
instruct the Varian interface to issue an interrupt signal to the 8080, which then
enters the appropriate subroutine and continues as previously described.

(d) *Interrupt handling.*   The previous sections have assumed the availability of
an interrupt control. Its implementation is as follows:

(i)   *8080-to-Varian.*   This is achieved by using the status lines of the 8080 which
      are set to indicate that an input/output instruction of a 'HALT' instruction
      has been executed. These status lines, when set, cause an interrupt to the
      Varian to be generated via the Varian interface. This eliminates the
      necessity for the Varian continually to monitor the status lines.

(ii) *Varian-to-8080.*   A specific external control instruction, when executed by
      the Varian, will cause the Varian interface to issue an interrupt signal to
      the 8080. When the 8080 acknowledges this signal, the 8080 is placed in a
      'WAIT' state. The Varian then sends a vectored 'RESTART' instruction to
      the 8080. This instruction will determine the location from which the 8080
      must continue execution, once it is released from the 'WAIT' state.

CONCLUSIONS

Assuming that there is a suitable minicomputer system available, the greatest
attractions of the concept proposed in this paper are the time and cost factors.
The system developed was urgently required to permit software development
and verification to take place concurrently with the development of an industrial microcomputer system. In terms of cost, the capital expenditure on the
system was of the order of £300 (including the cost of the microprocessor itself,
which amounted to £100 at that time). The system was developed, and preliminary control software written, within one month. Experience with the
system led to a certain amount of modification, but the main object of the
exercise was achieved in very short time. Since then, the simulation has proved
to be of great value in the development and verification of complex software.

Not only is the simulation readily available to the user, but he also has access
to minicomputer utility software.

The form of microcomputer software development aid proposed in this
paper certainly merits serious consideration by any organisation intending to
produce microcomputer-based systems.

ACKNOWLEDGEMENT

The authors wish to express their appreciation to the National Institute for
Metallurgy for sponsorship of the project, and to the University of Cape Town
for assistance in the production of this paper.

REFERENCES

[1]   Korn, G. A., 'A proposed method for simplified microcomputer programming', *Computer*,
       p. 43, (October 1975).
[2]   Kornstein, H., 'Developments in development systems', *Euromicro*, pp. 77–87, (1977).
[3]   Lowry, D. and Stofer, B., 'The 8002 — A new design tool for microprocessor users',
       Tekscope, **9**, No. 2, (1977).
[4]   Gray, G. T., 'A Microprocessor Development System', *M.Sc. Thesis, University of Cape
       Town*, (1976).
[5]   *VARIAN 620 Series Interface Manual*, Varian Data Machines, (1972).
[6]   *INTEL Data Catalog*, Intel Corporation, (1975).

APPENDIX 1: A BRIEF DESCRIPTION OF THE INPUT/OUTPUT STRUCTURE OF THE VARIAN 620 AND THE INTEL 8080

(a) *The Varian 620* [5]

This minicomputer uses four basic instructions to communicate with its
input/output bus. These are:

(i)   Output from Register 'R' to device 'D'. This sends the address bits selecting
       device 'D' to the input/output bus, followed by the 16 bits held in register
       'R'.

(ii)   Input to register 'R' from device 'D'. As for (i), except that the 16 bits on the
       input/output bus are transferred to the specified register.

(iii) Sense device 'D'. This checks the status of the device selected by the
       address bits specified by 'D'.

(iv)   External control to device 'D'. A pulse is sent to the device selected by the
       address bits specified by 'D'. In addition, the basic Varian has available
       eight priority-oriented interrupt lines, provided by means of a 'Priority
       Interrupt Module'. Direct Memory Access is implemented via the
       input/output bus and certain control lines.

(b) *The Intel 8080* [6]

Each instruction cycle of the 8080 is split into several machine cycles, with a
'SYNC' pulse to indicate the start of each machine cycle. During this 'SYNC'
pulse, status information is made available relating to the machine instruction
currently being executed. There are 8 different types of status indication.

A signal **DBIN** is produced by the 8080 to indicate when it is ready to receive data on the data bus for a 'Read' type of instruction. A signal **WR** indicates when data may be removed by the data bus. Following an external transaction request, the processor will enter into a 'WAIT' state until a 'READY' signal informs it that the request has been completed and permits it to continue. This effectively synchronises the 8080 with the external hardware.

Using the status information and the control lines described, the 8080 may be effectively controlled.

There are also additional control lines to the 8080 to provide for interrupts, initializing the processor, starting up the processor, and halting the execution of a programme.

MICROPROCESSOR IMPLEMENTATION OF A SIMPLE LOW-PASS FILTER

P. J. ALLEN and A. G. J. HOLT
University of Newcastle upon Tyne, England

INTRODUCTION

Digital filters find important applications in the fields of medical electronics, system control, missile guidance, sonar, radar and communications. They have certain advantages over their analogue counterparts which include immunity of their responses from changing component values caused by temperature or ageing, flexibility, availability of very low cut-off frequencies, exactly reproducible responses and compatibility with digital transmission systems. It is this last point and the accelerating use of digital techniques in communication systems which make it certain that we shall be seeing a lot more of the digital filter in the future[1].

The digital filter operates in an environment where samples are taken of continuous waveforms and are converted to binary values. The digital filter must process these streams of numbers and output similar 'filtered' number streams. The number output at any one time, nT (where $n = 0,1,2\ldots$ and T is the sampling period) depends on the type of filter that has been implemented. If this filter is non-recursive, the output number is calculated from past and present input numbers or, alternatively, the filter may be recursive in which case the past output numbers are used in the calculation to find the present output number, also.

Previously, a general-purpose computer or a specialized signal processor would have been used to implement a digital filter. This greatly reduced the area of application because of the high costs involved. However, the advent of the microprocessor has changed all that. As the cost of the microprocessor continues to fall, the digital filter is looking like a good economic proposition.

In the sections that follow, an implementation of a digital filter using the microprocessor is considered. The digital filter is derived from the simple RC-lag circuit shown in Fig. 1 using the z-transform[2].

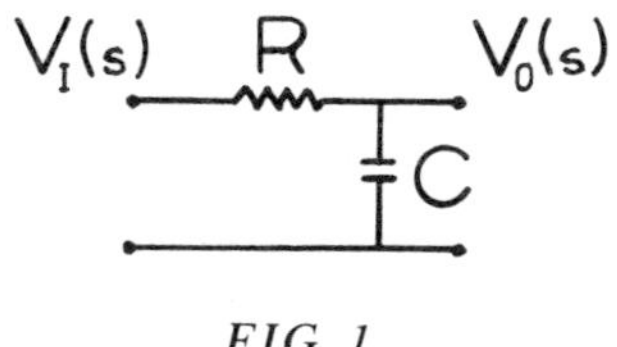

FIG. 1

121

ZERO-ORDER APPROXIMATION

The range of frequencies a digital filter can handle is limited by Nyquist's sampling criterion which states that the sampling frequency must be greater than twice the bandwidth* of the digital filter[3]. Since digital filters are bandlimited in this way and continuous, analogue filters are not strictly bandlimited, some form of approximation must appear when the digital equivalent of an analogue filter is derived. We shall use the zero-order approximation.

Consider the Fourier transform $H(jw)$ of the impulse response $h(t)$ of a continuous filter

$$H(jw) = \int_{-\infty}^{\infty} h(t).\exp(-jwt).dt \tag{1}$$

The zero-order approximation to $H(jw)$, denoted by $\bar{H}(jw)$ is

$$\bar{H}(jw) = \sum_{n=-\infty}^{\infty} h(nT).\exp(-jnwT)T \tag{2}$$

where T is the sampling interval, and also the interval of integration in the time domain.

Using the unit delay operator $z^{-1} = \exp(-jwt)$ we obtain

$$H(z) = T.\sum_{n=-\infty}^{\infty} h(nT).z^{-n} \tag{3}$$

which is the standard z-transform[3].

Assuming $h(nT) = 0$ for $t < 0$

$$H(z) = T.\sum_{n=0}^{\infty} h(nT).z^{-n} \tag{4}$$

We can use equation (4) to find the transfer function $H(z)$ of a digital filter which is the zero-order approximation to a continuous filter whose impulse response, after sampling, is $h(nT)$.

For the simple-lag in Fig. 1

$$H(jw) = \frac{1}{1 + jwRC} = \frac{a}{a + jw} \quad . \tag{5}$$

where $a = 1/RC$ = radian cut-off frequency.

Using Fourier transform tables[3]

$$h(t) = a.\exp(-at) \tag{6}$$

so that the sampled impulse response is

$$h(nT) = a.\exp(-anT) \tag{7}$$

---

*In this instance bandwidth is meant to convey the difference between the highest and lowest frequencies in the range.

Substituting in equation (4)

$$H(z) = T. \sum_{n=0}^{\infty} a. \exp(-anT). z^{-n} \tag{8}$$

$$= aT. \sum_{n=0}^{\infty} (\exp(-aT). z^{-1})^n \tag{9}$$

which is a geometric progression with sum

$$\frac{aT}{1 - \exp(-aT). z^{-1}} \tag{10}$$

Hence, the transfer function of the digital filter which is the zero-order approximation to the simple-lag in Fig. 1 is

$$H(z) = \frac{aT}{1 - \exp(-aT). z^{-1}} \tag{11}$$

The transfer function can be interpreted in a similar manner to the Laplace transfer function, that is, it is the ratio of the z-transforms of the input and output sampled data sets, $x(nT)$ and $y(nT)$ (i.e. the values of the inputs and outputs at the sampling instants) denoted $X(z)$ and $Y(z)$, respectively. Thus,

$$H(z) = \frac{Y(z)}{X(z)} \tag{12}$$

so that

$$\frac{Y(z)}{X(z)} = \frac{aT}{1 - \exp(-aT). z^{-1}} \tag{13}$$

therefore,

$$Y(z) = aT. X(z) + \exp(-aT). Y(z) z^{-1} \tag{14}$$

Taking the inverse z-transform and bearing in mind that a z^{-1} factor implies a time delay by one sampling period

$$y(nT) = aT. x(nT) + \exp(-aT). y([n-1]. T) \tag{15}$$

Hence, the output at time nT is calculated by multiplying the input $x(nT)$, at time nT by aT and adding it to the previous output $y(n-1)T$ scaled by $\exp(-aT)$. Equation (15) is an example of a linear difference equation.

THE IMPLEMENTATION

As an example of the design technique, let us consider the implementation of a digital filter approximating a simple-lag circuit with a $-3\,\mathrm{dB}$ frequency of 100 Hz.

Firstly, we must decide upon the rate at which we shall sample the input, continuous waveform. Our decision is affected by the approximation used. The

zero-order approximation is prone to errors, called aliasing errors, which result
from the periodic nature of equation (2). This can be seen more easily if we
separate equation (2) into its real and imaginary parts;

$$\bar{H}(j\omega) = T. \sum_{n=-\infty}^{\infty} h(nT) \cos n\omega T - jT. \sum_{n=-\infty}^{\infty} h(nT) \sin n\omega T \qquad (16)$$

from which we note that $\bar{H}(j\omega)$ is periodic over ω with period. $2\pi/T$. If $H(j\omega)$
has frequency components above π/T rads/sec. then there must be overlap
between the oscillations in $\bar{H}(j\omega)$ causing aliasing errors, as shown in Fig. 2.
We must choose the sampling frequency to be much greater than the cut-off
frequency so that aliasing errors are insignificant and, also to be more than
twice the highest frequency to be used (this second condition is from Nyquist's
sampling criterion). Assuming the highest frequency will be less than 500 Hz it
seems reasonable to choose the sampling frequency to be double the highest
frequency component so that the sampling frequency is a decade greater than
the cut-off frequency i.e. $f_s = 1/T = 1$ kHz.

Having obtained a value for T we can calculate the coefficients (aT) and
$\exp(-aT)$ which scale the current input number and previous output number,
respectively.

Hence,

$$aT = (2\pi \times 100 \times 0.001) = 0.6283186 \qquad (17)$$

and

$$\exp(-aT) = \exp(-2\pi \times 100 \times 0.001) = 0.5334881 \qquad (18)$$

Therefore, the tasks our microprocessor system must perform are:

  (i) Input of a sample
 (ii) Conversion of this sample to a digital value
(iii) Multiplication by 0.6283186 and 0.5334881
(iv) Addition of the two products
 (v) Output of the result and conversion to a voltage level
(vi) Storing of the result so that it is delayed by T seconds
(vii) Waiting until T seconds have elapsed since the sample was input.

A system that can perform all these tasks is shown in Fig. 3. The system is

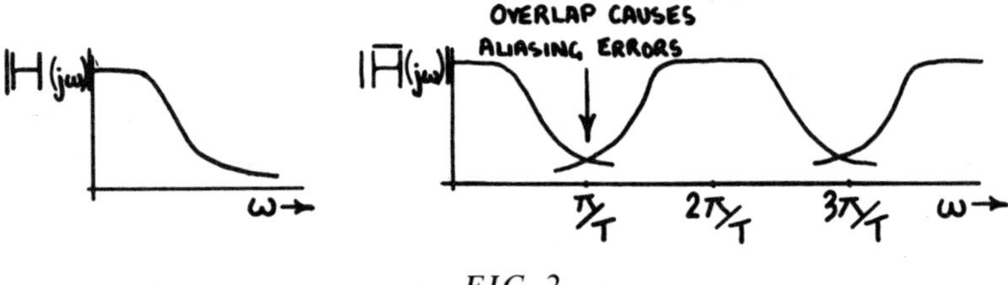

FIG. 2

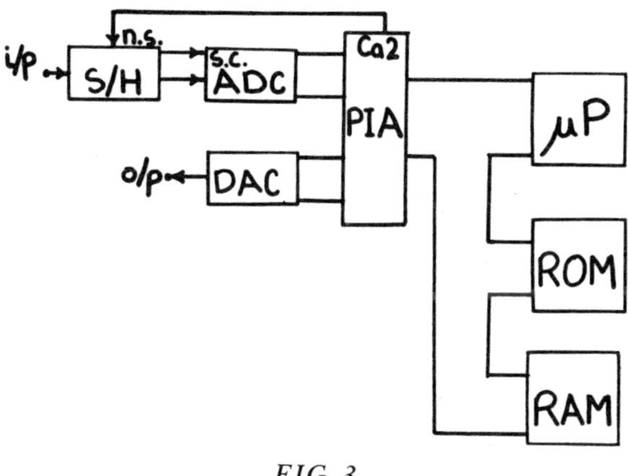

FIG. 3

based upon the Motorola M6800 microprocessor and the program for the system is written in the assembly language of this microprocessor and appears in the Appendix. For those who are unfamiliar with the M6800 we shall discuss how the system performs each task.

(i) Input of a sample[4]

The peripheral interface adapter (PIA) can be split into two halves, an A-side and a B-side each with 3 registers. The 3 registers are the control register (CR), data direction register (DDR) and input/output register (IOR). The CR allows access to either the DDR or the IOR depending on whether bit b_2 in the CR is set (IOR) or not (DDR). The CR also allows the two control lines (CA1 and CA2 or CB1 and CB2) on its side to be used in a variety of modes. The DDR makes the corresponding line in the IOR an output or input. As an example, if 10000001_2 was in the DDR then the two outside lines would be outputs and the rest inputs. The IOR is like a set of latches whose state depends on whether they have been programmed as inputs or outputs. If they are inputs then the number presented to them on their input/output lines can be loaded into the microprocessor. If they are outputs then the microprocessor can store a number to the IOR and this number will appear on the input/output lines.

The PIA is a memory mapped device which means that its registers appear as memory locations and can be manipulated in exactly the same manner. Therefore, no special input or output instructions are needed.

In this application the A-side of the PIA has been programmed as an input port to operate in the pulse-strobe mode. Thus, when the microprocessor loads the contents of the IOR into one of its two accumulators, as at line 54 in the program (Appendix), the most recent number corresponding to the output of the analogue-to-digital convertor (ADC) is input. Also, a signal (or strobe) is generated on control line CA2 which is used to command the sample and hold circuit (S/H) to take another sample. After the S/H has obtained a sample the ADC outputs a binary value corresponding to the amplitude of the sample.

The subroutine AD starting at line 115 in the Appendix is responsible for the initialization of the A-side of the PIA. The subroutine is called at the start of the program (line 36). The flow chart in Fig. 4 indicates the operation of this subroutine.

(ii) Conversion of the sample to a digital value
Once the S/H has acquired a sample of the continuous input waveform, the ADC begins converting it to a binary value. The time it takes to acquire the sample and convert it to a binary value should be less than the sampling period so that the ADC is not performing a conversion when the microprocessor is trying to read its output.

The binary value which the ADC outputs depends on the binary code employed. As positive and negative samples are possible, a bi-polar code must be used such as two's complement, offset binary or radix (-2). The M6800 uses two's complement arithmetic so this is the obvious choice. In this arithmetic system, the most significant bit (MSB) of the microprocessor word is a sign bit which is set for negative values and not-set for positive values. The rest of the word gives the magnitude of the number.

When the ADC finishes a conversion it stops and holds the number corresponding to the amplitude of the sample at its output (8 lines) which is connected to the input port of the microprocessor. This value is held for as long as there is no signal for it to start converting (SC).

(iii) Multiplication
A microprocessor only handles binary values, so we must convert the decimal numbers 0.6283186 and 0.5334881 to binary values before considering the

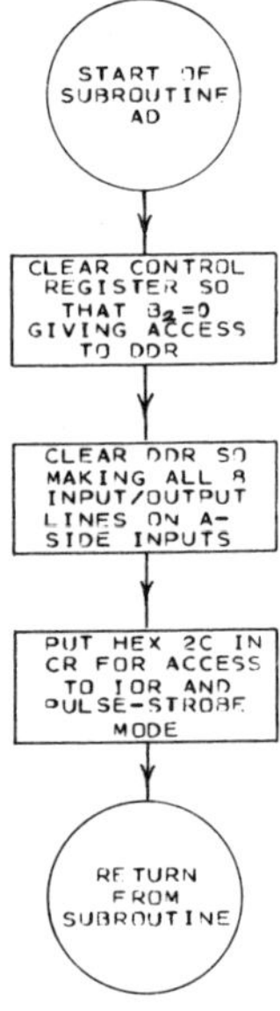

FIG. 4

question of multiplication. To do this we must imagine a fixed point in the microprocessor word. The situation of this point depends on the largest coefficient to be represented. If the coefficient has an integer part then sufficient bits to the left of the point must remain so that it can be represented. Also, one bit must be left to indicate the sign of the coefficient. As an example, $+7$ can be represented by 4-bits as shown in Fig. 5.

The numbers 0.6283186 and 0.5334881 have no integer parts so we need only leave one bit to the left of the binary point for the sign bit. To the right of the binary point the weighting is as shown in Fig. 6. Note that the smallest magnitude other than zero is 2^{-7} (0.0078125) which means we must represent our coefficients by the nearest multiples of 2^{-7}. Thus,

$$0.6283186 \doteqdot 1 \times 2^{-1} + 0 \times 2^{-2} + 1 \times 2^{-3} + 0 \times 2^{-4} + 0 \times 2^{-5} + 0 \times 2^{-6} + 0 \times 2^{-7}$$

$$= 0.625_{10} \, (0.1010000_2)$$

$$0.5334881 \doteqdot 1 \times 2^{-1} + 0 \times 2^{-2} + 0 \times 2^{-3} + 0 \times 2^{-4} + 1 \times 2^{-5} + 0 \times 2^{-6} + 0 \times 2^{-7}$$

$$= 0.53125_{10} \, (0.1000100_2)$$

Having to round the coefficients in this manner alters the filter's response as can be seen in Fig. 7. As the complexity of a digital filter increases, the effect of this rounding can cause instability[5].

Now we can consider multiplication. The M6800 has no special instructions for multiplication, so a subroutine must be written to perform multiplication. As we are using two's complement arithmetic, the ordinary multiplication procedure of shifting and adding when the multiplier bits are set, cannot be used. This is due to the cross-product terms introduced by the two's complement numbers[4]. To obtain the correct result, Booth's algorithm is used[4, 6]. Simply stated, the algorithm says:

(1) Test the transition of the multiplier bits from the right to left. Assume a 0 bit to the immediate right of the multiplier.
(2) If the bits are equal proceed to step 5.
(3) If there is a 0 to 1 transition, the multiplicand is subtracted from the accumulated product, then 5.
(4) If there is a 1 to 0 transition, the multiplicand is added to the accumulated product, then 5.
(5) Shift the product right by one bit keeping the MSB the same.
(6) Go to 1 for next transition.

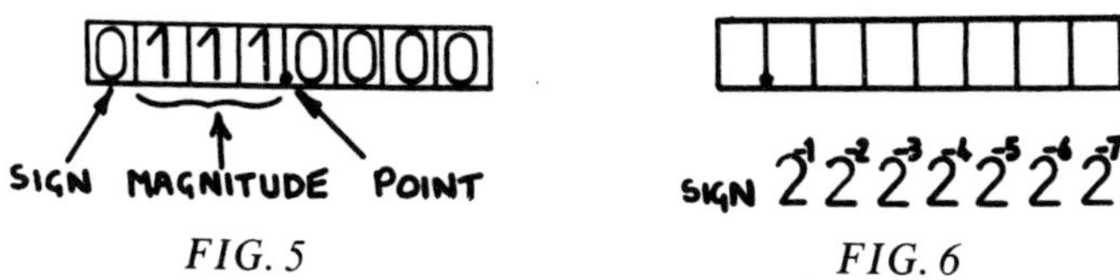

5.00
2.50
0.00
-2.50
-5.00
-7.50
-10.00
desired
actual
amplitude (dB)
0.00
10.00
20.00
30.00
40.00
50.00
60.00
70.00
80.00
90.00
100.00
log frequency
1hz
500hz

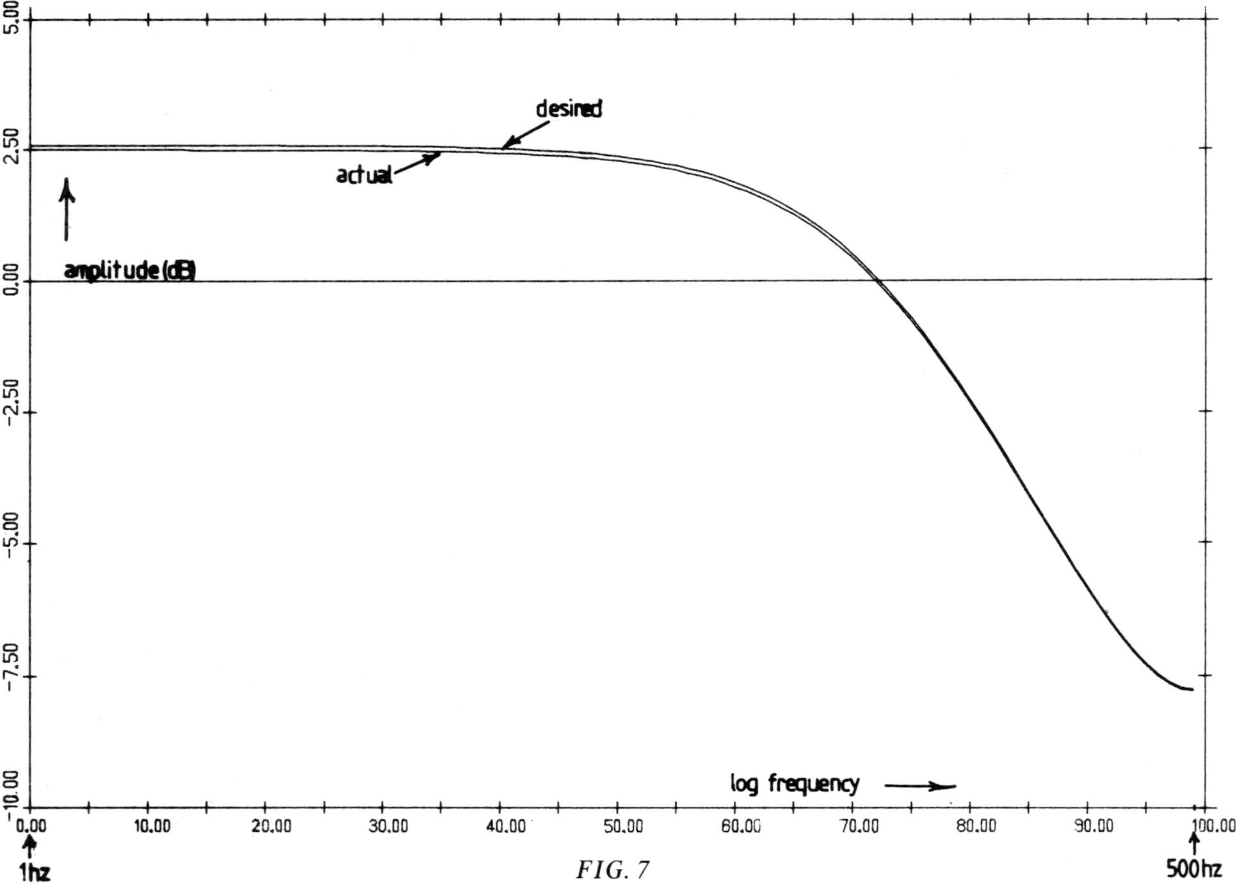

FIG. 7

A flow chart indicating the procedure used is shown in Fig. 8 and the relevant subroutine in the Appendix begins at line 149. The product is a two-byte number stored in locations 0006 and 0007 with label U.

The execution time of subroutine BOOTH is a problem. We have one millisecond to complete all the tasks. If we call BOOTH twice to perform the two multiplications, there is a possibility we may exceed this time limit. To avoid this problem we shall perform all the multiplications before filtering and store the products in two look-up tables (MULT 1 and MULT 2). Altogether there will be 512 products because the input is an 8-bit number with 2^8 (256) different values and there are two coefficients. To increase the speed of the filter program and reduce the amount of memory required, the two-byte products will be rounded to one byte. This rounding causes random errors in the output and is usually treated as noise[5].

The subroutine responsible for the creation of the look-up tables is called TABLE and begins at line 134 in the Appendix. The subroutine which rounds the products begins at line 182 and is called ROUND. Flow charts for these two subroutines are in Figs. 9 and 10. TABLE is called at lines 44 and 49 in the program after the coefficients have been loaded into the A accumulator and the starting addresses of the tables have been loaded into the index register, as required by the subroutine (note how easy it is to change the coefficients and hence the response).

The products in the tables are stored in order, so that to obtain $0.625_{10} \times 43_{10}$, for example, the location 43_{10} down from the starting address of the table would be examined. Therefore, to obtain the correct product, the starting address of the table is stored (in location labelled LOOKUP) and the number to be multiplied is added to the least significant byte of the starting address. If any carry results the most significant byte is incremented by one. The new address obtained from the addition is stored in LOOKUP and the index register then loads this value so that it is pointing at the required product. Indexed addressing (lines 70 and 88 of the program) is then used to access the product. As there are two coefficients, this procedure must be performed twice. The relevant parts of programming begin at lines 57 and 74 in the program. Note that a subroutine could have been used to access the product. The reason one was not is that subroutine calls take a long time to execute compared to other instructions, and as time is critical in the filter loop, subroutines should be avoided in it.

(iv) Addition of the two products

The two products are added together using a single instruction at line 88. The index register is pointing at one product and the A accumulator holds the other at this point in the program.

A problem that may arise with addition is overflow. If two 8-bit numbers are added together the result can be a 9-bit number. To avoid this, the input number can be divided by a power of 2 (since division by 2 is quickly performed in a microprocessor by shifting the contents of the accumulator or memory

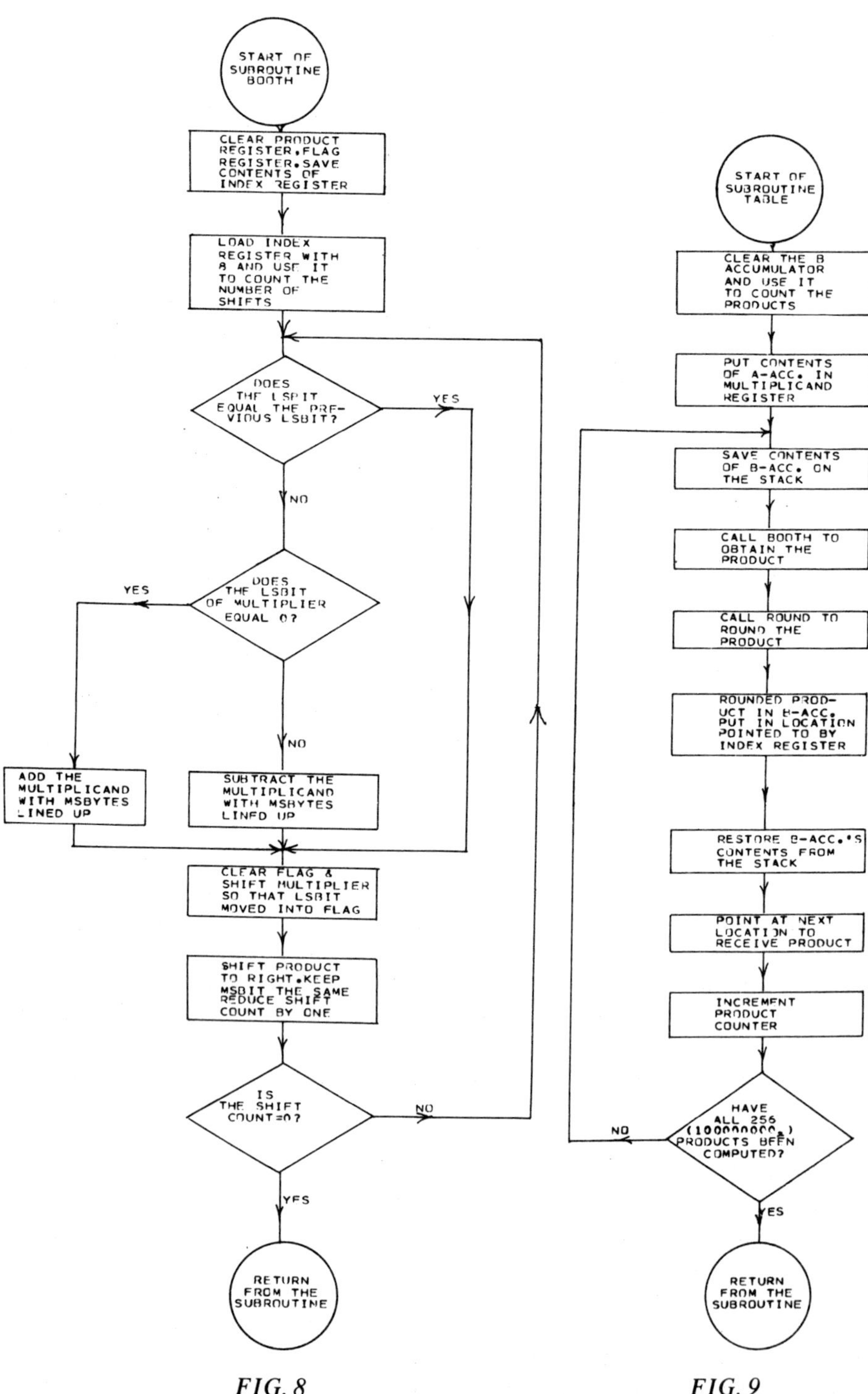

FIG. 8

FIG. 9

130

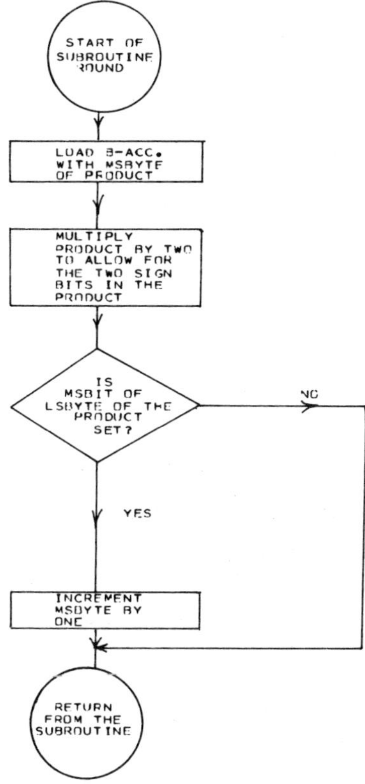

FIG. 10

location one bit to the right) thus reducing the range of magnitudes of the input value. As several sets of coefficients may be used so as to obtain different filter responses it is difficult, if not impossible, to predict the optimum power of 2 by which to divide the input number in this case. Therefore, no account has been taken of overflow in the program. If overflow does occur then the input voltage must be reduced.

(v) Output of the result and conversion to a voltage level
The microprocessor outputs the result in the A accumulator by storing the contents of this accumulator to the IOR of the B-side of the PIA. The IOR is connected to a digital-to-analogue convertor (DAC) which converts the two's complement number to a voltage level. The output of the result occurs at line 95 in the Appendix.

For the B-side of the PIA to act as an output port it must be programmed to do so. Subroutine DA is responsible for this initialization (line 123 in the program). The flow chart for this subroutine is in Fig. 11.

(vi) Storing the result
The number just output is needed to calculate the next output number.
Therefore, we must save this value either in memory or in one of the M6800
registers. As it can be accessed quicker in a register, it is saved in the B accumulator using the single instruction at line 92.

(vii) Waiting for the rest of the time to elapse
The system must sample the input every millisecond. Therefore, the filter loop
must last this length of time. To calculate how long a program will take to
execute, the time in machine cycles for each instruction must be found from a
reference card or programming manual[7] and the total time in machine cycles
can then be found. The actual time is found by multiplying the time in machine
cycles by the period of the clock waveforms. The period must be found as
accurately as possible using a frequency counter or oscilloscope.

Care must be taken when a conditional branch instruction is used. The
program should take the same time to execute regardless of the branch taken.
This is the reason for the no-operations at lines 61 and 79 in the program
which follows the branch if there is a carry out from the addition.

In the program the execution time to the output of the result (line 95) from
the start of the filter loop (line 54) is 79 machine cycles. Assuming a 1 MHz
clock, the execution time is 79 μs. After this the index register is loaded with a
value from locations labelled DELAY which controls the number of times the
HOLD loop is executed. The HOLD loop takes 12 microseconds to execute, so
we would like the remaining time to be a multiple of 12. Hence, a dummy
instruction is used at line 103 to make the execution time to the end of this
instruction 88 microseconds. Thus, 912 μs remain so that the value in DELAY
must be $(912/12) = 76_{10} = 4C_{16}$. The flow chart for this last part of programming is shown in Fig. 12 and a flow chart for the full program is shown in
Fig. 13. Note that the sampling rate can be altered very quickly by changing
the value in DELAY.

The response of the filter with a designed cut-off frequency of 100 Hz using
the coefficients in equations (17) and (18) can be seen in Fig. 14 together with
the response of a filter with the same sampling period but a 50 Hz cut-off
frequency. The actual cut-off frequencies were 106 Hz and 52 Hz, respectively.
The errors in the cut-off frequency can be attributed to coefficient accuracy,
aliasing errors, or an error in the sampling rate.

THE FUTURE
The implementation highlights some of the problems with using microprocessors in digital signal processing applications and some places where
designers can improve microprocessors. The chief problem with using microprocessors to implement digital filters is speed. If filters with large bandwidths
are to be designed, then the sampling frequency must be high. This means
programs must execute faster. We can see in our program that multiplication
takes a long time. as does accessing the products in look-up tables. However,

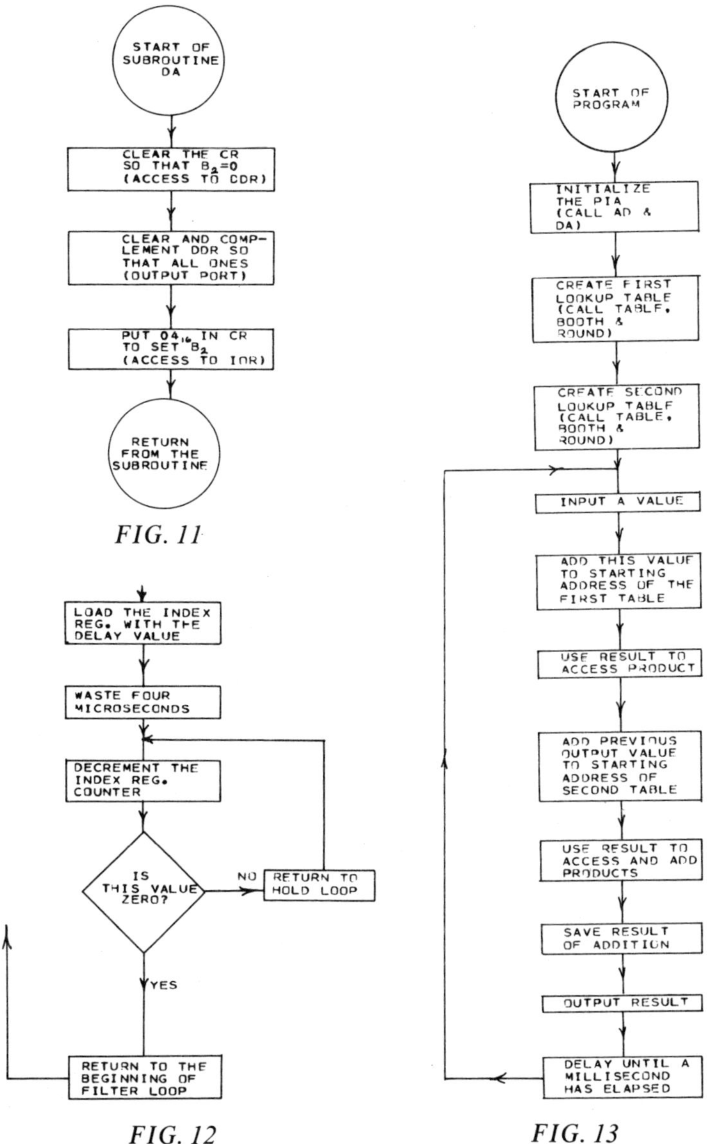

FIG. 11

FIG. 12

FIG. 13

the designers have already noted these problems and microprocessors are being provided with instructions to perform multiplication. This is usually an unsigned multiply facility but a few extra instructions can give a signed product. Also, index register manipulation is being improved, reducing the time to access data in tables[8].

Not only are the instructions sets of processors being improved. New versions of popular microprocessors are being offered, and recently-released devices also, with clock frequencies that are significantly faster than the older

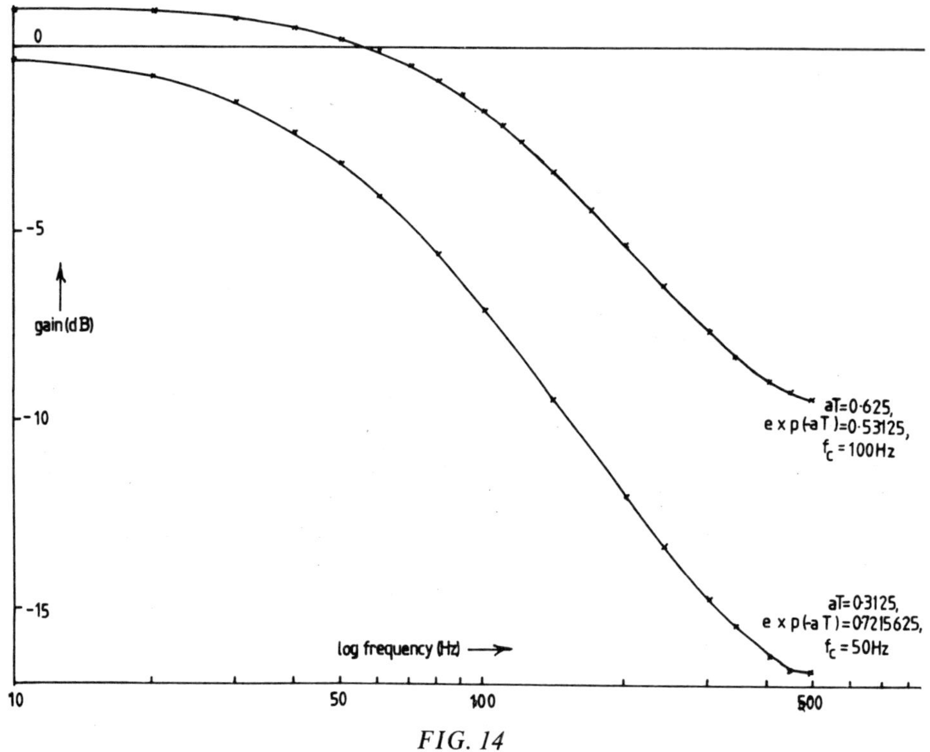

FIG. 14

microprocessors. This is mainly due to the developments in MOS technology and the adoption of bipolar and silicon-on-sapphire technologies.

The dynamic range of the filter and the accuracy of its response are affected by the wordlength. Using multiple-precision can cure these problems but it causes another; reduction in speed since more data must be handled. However, 16-bit processors are becoming available which greatly increases the dynamic range and precision over 8-bit processors.

Other points to note are the addition of analogue-to-digital convertors to microprocessors, making the front end of our system obsolete and the appearance of the single-chip processor with input and output ports, ROM, RAM, and CPU all on a single chip which will allow the package count of a digital filter to be reduced[8].

However, due to the particular tasks that a digital signal processor must perform, it is likely that the bit-sliced microprocessor will be favoured above all other processors. With bit-sliced microprocessors, the user microprograms the processors. This means that he can choose the instruction set, and, consequently, make the most efficient use of the system's architecture for his own application. Also, he can choose the wordlength of the processor by the addition of ALU slices, and lastly, the speed is very fast[9].

The future of digital filters is very bright now that the microprocessor has arrived.

134

REFERENCES

[1]   Terrell, M., Davenport, H. and Ross, M., 'The emerging world of digital filters' *Electronic Engineering*, pp. 26–31, (Mid-October 1977).

[2]   Jury, E. I., *Theory and Application of the z-transform*, Wiley, (1964).

[3]   Stearns, S. D., *Digital Signal Analysis*, Hayden Book Co., Inc., (1975).

[4]   Motorola, *M6800 Microprocessor Applications Manual*.

[5]   Liu, B., 'Effect of finite wordlength on the accuracy of digital filters — a review', *I.E.E.E. Trans. on Circuit Theory*, **CT-18** No. 6, pp. 670–677, (Nov. 1971).

[6]   Mick, J. R., *Digital Signal Processing Handbook*, Advances Micro Devices.

[7]   Motorola, *M6800 Microprocessor Programming Manual*.

[8]   Wiles, M. et al., 'Compatibility cures growing pains of microcomputer family' *Electronics*, pp. 95–103., (2nd February, 1978).

[9]   Alexandridas, N. A., 'Bit sliced microprocessors architecture' *Computer*, **11** No. 6, pp. 56–77, (June 1978).

APPENDIX

```
M6800 MICROPROCESSOR/370 ASSEMBLER                                    PAGE      1

TITLE:   SIMPLE RC LAG EQUIVALENT                          @ 14:17 ON NOV 28, 1978

   LOC     OBJECT CODE    STMT    MTS LINE#       SOURCE STATEMENTS

                            1       1.000               NAM    SIMPLE RC LAG EQUIVALENT
                            2       2.000         *THIS PROGRAM IS A DIGITAL FILTER PROGRAM.THE DIGITAL FILTER
                            3       3.000         *IS BASED ON THE SIMPLE RC LAG FILTER WITH A CUT-OFF FREQUENCY
                            4       4.000         *OF 100 HERTZ.THE DIGITAL FILTER IS IMPLEMENTED WITH A M6800
                            5       5.000         *MICROPROCESSOR AND HAS A SAMPLING RATE OF 1000 HERTZ WHEN
                            6       6.000         *THE CLOCK FREQUENCY IS 1 MEGAHERTZ.
                            7       7.000         *
                            8       8.000         *
            8008            9       9.000         PIAA     EQU    $8008     THE IOR OR DDR OF THE A-SIDE OF THE PIA
            8009           10      10.000         CRA      EQU    $8009     THE CR OF THE A-SIDE OF THE PIA
            800A           11      11.000         PIAB     EQU    $800A     THE IOR OR DDR OF THE B-SIDE OF THE PIA
            800B           12      12.000         CRB      EQU    $800B     THE CR OF THE B-SIDE OF THE PIA
                           13      13.000         *WE HAVE JUST GIVEN SYMBOLIC NAMES TO HEX ADDRESSES
                           14      14.000         *SO THAT IT IS EASIER TO FOLLOW THE PROGRAM
                           15      15.000         *
                           16      16.000         *
   0000                    17      17.000               ORG    $000C     THE STARTING ADDRESS OF THE PROGRAM
   0000    7E 020C         18      18.000               JMP    START
                           19      19.000         *THIS INSTRUCTION CAUSES A BRANCH AROUND RESERVED LOCATIONS
                           20      20.000         *
                           21      21.000         *
   0003    0001            22      22.000         Y        RMB    1         MULTIPLIER
   0004    0001            23      23.000         Z        RMB    1         MULTIPLICAND
   0005    0001            24      24.000         F        RMB    1         FLAG
   0006    0002            25      25.000         U        RMB    2         PRODUCT
   0008    0002            26      26.000         LOOKUP   RMB    2         LOOK-UP VECTOR
   000A    0100            27      27.000         MULT1    RMB    256       0.6125*INPUT TABLE
   010A    0100            28      28.000         MULT2    RMB    256       0.53125*OUTPUT TABLE
                           29      29.000         *SOME LOCATIONS IN RAM HAVE BEEN RESERVED FOR DATA STORAGE
                           30      30.000         *
                           31      31.000         *
   020A    004C            32      32.000         DELAY    FDB    $004C
                           33      33.000         *THIS 2-BYTE NUMBER CONTROLS THE SAMPLING RATE
                           34      34.000         *
                           35      35.000         *
   020C    BD 025F         36      36.000         START    JSR    AD
                           37      37.000         *A-SIDE OF PIA AN INPUT PORT NOW
                           38      38.000         *
   020F    BD 026B         39      39.000                  JSR    DA
                           40      40.000         *B-SIDE OF PIA AN OUTPUT PORT NOW
                           41      41.000         *
   0212    86 50           42      42.000                  LDAA   #%01010000
   0214    CE 000A         43      43.000                  LDX    #MULT1
   0217    BD 027A         44      44.000                  JSR    TABLE
                           45      45.000         *FIRST LOOK-UP TABLE HAS BEEN CREATED
                           46      46.000         *
   021A    86 44           47      47.000                  LDAA   #%01000100
   021C    CE 010A         48      48.000                  LDX    #MULT2
   021F    BD 027A         49      49.000                  JSR    TABLE
                           50      50.000         *SECOND LOOK-UP TABLE HAS BEEN CREATED
```

M6800 MICROPROCESSOR/370 ASSEMBLER   PAGE   2

TITLE: SIMPLE RC LAG EQUIVALENT   @ 14:17 ON NOV 28, 1978

```
  LOC    OBJECT CODE    STMT    MTS LINE#      SOURCE STATEMENTS

                         51      51.000        *
                         52      52.000        *
                         53      53.000        *THE FILTER LOOP PROGRAM BEGINS HERE
  0222    B6 8008        54      54.000        FILTER    LDAA   PIAA     INPUT OF A NUMBER
                         55      55.000        *
                         56      56.000        *THE FIRST LOOK-UP VECTOR IS TO BE CALCULATED
  0225    CE 000A        57      57.000                  LDX    #MULT1
  0228    DF 08          58      58.000                  STX    LOOKUP
  022A    9B 09          59      59.000                  ADDA   LOOKUP+1
  022C    25 03          60      60.000                  BCS    OVFL1
  022E    01             61      61.000                  NOP
                         62      62.000        *NEEDED FOR TIMING CONSIDERATIONS
  022F    20 03          63      63.000                  BRA    PO1
  0231    7C 0008        64      64.000        OVFL1     INC    LOOKUP
  0234    97 09          65      65.000        PO1       STAA   LOOKUP+1
                         66      66.000        *LOCK-UP VECTOR HAS BEEN FORMED
                         67      67.000        *
                         68      68.000        *USE INDEX REGISTER TO POINT TO PRODUCT AND LOAD PRODUCT
  0236    DE 08          69      69.000                  LDX    LOOKUP
  0238    A6 00          70      70.000                  LDAA   X
                         71      71.000        *ACCUMULATOR A HAS 0.625*INPUT IN IT
                         72      72.000        *
                         73      73.000        *THE SECOND LOOK-UP VECTOR IS TO BE CALCULATED
  023A    CE 010A        74      74.000                  LDX    #MULT2
  023D    DF 08          75      75.000                  STX    LOOKUP
  023F    DB 09          76      76.000                  ADDB   LOOKUP+1
                         77      77.000        *B ACCCUMULATOR HAS LAST OUTPUT SAMPLE IN IT
  0241    25 03          78      78.000                  BCS    OVFL2
  0243    01             79      79.000                  NOP
                         80      80.000        *NEEDED FOR TIMING
  0244    20 03          81      81.000                  BRA    PO2
  0246    7C 0008        82      82.000        OVFL2     INC    LOOKUP
  0249    D7 09          83      83.000        PO2       STAB   LOOKUP+1
                         84      84.000        *SECOND LOOK-UP VECTOR HAS BEEN FORMED
                         85      85.000        *
                         86      86.000        *POINT AT PRODUCT AND ADD IT TO PREVIOUS PRODUCT
  024B    DE 08          87      87.000                  LDX    LOOKUP
  024D    AB 00          88      88.000                  ADDA   X
                         89      89.000        *0.625*INPUT HAS BEEN ADDED TO 0.53125*OUTPUT
                         90      90.000        *
                         91      91.000        *SAVE THE RESULT
  024F    16             92      92.000                  TAB
                         93      93.000        *
                         94      94.000        *OUTPUT THE RESULT TO THE DAC
  0250    B7 800A        95      95.000                  STAA   PIAB
                         96      96.000        *
                         97      97.000        *
                         98      98.000        *
                         99      99.000        *THE MICROPROCESSOR MUST WAIT NOW UNTIL 1MSEC HAS ELAPSED
                        100     100.000        *IT DOES THIS BY LOADING THE INDEX REG. WITH A VALUE AND
```

137

138

APPENDIX (contd.)

```
M6800 MICROPROCESSOR/370 ASSEMBLER                              PAGE       3

TITLE:   SIMPLE RC LAG EQUIVALENT                          @  14:17 ON NOV 28, 1978

 LOC     OBJECT CODE     STMT    MTS LINE#     SOURCE STATEMENTS

                         101     101.000       *COUNTING DOWN TO ZERO.THE DELAY DEPENDS ON THE VALUE
 0253    FE 02CA         102     102.000                 LDX     DELAY
 0256    97 08           103     103.000                 STAA    LOOKUP    DUMMY INSTRUCTION TO MAKE DELAY EXACTLY 1MS
 0258    09              104     104.000       HOLD      DEX
 0259    27 02           105     105.000                 BEQ     CONTIN
 025B    20 FB           106     106.000                 BRA     HOLD
 025D    20 C3           107     107.000       CONTIN    BRA     FILTER
                         108     108.000       *
                         109     109.000       *
                         110     110.000       *THE NEXT SUBROUTINE MAKES THE A-SIDE OF THE PIA AN INPUT
                         111     111.000       *PORT.THE PORT IS PROGRAMMED FOR THE PULSE-STROBE MODE.
                         112     112.000       *THIS MEANS THAT LOADING FROM THE IOR CAUSES A SIGNAL ON
                         113     113.000       *THE CA2 LINE.THIS SIGNAL IS USED TO COMMAND THE S/H TO
                         114     114.000       *TAKE ANOTHER SAMPLE.
 025F    7F 8009         115     115.000       AD        CLR     CRA     BIT B2=0  ACCESS TO DDR
 0262    7F 8008         116     116.000                 CLR     PIAA    ALL 0'S IN DDR .INPUT PORT
 0265    86 2C           117     117.000                 LDAA    #$2C    CONTROL WORD FOR PULSE-STROBE MODE
 0267    B7 8009         118     118.000                 STAA    CRA     PUT IN CONTROL REGISTER
 026A    39              119     119.000                 RTS
                         120     120.000       *
                         121     121.000       *
                         122     122.000       *THIS SUBROUTINE MAKES THE B-SIDE OF THE PIA AN OUTPUT PORT
 026B    7F 800B         123     123.000       DA        CLR     CRB     BIT B2=0.ACCESS TO DDR
 026E    7F 800A         124     124.000                 CLR     PIAB    DDR ALL 0'S
 0271    73 800A         125     125.000                 COM     PIAB    DDR ALL 1'S.OUTPUT PORT
 0274    86 04           126     126.000                 LDAA    #$04
 0276    B7 800B         127     127.000                 STAA    CRB     BIT B2=1.ACCESS TO IOR
 0279    39              128     128.000                 RTS
                         129     129.000       *
                         130     130.000       *
                         131     131.000       *THIS SUBROUTINE FORMS THE LOOK-UP TABLES.THE STARTING ADDRESS
                         132     132.000       *OF THE TABLE MUST BE IN THE INDEX REG. AND THE COEFFICIENT MUST
                         133     133.000       *BE IN THE A ACCUMULATOR.
 027A    5F              134     134.000       TABLE     CLR     B       START AT ZERO
 027B    97 04           135     135.000                 STAA    Z       PUT COEFFICIENT IN MULTIPLICAND LOCATION
 027D    37              136     136.000       NEXTX     PSH     B       SAVE THE CONTENTS OF THE B ACCUMULATOR
 027E    BD 028C         137     137.000                 JSR     BOOTH   PERFORM THE MULTIPLICATION
 0281    BD 02C9         138     138.000                 JSR     ROUND   ROUND THE PRODUCT TO 1-BYTE
 0284    E7 00           139     139.000                 STAB    X       PRODUCT IN LOCATION INDEX REG POINTS TO
 0286    33              140     140.000                 PUL     B       RESTORE THE ORIGINAL CONTENTS OF B ACCUMULATOR
 0287    08              141     141.000                 INX             POINT AT NEXT LOCATION FOR PRODUCT
 0288    5C              142     142.000                 INC     B       INCREASE MULTIPLIER BY 1
 0289    26 F2           143     143.000                 BNE     NEXTX DO NEXT MULTIPLICATION IF MULTIPLIER IS NOT 256
 028B    39              144     144.000                 RTS
                         145     145.000       *
                         146     146.000       *
                         147     147.000       *THE NEXT SUBROUTINE IS BOOTH'S ALGORITHM FOR 2'S
                         148     148.000       *COMPLEMENT MULTIPLICATION
 028C    D7 03           149     149.000       BOOTH     STAB    Y       CONTENTS OF B ACCUMULATOR BECOMES THE MULTIPLIER
 028E    4F              150     150.000                 CLRA            CLEAR A ACCUMULATOR
```

M6800 MICROPROCESSOR/370 ASSEMBLER   PAGE   4

TITLE: SIMPLE RO LAG EQUIVALENT   @ 14:17 ON NOV 28, 1978

     LOC   OBJECT CODE   STMT   MTS LINE#   SOURCE STATEMENTS

     028F   97 C6   151   151.000   STAA   U   CLEAR UPPER PRODUCT BYTE
     0291   97 07   152   152.000   STAA   U+1   CLEAR LOWER PRODUCT BYTE
     0293   97 05   153   153.000   STAA   F   CLEAR FLAG
     0295   DF 03   154   154.000   STX   LOOKUP   SAVE THE CONTENTS OF THE INDEX REG.
     0297   CE 0008   155   155.000   LDX   #8   SET THE BIT COUNTER TO 8
     029A   96 03   156   156.000   LP1   LDAA   Y   GOING TO TEST TRANSITION OF BITS IN MULTIPLIER
     029C   84 01   157   157.000   ANDA   #1   SEE IF LSB IS SET
     029E   16   158   158.000   TAB   SAVE THE RESULT
     029F   98 05   159   159.000   EORA   F   SEE IF BITS ARE SAME
     02A1   27 11   160   160.000   BEQ   SHIFT   IF THEY ARE ONLY NEED TO SHIFT
     02A3   5D   161   161.000   TSTB   SEE IF BIT IS ZERO NOW
     02A4   27 08   162   162.000   BEQ   ADD   IF IT IS THEN 1 TO 0 MUST ADD MULTIPLIER
     02A6   96 06   163   163.000   LDAA   U   IF NOT 0 TO 1 MUST SUBTRACT FROM U
     02A8   90 04   164   164.000   SUBA   Z   SUBTRACTION OF MULTIPLIER FROM U
     02AA   97 06   165   165.000   STAA   U   SAVE ACCUMULATED TOTAL
     02AC   20 06   166   166.000   BRA   SHIFT   DO THE SHIFTING OPERATION
     02AF   96 06   167   167.000   ADD   LDAA   U   1 TO 0 TRANSITION IN BITS ADD Z TO U
     02B0   9B 04   168   168.000   ADDA   Z   ADD MULTIPLIER
     02B2   97 06   169   169.000   STAA   U   STORE ACCUMULATED TOTAL
     02B4   7F 0005   170   170.000   SHIFT   CLR   F   EMPTY FLAG
     02B7   76 0003   171   171.000   ROR   Y   CONSIDER NEXT BIT OF MULTIPLIER
     02BA   79 0005   172   172.000   ROL   F   PUT PREVIOUS BIT IN FLAG
     02BD   77 0006   173   173.000   ASR   U   SHIFT ACCUMULATED TOTAL RIGHT ACCOUNTING FOR SIGN
     02C0   76 0007   174   174.000   ROR   U+1   SHIFT SECOND BYTE OF PRODUCT TO RIGHT
     02C3   09   175   175.000   DEX   REDUCE THE BIT COUNTER BY ONE
     02C4   26 D4   176   176.000   BNE   LP1   CONSIDER NEXT BIT IF THERE IS ANOTHER BIT
     02C6   DE 03   177   177.000   LDX   LOOKUP   RESTORE THE CONTENTS OF THE INDEX REG
     02C8   39   178   178.000   RTS
                             179   179.000   *
                             180   180.000   *
                             181   181.000   *THIS SUBROUTINE ROUNDS THE 16-BIT PRODUCT TO 8-BITS
     02C9   D6 06   182   182.000   ROUND   LDAB   U   GET THE MSBYTE OF THE PRODUCT
     02CB   79 0007   183   183.000   ROL   U+1   MULTIPLY PRODUCT BY TWO TO ALLOW FOR THE 15-BIT
     02CE   59   184   183.020   ROL   B   PRODUCT BEING MADE UPTO 16-BITS BY AN EXTRA SIGN BIT
     02CF   79 0007   185   183.040   ROL   U+1   TESTING MSB OF LSBYTE NOW
     02D2   24 01   186   184.000   BCC   NORND   IF IT IS NOT SET DON'T ROUND
     02D4   5C   187   185.000   INCB   ROUND THE MSBYTE UP
     02D5   39   188   186.000   NORND   RTS
                             189   187.000   END

139

NEW FORMS OF OPERATION OBTAINED FOR THE Z-80 CPU

J. M. PÉREZ TOCA
Laboratorio de Sistemas, E.T.S.I.I., Universidad de Navarra, San Sebastian,
Spain

1   INTRODUCTION

Numerous microprocessors are available for the user from various manufacturers. From the standpoint of the designer, the selection of a suitable microprocessor involves investigating its hardware and software. Software investigation includes the examination of many features, including architecture (e.g. number of CPU registers, interface structures, interrupt capability, word length and speed) and programming flexibility.

The number of CPU registers is an important feature. These registers can reduce references to main memory and increase the computing speed. The degree of programming flexibility can be assessed by an examination of the instruction set.

The instruction set furnished by the manufacturer conditions the software design. This paper shows that the structure of the Z-80 CPU includes other capabilities than those listed by the manufacturers, enabling utilization of operation codes which have not been covered. This method is suggested to students and research teams for use with other microprocessors.

2   THE Z-80 CPU ARCHITECTURE AND THE NEW PRACTICAL DISPOSITION OF REGISTERS

The Z-80 CPU contains 208 bits of read-write memory. This is configured into eighteen 8-bit registers and four 16-bit registers. Those registers are classified in: two sets of 6 general purpose registers, two sets of accumulator and flags registers, one program counter, one stack pointer, one interrupt page address register, one memory refresh register and two index registers.

The index registers IX and IY are specially useful for programs using data tables, since the index registers can be used to point to the start location of any data table.

The Z-80 CPU can execute 158 instruction types with a total of 696 valid different operational codes.

However, it is possible to find 95 new codes nearly as useful as those defined by the manufacturers. The new object codes enable the definition of a new form of operation upon the registers, where each index register can be split into two 8-bit registers of free access, which can be operated in the same manner as the general-purpose registers. Those registers will be designated by HI and LI. HI contains the upper portion, and LI contains the lower portion of the index registers. HI and LI are practically identical to the other general-purpose registers with the following restrictions: they cannot perform rotations and shifts upon the bits of HI and LI, and it is not possible to perform operations between HI, LI and H and L.

Thus for those cases not requiring the use of index registers, the programmer can make use of four additional quasi-general-purpose registers.

3 NEW INSTRUCTIONS

The new instructions obtained are:
(a) Load of HI and LI from the A, B, C, D, and E registers.
(b) Load of A, B, C, D, and E from HI or LI.
(c) Load immediate of HI and LI.
(d) Load the contents of HI into LI and vice versa.
(e) Add, and add with carry, between the contents of HI or LI and the data in the accumulator.
(f) Subtract, and Subtract with borrow, between contents of HI or LI and the data in the accumulator.
(g) Increment, decrement, compare, AND, OR and EXOR between the contents of HI or LI and the data in the accumulator.
(h) The operation $r \leftarrow (r) + (r) + 1$, valid for all general-purpose registers.

4 NEW OP-CODES

These are given in Figs. 1 and 2. The following notation is used in the assembly language:
(i) r specifies any one of the following registers: A, B, C, D, E, H, L.
(ii) r^* specifies any one of the following registers: A, B, C, D, E.
(iii) n specifies a one-byte expression in the range 0-255.

The notation has been defined according to the MOSTEK Z-80 Assembly Language.

5 CONCLUSIONS

The new op-codes have been used with success in many programs. The results are reproducible without exception, and no errors have been detected. The new form of operation enables the programmer to configure the array of registers to carry out a particular application, by eliminating one or all of its index registers and replacing each by the HI and LI registers.

The new op-codes have the same formal structure as the 696 primitive operational codes and are easy to use. However, they will only be of use for this particular microprocessor as long as its design is unchanged. The manufacturer may alter this, so care should be taken to check that this does not happen while a set of new codes is in use.

MNEMONIC	SYMBOLIC OPERATION	FLAGS AFFECTED	OP CODE 7 6 5 4 3 2 1 0	HEX	NO OF BYTES	COMMENTS
LD HIX, r*	HIX ← r*	Same as	1 1 0 1 1 1 0 1	DD	2	r, r'
LD LIX, r*	LIX ← r*	LD r,r'	0 1 1 0 M r*	- -		000 = B
			M=0 : LD HIX,r*			001 = C
			M=1 : LD LIX,r*			010 = D
LD HIY, r*	HIY ← r*	"	1 1 1 1 1 1 0 1	FD	2	011 = E
LD LIY, r*	LIY ← r*		0 1 1 0 M r*	- -		100 = H
			M=0 : LD HIY,r*			101 = L
			M=1 : LD LIY,r*			111 = A
LD HIX, n	HIX ← n	Same as	1 1 0 1 1 1 0 1	DD	3	
LD LIX, n	LIX ← n	LD r,n	0 0 1 0 M 1 1 0	- -		
			n	- -		r* = A,B,C,D,E
			M=0 : LD HIX,n			
			M=1 : LD LIX,n			
LD HIY, n	HIY ← n	"	1 1 1 1 1 1 0 1	FD	3	
LD LIY, n	LIY ← n		0 0 1 0 M 1 1 0	- -		
			n	- -		
LD r*,HIX	r* ← HIX	Same as	1 1 0 1 1 1 0 1	DD	2	
LD r*,LIX	r* ← LIX	LD r,r'	0 1 r* 1 0 M	- -		
			M=0 : LD r*,HIX			
			M=1 : LD r*,LIX			
LD r*,HIY	r* ← HIY	"	1 1 1 1 1 1 0 1	FD	2	
LD r*,LIY	r* ← LIY		0 1 r* 1 0 M	- -		
			M=0 : LD r*,HIY			
			M=1 : LD r*,LIY			
LD HIX,LIX	HIX ← LIX	"	1 1 0 1 1 1 0 1	DD	2	
			0 1 1 0 0 1 0 1	65		
LD LIX,HIX	LIX ← HIX	"	1 1 0 1 1 1 0 1	DD	2	
			0 1 1 0 1·1 0 0	6C		
LD HIY,LIY	HIY ← LIY	"	1 1 1 1 1 1 0 1	FD	2	
			0 1 1 0 0 1 0 1	65		
LD LIY,HIY	LIY ← HIY	"	1 1 1 1 1 1 0 1	FD	2	
			0 1 1 0 1 1 0 0	6C		

FIG. 1   *Load group (new op-codes).*

MNEMONIC	SYMBOLIC OPERATION	FLAGS AFFECTED	OP CODE		NO OF BYTES	COMMENTS
			7 6 5 4 3 2 1 0	HEX		
ADD A, HIX	A←A+HIX	Same as	1 1 0 1 1 1 0 1	DD	2	
ADD A, LIX	A←A+LIX	ADD A,r	1 0 0 0 0 1 0 M	- -		
		"	M=0 : ADD A,HIX			
			M=1 : ADD A,LIX			
ADD A, HIY	A←A+HIY		1 1 1 1 1 1 0 1	FD	2	
ADD A, LIY	A←A+LIY		1 0 0 0 0 1 0 M	- -		
			M=0 : ADD A,HIY			
			M=1 : ADD A,LIY			
ADC A, HIX	A←A+HIX+C	Same as	1 1 0 1 1 1 0 1	DD	2	C, flag carry
ADC A, LIX	A←A+LIX+C	ADC A,r	1 0 0 0 1 1 0 M	- -		
			M=0 : ADC A,HIX			
			M=1 : ADC A,LIX			
ADC A, HIY	A←A+HIY+C	"	1 1 1 1 1 1 0 1	FD	2	
ADC A, LIY	A←A+LIY+C		1 0 0 0 1 1 0 M	- -		
			M=0 : ADC A,HIY			
			M=1 : ADC A,LIY			
SUB A, HIX	A←A-HIX	Same as	1 1 0 1 1 1 0 1	DD	2	
SUB A, LIX	A←A-LIX	SUB A,r	1 0 0 1 0 1 0 M	- -		
			M=0 : SUB A,HIX			
			M=1 : SUB A,LIX			
SUB A, HIY	A←A-HIY	"	1 1 1 1 1 1 0 1	FD	2	
SUB A, LIY	A←A-LIY		1 0 0 1 0 1 0 M	- -		
			M=0 : SUB A,HIY			
			M=1 : SUB A,LIY			
SBC A, HIX	A←A-HIX-C	Same as	1 1 0 1 1 1 0 1	DD	2	
SBC A, LIX	A←A-LIX-C	SBC A,r	1 0 0 1 1 1 0 M	- -		
			M=0 : SBC A,HIX			
			M=1 : SBC A,LIX			
SBC A, HIY	A←A-HIY-C	"	1 1 1 1 1 1 0 1	FD		
SBC A, LIY	A←A-LIY-C		1 0 0 1 1 1 0 M	- -		
			M=0 : SBC A,HIY			
			M=1 : SBC A,LIY			
DUPINC r	r←2*r+1	S, P/V, C	1 1 0 0 1 0 1 1	CB	2	
	(r←r+r+1)		0 0 1 1 0 r	- -		
INC HIX	HIX←HIX+1	Same as	1 1 0 1 1 1 0 1	DD	2	
INC LIX	LIX←LIX+1	INC r	0 0 1 0 M 1 0 0	- -		
			M=0 : INC HIX			
			M=1 : INC LIX			
INC HIY	HIY←HIY+1	"	1 1 1 1 1 1 0 1	FD	2	
INC LIY	LIY←LIY+1		0 0 1 0 M 1 0 0	- -		
			M=0 : INC HIY			
			M=1 : INC LIY			

FIG. 2   Arithmetic and logical group (new op-codes).

(continued overleaf)

MNEMONIC	SYMBOLIC OPERATION	FLAGS AFFECTED	OP CODE 7 6 5 4 3 2 1 0	HEX	N° OF BYTES	COMMENTS
DEC HIX	HIX←HIX-1	Same as	1 1 0 1 1 1 0 1	DD	2	
DEC LIX	LIX←LIX-1	DEC r	0 0 1 0 M 1 0 1	--		
			M=0 : DEC HIX			
			M=1 : DEC LIX			
DEC HIY	HIY←HIY-1	"	1 1 1 1 1 1 0 1	FD	2	
DEC LIY	LIY←LIY-1		0 0 1 0 M 1 0 1	--		
			M=0 : DEC HIY			
			M=1 : DEC LIY			
AND HIX	A←A∧HIX	Same as	1 1 0 1 1 1 0 1	DD	2	
AND LIX	A←A∧LIX	AND r	1 0 1 0 0 1 0 M	--		
			M=0 : AND HIX			
			M=1 : AND LIX			
AND HIY	A←A∧HIY	"	1 1 1 1 1 1 0 1	FD	2	
AND LIY	A←A∧LIY		1 0 1 0 0 1 0 M	--		
			M=0 : AND HIY			
			M=1 : AND LIY			
OR HIX	A←A∨HIX	Same as	1 1 0 1 1 1 0 1	DD	2	
OR LIX	A←A∨LIX	OR r	1 0 1 1 0 1 0 M	--		
			M=0 : OR HIX			
			M=1 : OR LIX			
OR HIY	A←A∨HIY	"	1 1 1 1 1 1 0 1	FD	2	
OR LIY	A←A∨LIY		1 0 1 1 0 1 0 M	--		
			M=0 : OR HIY			
			M=1 : OR LIY			
XOR HIX	A←A⊕HIX	Same as	1 1 0 1 1 1 0 1	DD	2	
XOR LIX	A←A⊕LIX	XOR r	1 0 1 0 1 1 0 M	--		
			M=0 : XOR HIX			
			M=1 : XOR LIX			
XOR HIY	A←A⊕HIY	"	1 1 1 1 1 1 0 1	FD	2	
XOR LIY	A←A⊕LIY		1 0 1 0 1 1 0 M	--		
			M=0 : XOR HIY			
			M=1 : XOR LIY			
CP HIX	A-HIX	Same as	1 1 0 1 1 1 0 1	DD	2	
CP LIX	A-LIX	CP r	1 0 1 1 1 1 0 M	--		
(Compare)			M=0 : CP HIX			
			M=1 : CP LIX			
CP HIY	A-HIY	"	1 1 1 1 1 1 0 1	FD	2	
CP LIY	A-LIY		1 0 1 1 1 1 0 M	--		
			M=0 : CP HIY			
			M=1 : CP LIY			

FIG. 2 (contd.)   Arithmetic and logical group (new op-codes).

QSIM — A SOFTWARE EXPERIMENT BASED ON A MICROPROCESSOR EVALUATION KIT

*M. G. HARTLEY† and J. P. ALBERTI**
†Department of Electrical Engineering and Electronics, University of Manchester Institute of Science and Technology, England
**Datakor (PTY) Ltd., Johannesburg, South Africa*

INTRODUCTION

Microprocessors were introduced for the first time into the Department of Electrical Engineering at the University of the Witwatersrand, Johannesburg, in 1976. In that same year one of the authors, M. G. Hartley, on leave from U.M.I.S.T., Manchester, provided a course of lectures on simulation of systems involving stochastic processes. Accordingly, a need arose to provide a laboratory experiment to illustrate the lecture material. The authors, in devising such an experiment, decided to use the opportunity to provide, at the same time, a demonstration of the capability of microprocessors for students new to this subject area. The result is the 'stand-alone' queueing simulation system described in this paper. In discussing the design and implementation of this experiment the authors hope to illustrate how any common microprocessor evaluation kit may be used as the basis of one or other of a series of economical experiments, in addition to its primary function of providing 'hands-on' experience of a small microcomputer system.

Physical situations involving a queue or a set of queues are very common. In general, a queue will form whenever the demand for a service exceeds the current capacity to provide that service. The term 'queueing system', therefore, may be applied to a host of different situations where a demand exceeds a supply. Examples of queueing systems include vehicles in a traffic network, people waiting at a post-office counter, warehouse goods awaiting delivery and jobs awaiting processing in a computer system. If such queueing systems were trivial, it would be unnecessary to give them further consideration. In practice, however, the performance of a queueing system is critical. An inadequate service capacity results in long queues which in turn are likely to have economic and social consequences in many practical situations. An excessive service capacity results in unnecessary idle time, which is a direct financial burden, and may also have other far-reaching effects. From this it is clear that, in many

---

The work was carried out in the Department of Electrical Engineering at the University of the Witwatersrand, Johannesburg.

queueing situations, optimum design can only be achieved after careful consideration has been given to the behaviour of the particular system involved.

The only feasible technique for studying the behaviour of many complicated queueing situations is simulation. Full-scale trials on the real system are often impracticable, either because no physical system yet exists or because of the risk associated with an unsuccessful trial. The only other alternative is mathematical analysis. Unfortunately the mathematical description and analysis of all but the simplest systems is not feasible.

Simulation may be achieved in various ways, but in recent years a preference for digital simulation, as opposed to analogue simulation, has become evident. Here software simulation plays a significant role with a program, run on some form of computer system, used to model the performance of the system under consideration. Accordingly it was decided in this case to use a microprocessor system to illustrate, via simulation, various aspects of queueing systems. Most such systems involve inputs and outputs having certain random properties. Within a simulation, the modelling of these inputs and outputs is achieved by generating random events according to the required probability distributions. Thus special emphasis was devoted to simple techniques for the generation of random events according to different probability distributions.

An Intel SDK-80 stand-alone microprocessor system was used as the basis of the queueing simulator. The approach was to provide the simulation system as an addition to the SDK-80 microprocessor development kit, thus enhancing the value of this kit, without diminishing its educational capability in the area of microprocessor evaluation.

To achieve the enhancement goal, the simulation system, known as QSIM (Queueing SIMulator), is stored on a 1K EPROM (Erasable Programable Read Only Memory) which may be plugged into any standard SDK-80 kit. The operation of QSIM is controlled by the user via the Intel SDK-80 Monitor Program provided on another EPROM, which is supplied as a standard item with the kit. Communication with the user is achieved by the terminal connected to the SDK-80, which may be either a teletype or a visual display unit (VDU). The result of this approach is an experimental facility which is versatile, transportable and may be added to any standard SDK-80 at the cost of a single 1K EPROM.

The simulation software, QSIM, is divided into three sections. The first is the simulation executive program which controls the system by managing the simulation modules. These simulation modules form the basic structure of a generalised queueing system having a maximum of four queues. The second section of software comprises a number of subroutines which may be selected to provide module characteristics. It is in this way that a generalised structure may be set up to simulate many different queueing systems. The final section of software consists of a number of programs designed to allow the user to examine, in detail, the performance of some of the simulation subroutines. Here, particular emphasis is placed on the performance of random event and random number generators.

The procedure for inputting data and setting up a simulation has been kept extremely simple. This demands from the user a measure of understanding of the microprocessor, the monitor program and the simulation software. This approach is consistent with the educational aims of the work. The complete system provides the opportunity for simple experimentation in the areas of microprocessor programming, queueing systems and their simulation, and also in random event generation.

THE SIMULATION MODEL

Fig. 1 shows a block diagram of the system which forms the basis of the simulation model. An epoch-by-epoch approach is adopted[1] in which each element of the model is inspected at frequent and regular intervals and updated as necessary. Such would be the case, for example, when an arrival at the input generator is allocated a specific queue according to an appropriate algorithm, or when a queue is decremented on a departure. A model of the sort illustrated would represent the situation at a post-office, bank or supermarket where customers arrive at random, select a queue on what seems to them a logical basis, wait in a queue for service, conduct transactions which take various times and then depart. The model shown offers the additional feature of queue-switch which permits customers to change their queue while waiting-in-line. The requirements of the various elements of the model, together with their implementation, are discussed in turn below. In order to allow for the possibility of repeated sets of experiments under controlled conditions, provision must be made for arrival patterns to be repeatable. Accordingly, pseudo-random rather than random generators are used throughout. In this way, the Monte Carlo technique, involving repeated tests and a statistical approach, is facilitated.

Input generator

In specifying the input generator, the problem is to determine which probability distributions are needed to represent inter-arrival times corresponding to real situations.

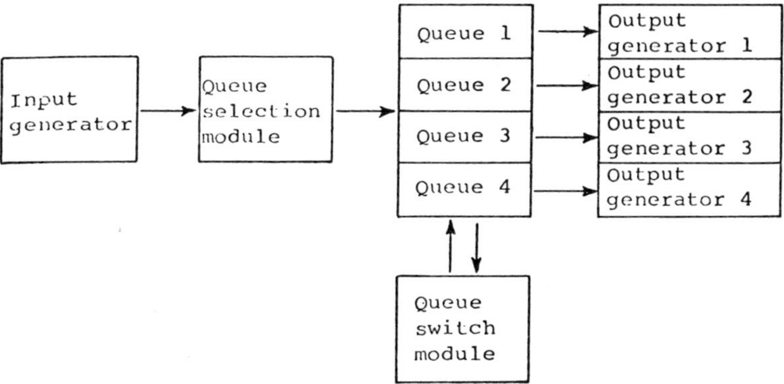

FIG. 1   The simulation system block diagram.

The post-office and similar situations, for example, call customers from an ostensibly infinite population. The probability of a customer input is therefore not affected by the number of people already waiting. This observation leads to the common assumption that the random arrival of customers may be described by a Poisson distribution, since in this process there is a constant probability that an event will occur in a certain period of time irrespective of past history. Thus if $P_n(t)$ is the probability of n events occurring in a time interval t, then the process may be described by the following equation:

$$P_n(t) = \frac{(\lambda t)^n e^{-\lambda t}}{n!} \text{ for } n = 1, 2 \dots .$$

The corresponding probability distribution of inter-arrival times exhibits a negative exponential characteristic of the form $\lambda e^{-\lambda t}$ with mean arrival rate of λ arrivals per unit time.

In some cases the arrival pattern might be such that it would be represented by a pseudo-random event generator with a rectangular distribution of inter-event gaps. This might be the case when modelling the performance of an assembly line for which small variations between individual items, bicycles with a variety of accessories for example, resulted in arrivals at inspection and final test which could be represented by a rectangular distribution of inter-arrival times.

In certain other cases it is likely that arrivals will be regular, with some flow rate determined by the production process itself. This would be true of a production line manufacturing uniform articles.

In order to achieve the above distributions, a subroutine is provided to model a Poisson pseudo-random event generator while a further routine yields pseudo-random arrivals with a rectangular distribution. Both these exploit the properties of m-sequences [2,3] achieved through the use of shift-registers with linear feedback. A regular event generator is also provided.

Queue selection

In situations such as that of the post-office, two main queue selection mechanisms may be recognised. The first case corresponds to each counter providing a full range of service. Here it is fairly reasonable to assume that each new arrival will join the shortest queue. Sometimes the service provided to each queue is specialised. Here the queue which a new arrival joins depends on his business and not the state of the queues themselves. This implies that individual customer inputs will be divided randomly among the queues but according to some predictable numerical ratio.

Thus, for this module, a choice of two functions is provided. One increments the shortest queue when an input occurs, the other divides input events randomly, but in some selective ratio.

Queue switch

A more difficult aspect of queueing systems concerns the possibility of a customer switching queue in the hope of more rapid progress. Little systematic research work has been reported in this area but intuitively some reasonable ideas can be put forward. Firstly, it is reasonable to assume that the last members of the longest queue are most actively interested in finding a better queue and thus most likely to make a move to the shortest queue. This move could be based on the difference in length of the two queues in question, their relative rates of progress or a combination of both these factors. The above situations involve people. In other cases there will be no interaction between queues, as in the case of multiple assembly lines which are essentially independent from each other.

The subroutine provided for queue interaction operates in such a way that if the differences in length between the longest and shortest queue is greater than, or equal to, a preset value, then the longest queue is decremented and the shortest incremented by one. The action is repeated until all the differences are less than the specified value. Alternatively, the switch procedure may be rendered inoperative.

Output function

In some situations a negative exponential or Poisson distribution of service times is appropriate. This applies when the probability of a short service time is high, while longer service times occur with decreasing probability. In many other circumstances it is likely that there will be some minimum and some maximum service time. It is also likely that the distribution of inter-departure times between these two limits will be fairly uniform. This implies a rectangular distribution of inter-departure gaps. When the service provided to each queue is specialised, the service times for a particular queue will be approximately equal. The extraction function would therefore be regular with an average flow rate determined by the service provided.

Accordingly, three subroutines similar to those provided for the input generator will be required.

The overall scheme

The basic block diagram of Fig. 1. may now be re-examined. The constituent modules are generators for input and output functions, a queue selection module, a set of queues and a queue switch module. This will be entirely a software simulation executed through the microprocessor system. A choice of subroutines for each module allows different situations to be modelled.

A module and subroutine approach is used for three main reasons. Firstly, it allows the simulation to be set up easily by defining which modules are to be active and which subroutines are to perform the modular functions. Secondly, it permits examination in detail of individual subroutine performance in order to lead to a better understanding of the components of the simulation system. Lastly, a user is able to write his own additional software subroutines and to incorporate them in the simulation. Fig. 2. shows a simplified flow diagram of the overall simulation process.

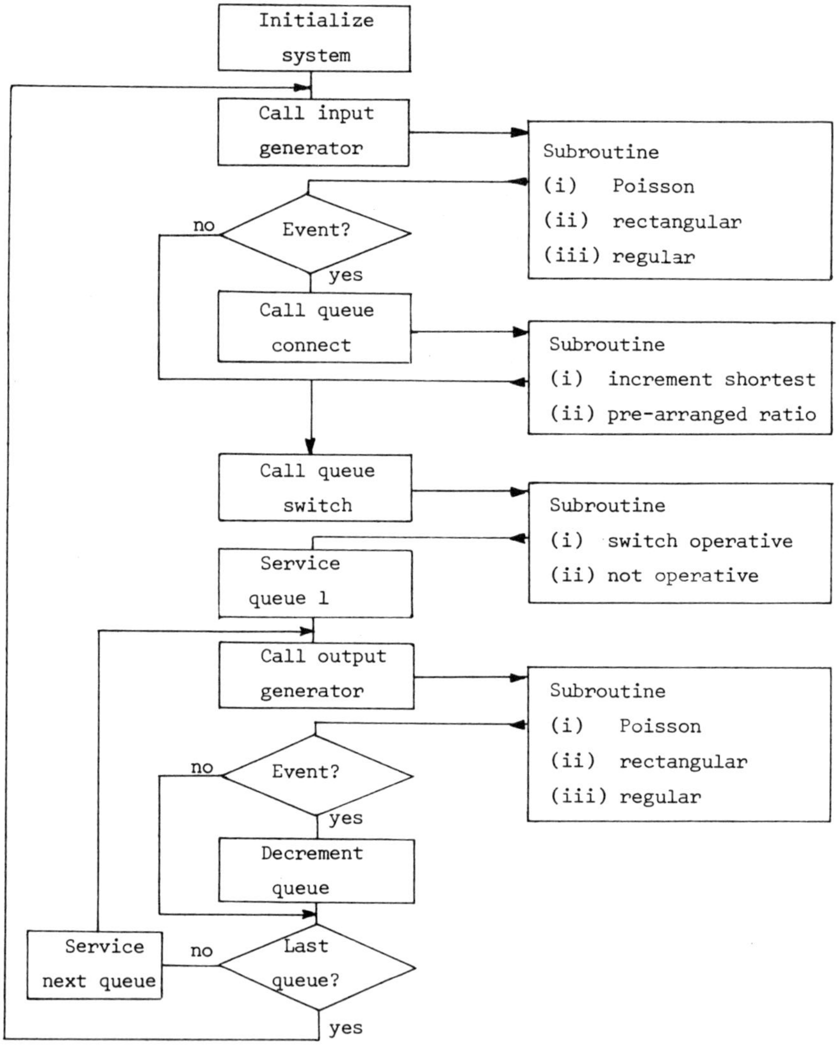

FIG. 2   Simulation flow diagram.

SOFTWARE IMPLEMENTATION OF THE MODEL

The entire body of software developed for the model is named QSIM. The executive is that part which provides overall control by managing the modules and subroutines already mentioned, which constitute the particular model under investigation. There are also a number of utility programs which allow detailed examination of certain features such as the properties of the random generators. Such programs constitute an important part of the individual facility.

150

The simulation executive

The executive program provides overall control during a simulation run. This program may be divided into two sections. The first section, referred to as the Run Control Program, is responsible for the simulation clock and also for organising periodic output, under Monitor Program supervision, of the queue system state. This program, therefore, controls the length of, and the output from, a simulation run. The control of a simulation run is achieved by setting two parameters, STP (step size) and STPNO (step number). These values would be set up before the simulation, using the Intel Monitor. During operation, the PRINT subroutine is called at regular intervals in the progress of the simulation. Each time PRINT is called, the contents of the clock or epoch counter (CLOCK) as well as the length of each queue are outputted via the terminal. The step size or number of epochs to be simulated between print-outs, is determined by STP. The total number of steps simulated is set by STPNO. This implies that a total number of (STP) × (STPNO) epochs are simulated. During the simulation, print-out of queue system state will occur after (STP), 2(STP), ... (STPNO)(STP) epochs.

The second section is the Update Control Program which manages the actual updating of the queue system during each epoch. Fig. 3 illustrates the situation. The process begins by calling the input random event generator module, RGIN. If an event has occurred, the queue connection module, QCON, is called. After this, or if no event occurred, the queue switch module, QSWCH, performs its function. The next step is to service each queue in turn. Firstly for queue 1, the output random event generator, RGO1, is called. If an event occurs, the queue is decremented by the queue extraction module, QEXTR. If no event occurs, it is checked to see if the queue just serviced is the last active queue in the system or not. This is achieved by examining the value of QNO which, before the simulation, was set up to be the number of queues required in the system. This process is repeated until all the queues have been updated. After the queue update procedure is completed, each active queue is checked to see if any queue length has reached its maximum value. If any queue has reached the length of 255 decimal (FF hex.), the simulation is automatically terminated. Before termination, however, the PRINT subroutine is called, which causes final queue state to be printed-out. Control then passes back to the Monitor. If all queue lengths are within limits, control passes back to the Run Control Program and the simulation continues.

There are five random event generator modules in the system. It is possible to define each one of these as providing a Poisson, rectangular or regular function. Associated with each event generator module, RGIN, RGO1, ... RGO4, is a data block. This data block stores, for the particular module, feedback shift register contents, intermediate data during processing as well as information pertaining to the settings put on the generators before the simulation run. Each subroutine, POISS, RECT, REG, can make use of these data blocks, although in a different way. The data block is updated by the generator subroutines during each epoch, and stores the state of that particular

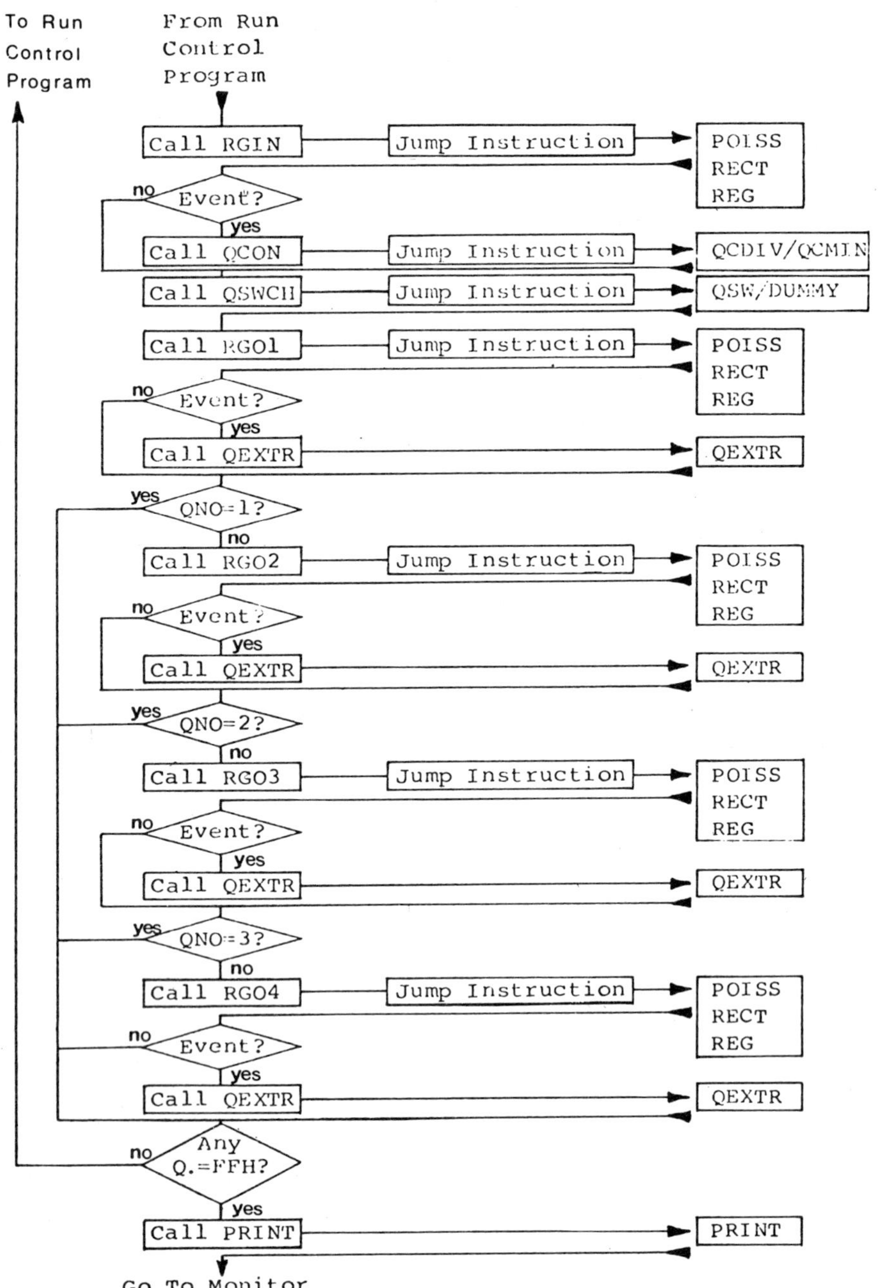

FIG. 3 *The update control program with associated subroutines.*

generator until the next epoch. Since no information is stored in the subroutines themselves, they may be used, with different settings, by more than one generator module during a simulation.

Utility programs
The software includes a number of programs which are not part of the actual simulation system but which are important from an educational point of view. These programs have been designed to help investigate and display data from the random event generators.

System configuration and operation
This was the system chosen to support the QSIM software. It is engineered on a single board and facilities include the following:

(i)   8080 CPU 8-bit word-length
(ii) System controller
(iii) Monitor program mounted on 1K EPROM at address range 0000 to 03FF (hexadecimal). The monitor includes the software necessary to support communication with the teletype or VDU. This is a particularly important consideration. Monitor-functions include display of selected area of memory and CPU register contents, initiation of user programs, modification of contents of memory or registers and finally input of hexadecimal data from console (teletype or VDU) to memory.

The above listing indicates the importance of the Monitor to the model. Without it QSIM would be inoperative. It must be appreciated that the simulation software provided is non-interactive. In other words, there are no prompts or questions from the system before or during simulation. It is therefore necessary to set up all the data defining a simulation before the simulation is run. This setting up is done at a very basic level. The user himself must insert the desired values into memory locations specifically allocated. To achieve this the Monitor Insert Instruction is used. This takes the form:

I{Address}
{Data String} (ESC)

The data string must consist of hexadecimal digits. The first two digits (corresponding to the first 8-bit word) are inserted into the location specified by {Address}. The next two digits in the data string are inserted into the following memory location and so on until the escape key (ESC) is pressed.

The simple operating method used has a number of advantages over a more sophisticated mechanism. Although setting up by this means is more tedious, a close contact between user and system is maintained. The user is forced to appreciate certain aspects of the simulation software and is introduced to the Intel Monitor. Interacting with the system at a basic level places more emphasis on the operation of the simulation, rather than just on the end results. This approach is consistent with the educational objectives of the work.

Another factor to consider is that a comprehensive high-level setting-up procedure could not be supported, together with QSIM, on 1K of EPROM.

Once the data has been set up, the simulation can be started by using the Monitor Go command. This instruction takes the form:

G {Entry Point}

The effect of this command is to pass control to the memory location specified by {Entry Point} and the simulation follows:

(iv) RAM. A section of RAM (256 locations) corresponding to addresses 1300 to 13FF is reserved for the use of the Intel Monitor. A further section of RAM at addresses 1200 to 12FF (256 locations) is used by QSIM.

(v) USART (*U*niversal *S*ynchronous *A*synchronous *R*eceiver *T*ransmitter). This is a serial interface unit to the console device.

(vi) Cannon connector. This plug provides the physical interconnection to the power supply and console device.

The only device additional to the SDK-80 kit required for the implementation of the model is a single 1K EPROM programmed with the routines of QSIM and located in the socket corresponding to the addresses 0400 to 07FF. A memory map is shown in Fig. 4. The locations designated 'optional user RAM and EPROM' are available for the execution of additional and more ambitious experimental work.

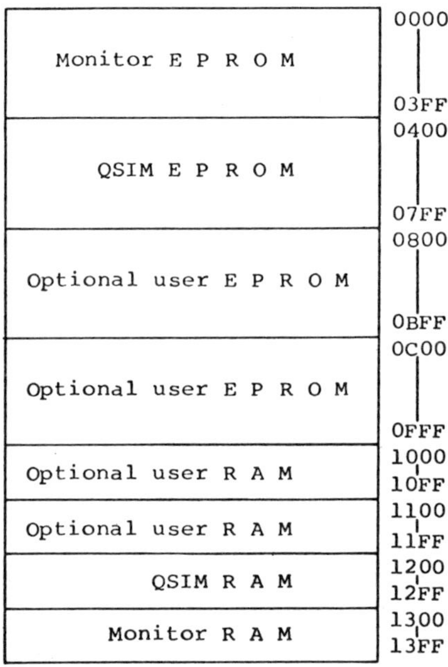

FIG. 4   The SDK-80 memory map.

CONCLUSIONS

An Intel SDK-80 stand-alone microprocessor system has been used as the basis
of this queueing simulator. The obvious educational value of the microprocessor kit used was recognised, and this fact influenced the approach to the
work. The approach was to leave the hardware of the SDK-80 completely
unmodified and to provide the simulation system as a software addition. The
simulation software, known as QSIM, has been provided on a 1K-byte
EPROM which may be plugged into any SDK-80. The operation of QSIM is
controlled by the user via the Intal Monitor program, and communication is
achieved by the terminal, teletype or VDU, which is connected to the SDK-80.
As a result an economical and versatile experiment is now available. Clearly
this approach could be used with advantage for widely disparate software
experiments.

ACKNOWLEDGEMENTS

The work described in this paper was carried out in the Department of
Electrical Engineering at the University of the Witwatersrand. The authors
would like to thank both Professor Hanrahan and Mr. M. B. Dewe (now in
the Department of Electrical Engineering at the University of Canterbury,
Christchurch, New Zealand) for their encouragement and help.

REFERENCES

[1]   Hartley, M. G., Ed., *Digital Simulation Methods*, Peter Peregrinus. London, (1975).
[2]   Hartley, M. G., 'Development, design and test procedures for random generators using
        chaincodes', *Proc. I.E.E.*, **116**, pp. 22–26., (1969).
[3]   Hartley, M. G., 'Evaluation of performance of random generators employing chaincodes',
        Proc. I.E.E., **116**, pp. 27–34., (1969).

PRACTICAL TEACHING OF MICROPROCESSORS FOR POSTGRADUATES IN ELECTRICAL POWER SYSTEMS

J. V. H. SANDERSON, W. S. KWONG* and C. K. NG†*
**Department of Electrical Engineering and Electronics, University of*
Manchester Institute of Science and Technology, England
†Formerly with U.M.I.S.T., now with G.E.C. (Measurements) Ltd, Stafford,
England

INTRODUCTION

It is only in the last ten years that transistorised equipment has been widely used in power systems. This delay was as a result of reluctance to use modern electronic technology where previously electro-mechanical instruments had been used satisfactorily. It is just a little surprising, therefore, that digital equipment has become accepted during the last three years or so. For example, earlier experience with digital frequency meters had been disappointing. These suffered from electrical interference when installed in the particularly noisy environment of an electrical substation. The interference problems were eventually solved using isolation transformers, RF filters, and optical isolators in the production of digital equipment which has performed well in a growing number of substation installations. The solution of the interference problem was a breakthrough. It permitted manufacturers to offer, with confidence, microprocessor-based equipment which had significant advantages in terms of cost, size and performance over conventional electro-mechanical and electronic alternatives.

The main applications of microprocessors in substations are:

(i) *Auto-reclose switching* — a sequence of switches and isolators are opened and closed in order to isolate a faulty circuit yet maintain supplies to healthy circuits and to circuits which are temporarily faulty.

(ii) *Metering* — data is collected from a number of metering points. Power and power factor are calculated and a hardcopy log is produced.

(iii) *Event recording* — a record is maintained of equipment status, e.g. circuit breakers, isolators, relays, air pressures.

(iv) *Protection relays* — current and voltage signals are processed digitally to determine the positions of faults on transmission circuits. This application is still very much at the research and development stage although one manufacturer has recently marketed a digital relay.

156

AN EDUCATION GAP

Very few power system engineers are highly trained in electronics and even fewer are proficient in digital electronic processing. There is, therefore, a gap in the knowledge that power system engineers have about digital equipment and this is knowledge which they need in order to make full use of such equipment. This is true of the users of digital equipment (the electrical utilities) and also, to a lesser extent, of the manufacturers of power system instrumentation. It was once thought that utilities would purchase digital systems on a turn-key basis and would not require detailed knowledge of the functioning of the systems that were installed. This has not, however, been the experience. The utilities have made bold attempts to learn about the new technology so that they can play a full part in the specification of new equipment. In addition, they wish to be able to maintain installations to the extent that simple modifications to hardware and software can be implemented if desired without assistance from the manufacturer.

There is clearly a demand for educational institutions to help fill some of the gap in the education of power system engineers. Certain universities and colleges can and do offer suitable courses in microprocessor technology. The post-graduate courses in Power System Engineering at U.M.I.S.T., which have been running successfully for many years, now include appropriate subjects on computer applications. This paper describes a laboratory teaching equipment which is used for practical training, and which supplements formal lectured material in these courses. The teaching equipment consists of a substation simulator controlled by a microcomputer. The aim is to provide students with some basic understanding of how a microcomputer functions, and to appreciate applications such as auto-reclose switching and event recording in power systems.

MITE HARDWARE

MITE is a *Mi*croprocessor *T*eaching *E*quipment. This acronym also reminds one of those obedient black multipeds (also known as integrated circuits) which now inhabit every item of digital equipment!

MITE is based on a proprietory microcomputer of type PERM[1] (Programmable equipment for relaying and measurement) as used widely in substations in the U.K. power system. PERM is based on the INTEL 8008 microprocessor and consists of power supply, CPU (central processor unit), PROM (programmable read only memory), RAM (random access memory), and timer units and a communications unit for input-output functions. The opto-isolators used in practice in a substation installation are not included since they are unnecessary in a laboratory environment.

The whole equipment (Fig. 1) requires 0.83 m (height) of standard rack (0.48 m wide). PERM itself occupies 0.13 m of the rack height. To complete the equipment, an input-output peripheral is required. A teletype or VDU is suitable. The upper 0.7 m of rack is occupied by the substation simulator. This is constructed as a mosaic panel using twenty three building units. Up to

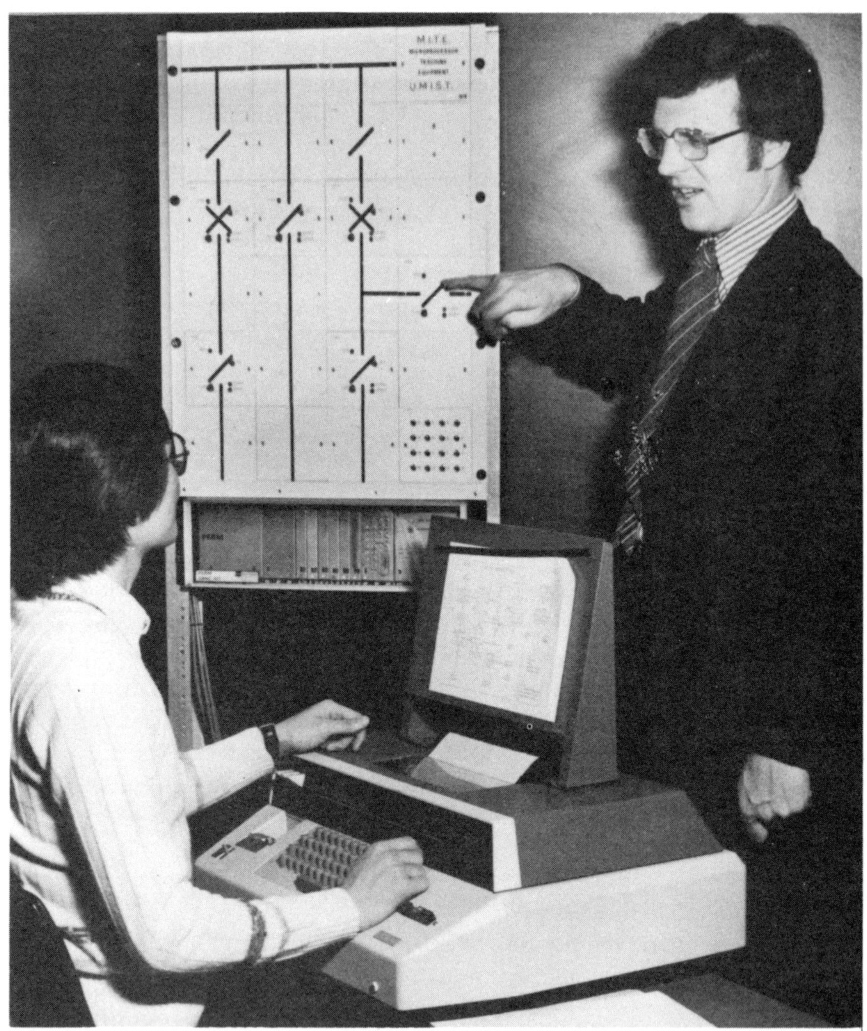

FIG. 1   Overall view of MITE showing substation simulator and PERM
microcomputer.

sixteen of these may be made to simulate a circuit breaker or an isolator
(Fig. 2). This simulation is achieved using electronic circuits which are potted in
resin for durability and which have LEDs (light emitting diodes) and switches
protruding through the engraved facia of each unit. This facia is removable and
reveals potentiometers which can be adjusted to alter the response time of the
circuit breaker/isolator. By adjusting these potentiometers and changing the
plastic facia, a circuit breaker can become an isolator since the simulator circuit
is basically the same for each. Connections are made from these circuits to
PERM so that the latter can close a 'circuit breaker' or open an 'isolator'. The

158

FIG. 2   A mosaic unit used in construction of substation simulator. The potted electronic circuit is identical for circuit breaker and isolator units.

'open circuit breaker' and 'close isolator' operations are performed manually by operating a push button on the front panel. In practice, of course, the 'open circuit breaker function' is achieved by the protection relays which operate independently from PERM. One of the LEDs on each panel shows the presence of a command from PERM, and the other two show the status of the simulator, e.g., 'circuit breaker closed' and 'circuit breaker not open'. PERM is supplied with corresponding inputs from the simulators so that the computer also knows the status of the substation plant. A plant failure can be simulated by moving the FAIL switch on the corresponding mosaic unit.

Additional inputs to PERM are represented by an array of switches. These correspond to the protection relay states on the four transmission lines and on the busbars, the air pressure relays which must indicate correctly for a switching sequence to be undertaken by PERM and various subsidiary inputs. Finally, a potted circuit is provided to simulate up to six 'check synchronism' relays. PERM must check before closing a circuit breaker that the voltages on either side of it are in synchronism.

SOFTWARE

The software used within PERM is in two parts and is structured in a modular manner. The first part consists of a number of standard subroutines (called *Sections*) which are used in every software design for a substation. These include the *Starter, Input, Output, Update Data, Update Timer, Self Checking* and *Event Recording* routines.

The second part consists of a number of subroutines called *Sets*. Each *Set* is a
standard program written to deal with a part of a substation. For example, *Set*
31 deals with a circuit breaker and a busbar isolator. When *Set* 31 is called
together with *Set* 11 (a line and line isolator), the program associated with a
single circuit e.g. *Line* 1 (Fig. 3) is complete. The software can thus be tailored
to a particular substation configuration by calling the standard *Sets*
accordingly.

This modular structuring of the software is a recent advance in programming
for automatic switching application[2]. By using this scheme, the engineering
time spent on program writing, de-bugging, flowcharting and documentation
can be greatly reduced. It also enables engineers and students to appreciate the
organisation of the software without the need to understand the detailed
machine code within the software modules.

THE TEACHING SCHEME

The MITE equipment is designed for teaching not only M.Sc. students who
enrol on the Power System Engineering Courses at U.M.I.S.T. but also for in-
service training of engineers from industry.

Students are prepared for the MITE project by attending an examinable
course of ten lectures. The object of the course is to educate participants to the
point where they can participate in the specification of microprocessor systems
for power system applications.

The present provision for M.Sc. laboratory time allows 4 × 3-hour practical
sessions per project. The plans to offer in-service training for engineers from
industry provide for a more leisurely 4 × 6 hours of laboratory time. This is a
more appropriate period of learning on the equipment.

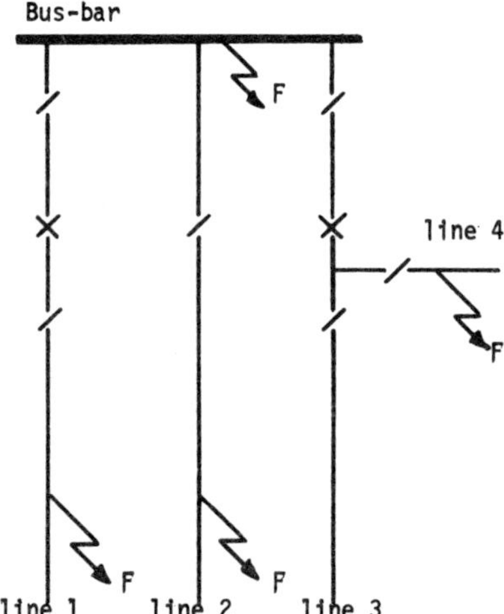

FIG. 3   *Positioning of fault F for delayed auto-reclose study*
— × — circuit breaker, —/— isolator.

During the first practical session on MITE, the M.Sc. students are allowed to examine the PERM hardware. The printed circuit boards are removed from the rack and the components are identified. The purpose of this is to clear the mystery of 'what is inside a computer'. The students then interrogate PERM by using a monitor program which enables instructions to be given from the teletype keyboard. In this way they can examine the contents of PROM and can examine and change the contents of RAM. In addition, the monitor program, which is itself resident in PROM, allows memory to paper tape dumps, paper tape to memory loads and program start commands to be performed. The exercises that can be performed during the first three-hour session are various and no fixed goals or firm objectives are set. The demonstrator, who needs to provide close supervision at this stage, can easily modify demands based on the learning rates which he observes. The most important aim is to instil some confidence into the students by removing as much of their ignorance as possible. The students are encouraged to explore various possibilities and in this way to learn for themselves. For example, contents of memory locations in RAM can be examined and changed (using the monitor) and the students can prove this for themselves. Locations in PROM can be examined but not changed. However, a significant proportion of students try to change a PROM location as they did with RAM. When this happens they are reminded that irradiation with ultra violet rays is necessary to release the trapped charges which represent the information in PROM.

PERM includes a timer card which is used by the monitor to keep the time of day. The demonstrator explains that the monitor's clock was set accurately earlier in the day and they are invited to check their wrist watches by asking PERM for the current time. This simple lesson is used to introduce the concept of *real time*. The operation of the *real time clock* is explained and the functioning of an *event recorder* is demonstrated by arranging for MITE to record the time of day and print a warning message when a 'Low Air Pressure' switch is depressed on the simulator. The operation of the input and output interfaces are also investigated. The students choose an isolator on the mosaic panel and after referring to the reference paper, cause the computer to issue an open command to that isolator. The LED for the isolator momentarily glows as the command is received, and after the delay which is preset in the simulator to be 30 s., the opened and closed LEDs reverse their status. Inputs to PERM can be examined and tested in a similar way.

The ideal size of student group is two because this allows the students to take turns at operating MITE. Since good concentration is difficult to maintain for three hours, a periodic re-shuffle of seats is quite desirable. Unfortunately, the M.Sc. laboratory timetable allows only five projects to be run consecutively and so the group size is extended to three in order to allow fifteen students instead of ten the opportunity of the experience. The increased group size is manageable and is not thought to degrade the learning rate of the students significantly.

During the second three-hour session the demonstrator shows that, when a fault occurs on the power system and this is detected by the protection relays (simulated by moving a switch of the mosaic panel), PERM correctly controls a sequence of circuit breaker and isolator operations. This sequence should restore power to the faulty line and, if the fault is still present, isolate the faulty line and restore supplies to the adjacent healthy circuits. This short demonstration serves to remind the student of what the equipment does. The remainder of the session is devoted to learning about the software, i.e. how it is structured with starter and update sections, timer and flags. The function of the sets and sections are also explained. The existence and importance of the self-check routines are also learned at this stage of the project. These are concerned with ensuring that a fault in the PERM electronics does not result in an incorrect command being issued to the substation plant. For example, a circuit breaker must only be instructed to close if the voltages on the circuits it is about to join are in near synchronism. It is just conceivable that a fault within the computer could cause this action to be taken without the necessary conditions being satisfied. The utilities who purchase PERM regard self-checking as being most important and a feature of software which is not included in many other microprocessor systems.

By the close of the second session the students should have followed the *delayed auto-reclose scheme* (DAR) in steps, and should have a good understanding of the operation for a single line reclosure (fault on line 1, Fig. 3).

During the third session they follow the other DAR cases in steps by calling in the appropriate *subroutines* and *sets*. The cases considered are:
(i) Mesh corner reclosure (fault on line 4, Fig. 3).
(ii) Reclosure involving two circuit breakers (fault on line 2, Fig. 3).
(iii) Busbar zone protection.
(iv) I/O failure, low air pressure, breaker failure.

The fourth and final session is concerned with programming and software.

The students are taught how data are input and output using memory-mapped instructions, how the teletype is concerned with ASCII code characters and how these are generated by PERM. The students then write a program concerned with timing which is used in the subsequent exercise on auto-switching.

In the final exercise, the students working together as a group write a simple program which reads in the status of a circuit breaker, a line isolator and a protection relay. The program initiates an auto-reclosure sequence when a circuit breaker trips after having supplied load for more than 4 seconds. Otherwise, the program causes the line isolator to open. This reclosure scheme designed by the students is bound to be simple and incomplete but it is nevertheless a worthwhile exercise. The students are encouraged to criticize their scheme, to explore every deficiency and to suggest improvements.

In the present form, the teaching scheme requires a particularly specialised type of supervision for all but the first of the four three-hour sessions. The demonstrator must have general expertise in microprocessors and particular expertise in the software used in MITE. In addition, knowledge of power system switching is required. It is recognised that reliance on such supervision represents a basic weakness in a teaching scheme and so it is the intention to prepare a comprehensive guide to the procedures involved. This will be based on the first year of teaching the material to the M.Sc. course which was completed in March 1979.

CONCLUSIONS

Digital equipment, and especially microprocessor equipment, is becoming widely used in power systems, a situation which was not envisaged ten years ago. There is a shortage of engineers who have knowledge of such equipment and there is a strong need for suitable post-graduate teaching in this area.

A worthwhile amount of appreciation of microprocessor systems can be taught to post-graduate students who have no pre-knowledge of the technology, and this can be achieved within ten hours of formal lectures and twelve hours of practical sessions. Students who receive this training obtain the confidence and the basic knowledge required for them to participate in the purchase of such equipment. They also obtain the necessary experience to appreciate what is involved in the detailed system engineering of microprocessor installations.

ACKNOWLEDGEMENTS

The authors are grateful to the following:

(i) G.E.C. (Measurements) Ltd., Stafford, England, for material support and advice.
(ii) The Central Electricity Generating Board (North West Region) for consultations at the planning stage.
(iii) Mr. Peter Thompson, who was concerned with the construction of the substation simulator in the departmental workshops at U.M.I.S.T.

REFERENCES

[1]   G.E.C. (Measurements) Ltd., Stafford, England, *Programmable Equipment for Relaying and Measurement, Publication* R5174.
[2]   Cottam, W. A., 'A New Method of Developing Microprocessor Software for Automatic Switching', *M.Sc. Dissertation, U.M.I.S.T.*, (1977).

MICROPROCESSOR SHORT COURSES FOR INDUSTRY

T. J. TERRELL and R. J. SIMPSON
Systems and Instrumentation Division, Preston Polytechnic, England

1 INTRODUCTION

Microprocessor technology has developed at a rapid pace over the past few years [1], and the effects are far-reaching in almost every industry. One result of this has been an ever-increasing demand for courses on microprocessors. The demand shows no sign of abating, especially with the widespread coverage given by the mass media to the social and technological implications of microprocessor systems. Furthermore, great interest has recently been generated by the Department of Industry [2] in the U.K., who offer financial assistance for three categories of support, namely, under the headings *Industrial Awareness and Training, Feasibility Studies and Consultancy Support*, and *Microprocessor Application Support*.

At an introductory level we have been involved with two main types of user (or potential user), the undergraduate engineering student and the practising engineer. We have adopted a 'hands on' approach to the teaching of microprocessors, which is similar to the method described by Lee [3]. In this paper we describe in detail the various aspects of the planning, organisation and operation of our microprocessor short courses for the practising engineer or technician. However, it should be noted that many of the details concerned with the teaching aspects of these courses are equally appropriate and applicable to electrical engineering undergraduate courses.

The microprocessor short courses we have organised and presented may be categorised under two broad headings: *Open* and *Closed*. We define an *Open* course as that for which any student may enrol, this may be contrasted with a *Closed* course which is restricted to participants from one industrial organisation. Many institutions offer the former type, as is evident from an abundance of course publicity, and brief details are readily available from course brochures. However, it is a pity that details of the latter are normally restricted to the parties concerned, because, in general, this information could prove useful to students and teachers involved in microprocessor education. In this paper, one of our aims is to ameliorate this deficiency by discussing, in particular, our experiences in operating *Closed* short courses.

Our initial courses were all of the fixed duration *Open* type, similar to those offered by many other institutions. These courses were of the B type as shown in Table 1. Some participants of these courses felt that stronger links should be developed between our polytechnic and their respective industrial organisations.

TABLE 1 *Summary of courses*

Course code	Title	Main aims	Typical categories of course members	Course capacity (max. number)	Course duration
A	Microprocessor appreciation	General introduction to the basic concepts . of microprocessor systems	General engineering background	25–30	half day
B	Introduction to microprocessor systems	Introduction to structure of microprocessor systems: hardware and software aspects	Engineers with specialist electronic back-ground	12	1 day
C	as B	As B but less depth of treatment	Engineers with non-specialist electronic back-ground	12	1 day
D	Project course	To extend the basic knowledge gained in courses B or C	As B or C	12	3 × 1 day
E	Extended project course	As D but more demanding	As B or C	12	6 × 1 day

In subsequent discussions with industry it became apparent that there was a demand for other types of microprocessor courses, and as a result, a series of meetings was undertaken, embracing a wide spectrum of personnel (managers, technicians, engineers, etc.) in order to identify specific needs.

As a result of these discussions, several different types of courses have been conceived, and brief details are summarised in Table 1. Selection of the appropriate course(s) may be achieved by following the flow chart shown in Fig. 1, which should be read in conjunction with Table 1.

2   PLANNING OF CLOSED COURSES

It was felt that in order to formulate the appropriate *Closed* courses, organised planning was necessary. The authors' approach, in tackling this problem, was to adopt the method illustrated in flow chart form in Fig. 2. This structured approach has proved successful in formulating the courses and their contents.

In an attempt to optimise the educational value of the courses we have included 'feedback loops' as shown in Fig. 2. Necessary changes concerned with the planning of the course contents are accommodated by loop 1. Furthermore, any necessary changes arising out of course operation are accommodated by loop 2. The latter is an on-going iterative process which can only operate

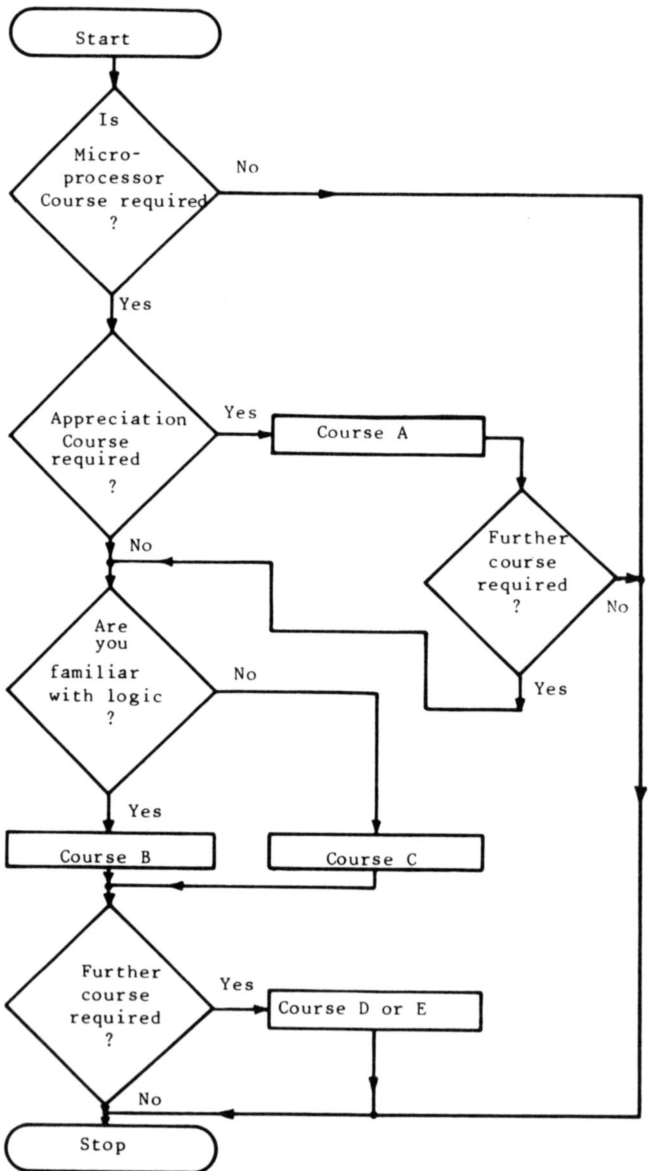

FIG. 1   Flowchart for course selection.

successfully when the selection process in Fig. 1. is implemented correctly. In practice, this implies very close collaboration between course organisers and the industrial organisation.

We have found that our approach has assisted the formulation of projects relevant to specific industries. These are then included in the planned courses as

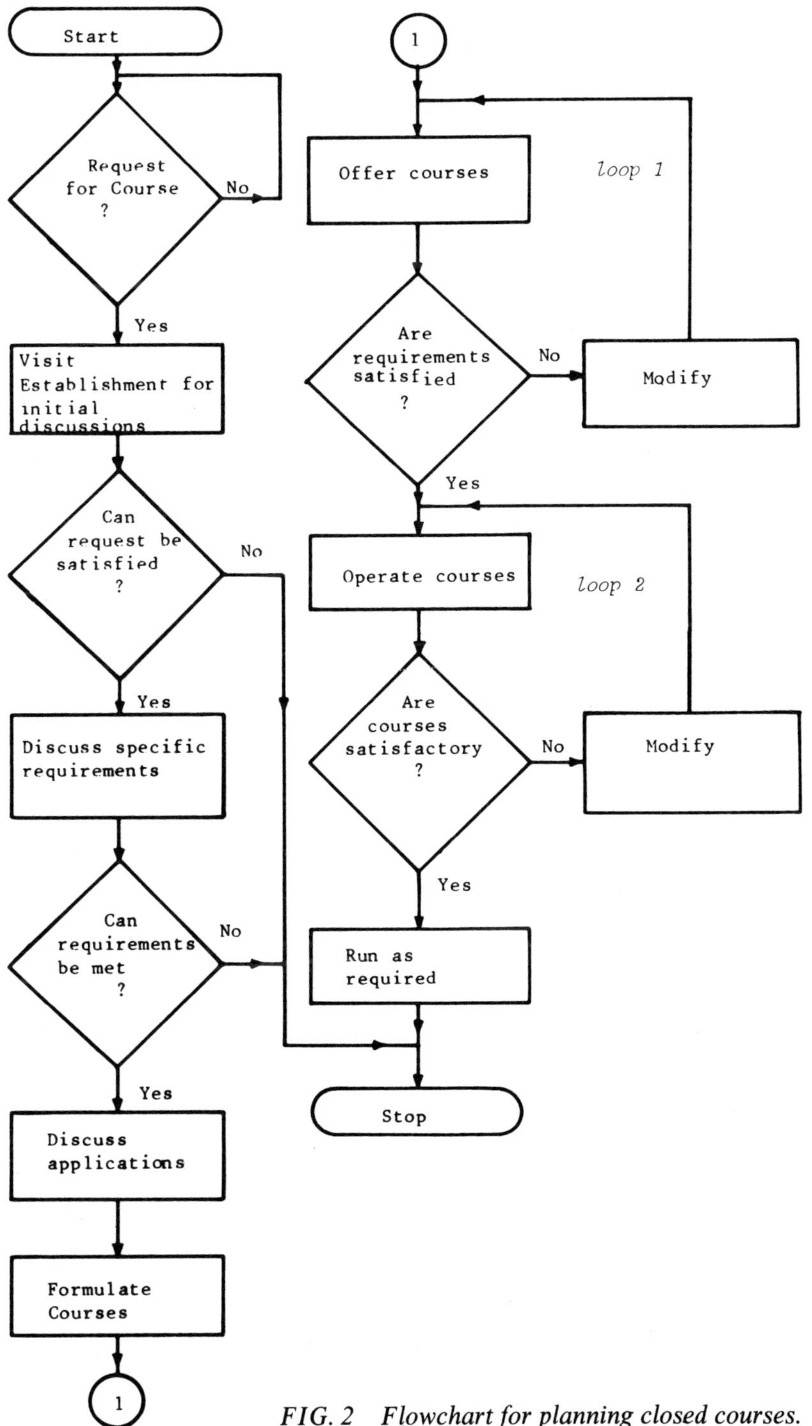

FIG. 2   Flowchart for planning closed courses.

demonstration material for courses B and C, and as projects to be developed
further in courses D and E. For example, for the aerospace industry, projects
may involve digital filters or engine start-up routines, whereas, in contrast,
transducer linearization projects may be appropriate for the temperature
control industry.

3   COURSE ORGANISATION

Whilst it is obviously necessary to have adequate resources available, in order
to implement planned courses, we consider from our experiences that the
essential resources are:
(i)   teaching aids and laboratory equipment,
(ii)   sufficient and suitable accommodation (classroom and laboratory),
(iii) adequate staffing, and
(iv)   documentation.

In addition we believe it is desirable to have cross assembler, simulation and
microprocessor development systems. The 'hands on' philosophy dictates that
a microprocessor teaching aid and associated peripheral are available to all
course members. In practice, in our courses, participants work in groups of
two, each group having a dedicated teaching system for their exclusive use
throughout the course. The system consists essentially of a teaching aid,
described in Sec. 4.2.2, and a teletype. The approximate cost of a system is
£1500 and, with limited resources, we could only provide six systems. This
consequently restricts course membership to 12 (see Table 1).

An advantage of having a restricted course membership is that we can
readily provide appropriate accommodation. We use a small room for lectures,
which helps to promote a congenial atmosphere. This, we believe, is a desirable
feature for short courses of the type we offer, and helps to develop the appropriate rapport between lecturer and student. Also we are fortunate that we can
use an adjacent teaching laboratory for the practical demonstrations and
laboratory exercises.

We can provide adequate staffing of the courses because over the past few
years we have built up our expertise in microprocessor system development
and research. We currently have an enthusiastic microprocessor team consisting of four staff, all being involved with the courses.

We provide documentation in the form of duplicated course notes to cover
the essential contents of the lectures and the teaching system. For the duration.
of the corse each student is provided with a programming manual.

We have an Exorciser and microprocessor development system available in
the laboratory for student use as appropriate. In addition, simulation facilities
are available on the Polytechnic's interactive Prime 300B via a teletype located
in the laboratory.

4   DETAILS AND OPERATION OF COURSES

By referring to Table 1 it can be seen that the five courses may be categorised
under the three broad headings: *Appreciation* (A), *Introduction* (B and C) and

Project (D and E). The essential differences are in course content and presentation.

4.1 *Course A*

This course is normally attended by personnel with a general engineering and/or management background. The main objective is to provide an awareness and appreciation of the basic concepts of microprocessor systems. The course consists of a lecture/demonstration and question/answer session. Unlike the other courses it does not require the adoption of the 'hands on' philosophy. Therefore course membership is readily increased to between 20 and 30, which still permits appropriate student participation in the question/answer session. We have found that this course often serves as a feeder to the *Introduction* type courses (see Fig. 1).

During the lecture session we explain, without recourse to too much detail, the essential features of a microprocessor system and its capabilities and limitations. We have found, from experience, that substantial visual support material is appropriate for conveying the concepts of microprocessor systems. The visual aids we use include:

(i)   selection of digital system hardware to portray developments over the past 20 years.

(ii)   microprocessor system hardware, including MPU, PIA, EPROM, RAM, etc.

(iii) Slides and overhead projector diagrams.

The portrayal of the digital system hardware development helps to put the microprocessor in perspective, especially when a practical system configuration is described. The participants on the course are very receptive to a presentation making extensive use of slides and the overhead projector in preference to a 'chalk and talk' approach. Therefore we use this method to present the basic ideas associated with topics such as number systems, memory mapping, and peripheral interfacing. System operation (programmability) is illustrated by means of simple practical demonstrations based on the teaching aid (see Sec. 4.2.2). We generally use a logic sequence control operation and a binary code conversion at this stage.

4.2 *Courses B and C*

At the outset of these courses it is pointed out that microprocessors are frequently employed in a specialised role, for example, in sequence controllers, signal processors (digital filters) and instrumentation systems. Inclusion of a practical demonstration serves as a focal point for promoting a brief, but thought provoking, question and answer session, thereby allowing student participation at an early stage. The demonstration uses the teaching aid which is based on the M6800 evaluation-kit, (see Sec. 4.2.2). In describing the demonstration opportunity is taken to draw the students' attention to:

(a)   the hardware (MPU: RAM: ROM: PIA etc.),

(b)   the software (source program; editor; assembler)

(c)   the MIKBUG firmware, and

(d)   the peripherals and interfaces.

The inclusion of a practical, albeit simple, demonstration has the advantage of stimulating the students' interest, and in addition allows microprocessor terminology to be introduced and explained. Furthermore, the demonstration affords the opportunity to stress that the engineer concerned with the development and implementation of microprocessor systems, must have a good working knowledge of hardware, firmware and software.

Having whetted the students' appetite for more detailed information and aroused an interest in microprocessors and their applications, attention is then given to presenting lecture material which prepares the students for the important laboratory ('hands-on') phase of the course. The laboratory-based instruction is, in the authors' opinion, an important part of the course because it provides the student with:

(i)   the facilities (M6800 teaching-aid, VDU or Teletype, peripheral LSI circuits, etc.), and

(ii)   the opportunity to investigate, verify and develop lecture/tutorial material. However, before embarking upon the laboratory phase of the course, some prerequisites are required, as outlined in the following section.

4.2.1   *Prerequisites for the laboratory-based instruction.* Lecture material, which is concerned with the prerequisites for the laboratory-based instruction, is presented in the order listed below:

(a)   Number systems — binary, octal and hexadecimal number systems are described and demonstrated using the M6800 teaching aid.

(b)   A minimum system configuration is described.

(c)   The evaluation-kit memory map is explained.

(d)   A basic programming model of the M6800 is explained.

(e)   The M6800 addressing modes are explained.

(f)   The M6800 Instruction Set is presented, and examples are included to emphasise the operation, condition codes and addressing modes.

(g)   The MC6820 PIA initialisation and programming is explained and demonstrated.

Once the students have studied the lecture material outlined above, they are ready to undertake the laboratory phase of the course.

4.2.2   *Laboratory-based instruction.* In the laboratory we make substantial use of our teaching aid, which has been developed from the basic M6800 evaluation-kit, see Fig. 3. The system contains MIKBUG[4] firmware, and Address, Data and Control signals are brought out to 2 mm sockets. In addition, LED displays, switchable logic levels and DIL sockets are provided. Hence it is possible for the students to 'patch-up' a variety of relatively simple laboratory exercises and mini projects.

The first task for the students is to investigate the MIKBUG routines using the teaching aid and a teletype. They then undertake a set laboratory assign-

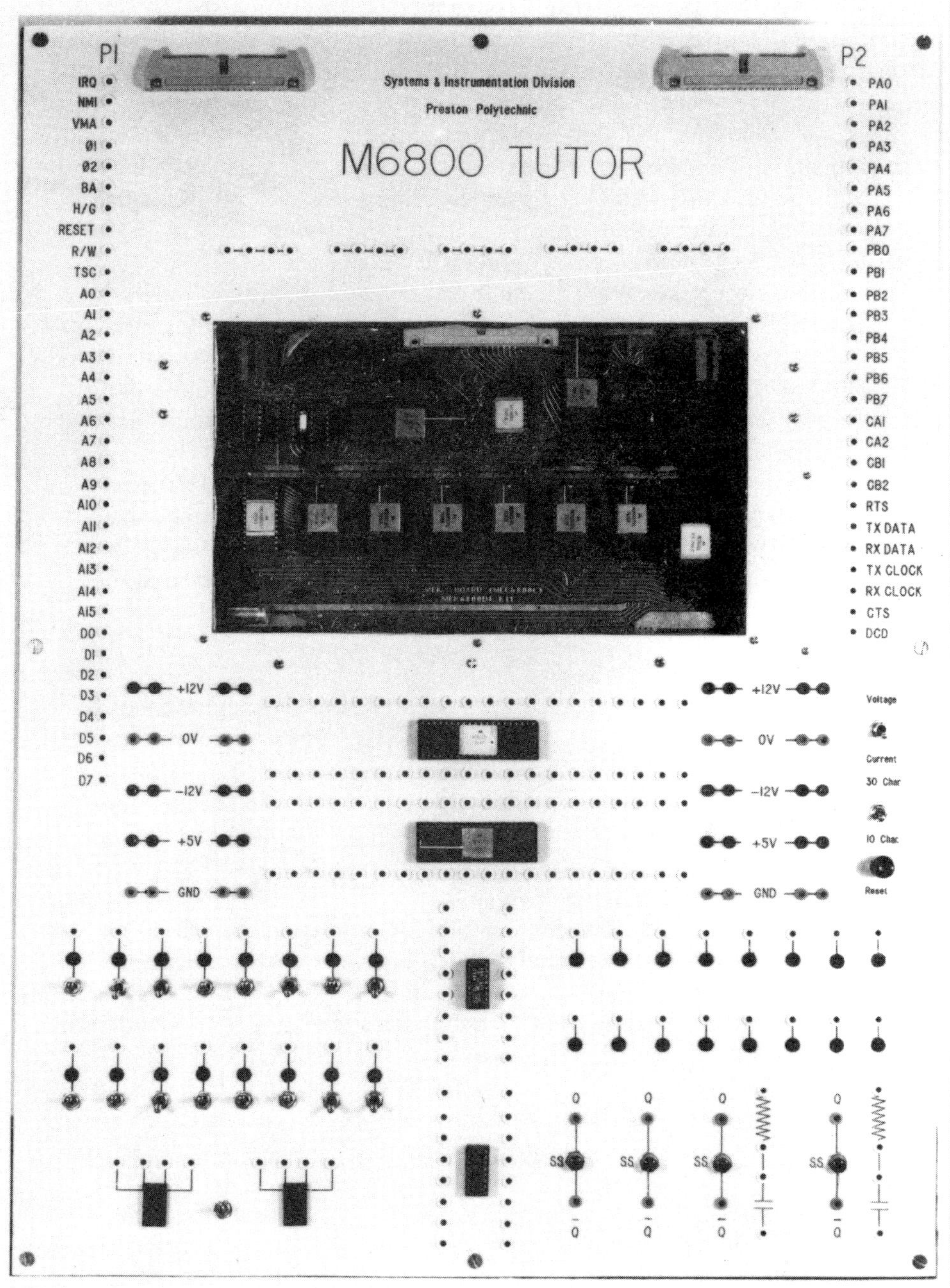

FIG. 3   The teaching aid.

ment which is designed to develop the students' knowledge of microprocessor programming using the various addressing modes. This concludes the material covered in a C course. However, we have found that for the B courses we can extend the assignment to include initialisation and use of the MC6820 PIA.

4.3   *Courses D and E*

The main aim of these courses is to extend the basic knowledge gained in courses B and C. This is achieved by undertaking a practical project which involves the student in the design, programming (including use of cross assembler) and implementation of a microprocessor-based system.

A typical project is a lowpass digital filter realization[5]. In this case the students are given a specific linear difference equation as the starting point, and they proceed to develop the appropriate flowchart and a corresponding program. The project does, by necessity, require A/D and D/A conversions under microprocessor control, coupled with the correct PIA initialisation and operation, and consequently provides a stimulating challenge.

It is worth noting that students are not given any supporting detailed laboratory instructions. Normally we allow the students to formulate their own programs and method of system implementation, thereby encouraging them to use their initiative and judgements. We consider, for these courses, that the lecturer's main role is to act as consultant and advisor.

5   CONCLUDING REMARKS

We have shown in this paper that our programme of microprocessor short courses has developed from a single one-day course, sometimes offered as 4 × 2 hr. evening course, to the current package of five courses designed to meet the requirements of industry that we have identified. We believe that course organization and operation, to satisfy the needs of local industry, is an important and essential role of polytechnics, and we have consequently attempted to satisfy the demand for microprocessor courses.

We are very encouraged by the reaction of industry and students to the courses and we find that the demand for such courses seems to be increasing further.

Our undergraduates receive approximately the same material covered in the B and D type courses, and this forms part of their normal undergraduate lectures under the subject title Digital Systems. Some useful industry-supported undergraduate projects are presently being undertaken. These have evolved as a result of our discussions with industry concerning the courses and applications.

An important and stimulating aspect of operating courses is that we have forged strong links with specialist departments within industry and this has led to consulting work and joint industry-polytechnic research projects. In addition, academic staff have an increased awareness of current industrial trends and applications of microprocessors.

We recognise that all our courses are intensive. However, from experience, we believe that we make a useful and effective contribution to microprocessor education for industry.

6 REFERENCES

[1] Powner, E. T., Escuder, M. A., Depledge, P. G. and Best, P. J., 'Introduction to microprocessor systems — Parts 1, 2 and 3' *I.J.E.E.E.* **14**, (1977).

[2] *Microprocessor Applications Project — Consultants (MAPCON)*, Department of Industry, Warren Spring Laboratory, Stevenage.

[3] Lee, I., 'Hands-on approach to microcomputer education', *Proc. I.E.E.E.*, **64**, No. 6, (1976).

[4] *M6800 Programming Reference Manual, M68PRM(D)*, (November, 1976).

[5] Yaacob, M., 'Digital filtering using a microprocessor', *M.Sc. Dissertation, U.M.I.S.T.*, (1977).

THE PROVISION OF COMPLETE MICROPROCESSOR ENGINEERING SERVICES BY A UNIVERSITY DEPARTMENT

E. T. POWNER
Department of Electrical Engineering and Electronics, University of Manchester Institute of Science and Technology, England

1   INTRODUCTION

The Department of Electrical Engineering and Electronics at the University of Manchester Institute of Science and Technology was the first university establishment to create an autonomous Microprocessor Engineering Unit, (MEU), separately staffed and wholly devoted to the research, teaching and application of microprocessor and microelectronic circuit techniques. Such activity was a natural extension of the vast experience previously gathered in the digital processes and computer application fields.

The development of stored-program calculators and microprocessors, by innovation of memory technology into the powerful single-chip microcomputer and processing elements available today, demands that special attention be paid to all facets of its fabrication and application. Microprocessor technology has penetrated all fields in the home, commercial and industrial environments, currently assuming a very important and dominant position. As a consequence, the activities of the Microprocessor Engineering Unit are wide-ranging and embrace many disciplines. Co-operation with personnel and colleagues having expertise in fields complementary to Electrical Engineering and Electronics makes the Microprocessor Engineering Unit a fully-integrated group, able to meet the increasing demands for consultancy, testing, prototyping, research and development, especially from the industrial sector, taking into account the economic and social implications.

2   RESEARCH

A large fraction of the Microprocessor Engineering Unit activity is devoted to the primary areas of research and advanced development associated with microprocessors and microcomputer systems. Research pursuits provide academic excellence, expertise, innovation and contributions to knowledge in the microprocessor and related fields. This in turn leads to good teaching from an authoritative base and competence in applying the derived techniques and thoroughly-researched design methodologies to the many practical situations which arise daily in industry.

Approximately 60 full-time staff and personnel are associated with the Microprocessor Engineering Unit, in conjunction with the Digital Electronics

Group, researching and investigating microprocessor techniques and system behaviour. It is inappropriate here to discuss individual research projects but some indication of the range and depth of experience in the microprocessor field is given in the following spectrum.

(i)   *Multiprocessor Systems.* Operation, interconnections, distributed systems, communication protocols, performance evaluation, reliability, fault-tolerant computing.

(ii) *Single-Chip Microprocessor/Microcomputer Systems.* Interfacing configurations, peripheral components operation in hostile environment, automated procedures, intelligent instrumentation, bit-slice processors, special purpose machines, P.L.A., emulators and controllers.

(iii) *Microprocessor System Design Methodology.* Computer-orientated tools and conversational techniques to assist and enhance methods of design and evaluation of microprocessor systems.

(iv) *Software, Languages, Simulation.* Assemblers, simulators, interpreters, cross products, concurrency, system modelling, procedure and special application-orientated languages.

Association with solid-state electronics personnel allows access to investigations of microelectronic circuit and device technology, material properties, post-manufacture performance and semiconductor fault investigation.

The research programmes arc directed towards both long and short term objectives relating to the above fields of investigation.

3   TEACHING AND INSTRUCTION

The Microprocessor Engineering Unit, in conjunction with the Digital Processes Research Group at U.M.I.S.T., is responsible for all of the microprocessor and digital courses both of a full-time and short-duration nature.

A summary of the type and variety of courses is listed below. Outline details only are given since the aims and contents of courses typical of this list are described in other papers[1, 2, 3] of this volume.

Full-time courses

Undergraduate degree courses in Electrical Engineering and Electronics include modules and options on microprocessors. At post-graduate level a one-calendar year master's degree course in Microprocessor Engineering and Digital Electronics provides thorough training and practical experience in microprocessor system design and application. Many candidates are seconded from industry via private or government-sponsored support schemes.

Short-duration courses

These are intended primarily for people from industry requiring rapid acquisition and training in a variety of microprocessor skills including:

(a)   *Initial appreciation of microprocessor technology.* One-day course suitable for businessmen and technical executives covering the potential, awareness, market forces and penetration of microprocessors.

(b)   *Introduction to microprocessor system design.* A three-day course covering
       the introductory principles of programming and microprocessor appli-
       cations with some practical experience.

(c)   *Application and utilisation of microprocessors.* A three-day/one week
       conversion course for engineers, giving a wide range of examples, demon-
       strations and hands-on experience of programme development and
       system construction.

(d)   *Advanced topics.* One/three days covering advanced techniques associated
       with program design/structuring, interrupt processing, real-time control,
       input/output interfacing, etc.

(e)   *Seminars.* Half/one day discussion and information exchange on special-
       ised aspects of microprocessor structures, behaviour and design
       methodology. Experienced engineer participation.

(f)   *Colloquia.* Half/one day lectures and presentations with the theme of
       microprocessor application to particular situations or industries e.g.
       medical, oil, food, process control, hazardous environments, etc.

Medium term courses

These are intended to provide in-depth training and experience in microprocessor system design skills. Typically lasting up to 10 weeks, personnel seconded
from industry combine hardware and software skills, often working on projects
immediately related or useful to their own particular sector of industry.

4   INDUSTRIAL SERVICES

The Microprocessor Engineering Unit in addition to its research and teaching
functions has comprehensive facilities for microprocessor project-based:

(i)   consultancy services
(ii)   advanced development and applications
(iii)   advisory and test services.

   A long and well-established U.M.I.S.T. tradition of close involvement and
association with industry throughout the years has provided a valuable
foundation, based on confidence and capability in the digital processes and
computer applications field, to be extended in the microprocessor direction.
   Vigorous research activity and accumulated experience with academic
colleagues and industrial concerns integrated over a long time period helps
both old and new industries to develop and exploit the latest microprocessor
technology in relation to its particular products or systems.
   The MEU at U.M.I.S.T. is in the rare position of being close to the needs of
industry, backed by academic and technical staff, all having had industrial and
research experience, offering knowledge and services as summarised below:

(i)   *Consultancy services*

Independent, confidential and speedy advice is offered on all aspects of microprocessor components, systems and applications. The service covers detailed
discussions of customer requirements, and, for a mutually-agreed fee, the

necessary appraisal, evaluation or experimental work in order to provide a detailed report. Such a report would typically describe how the customer needs can best be met with the available technology, the expected results likely to be achieved from the proposed system and the costing involved in producing a microprocessor-based equipment for manufacture or production.

(ii) *Advanced development and applications*
In addition to the above, the Microprocessor Engineering Unit is well-equipped to carry out the software and hardware development for the construction and operation of microprocessor-based instrumentation or control systems to customer-agreed specifications. Systems of a high standard of workmanship and presentation are utilised to provide an end-product in pre-production prototype form, suitable for installation and testing on site or in the customer's premises. Flexibility is the keynote of MEU operation and arrangements with industrial organisations vary from letters of intent to formally-agreed contracts.

(iii) *Advisory and test facilities*
The facilities of the Microprocessor Engineering Unit include a wide range of specialised test equipment for microprocessor system performance monitoring, evaluation and trouble-shooting. Often organisations do not possess such equipment or cannot justify their purchase on economic grounds. Access to such facilities is available, and on-site investigations have been arranged.

5   FACILITIES
Many concerns offering advice on microprocessor matters are confined to one or two families of microprocessor. The Microprocessor Engineering Unit has extensive facilities for the software and hardware development of over 12 different microprocessor types ranging from the small 4 bit to the more powerful 8 and 16 bit systems of leading manufacturers including

(i) Full development systems with twin floppy disc, VDU, teletypewriter and printer support for

Intel	4040, 8080, 8085, 8748, 8086.
Motorola	6800, 6802, 6809.
Zilog	Z80.
Texas Instruments	9900, 9940 series.
DEC	LSI-11 series.

(ii) Prototype development kits and single board computers for all the above range plus
   National Semiconductors SC/MP.
   A.M.D./National Semiconductors 2900 Bit Slice series.

(iii) Special test equipment includes facilities for
   PROM programming and simulation
      1702, 2708, 2716, etc. STAG, ITT.
   In-circuit emulation ICE-85.

Logic state analysers — Hewlett Packard, Tektronix, Systron Donner.

Such a range of equipment enables the Microprocessor Engineering Unit to offer services which are independent of any specific manufacturer or supplier. Experience enables comparisons to be made between processors, and thus advice can be given which, in addition to being confidential, is unprejudiced and best-suited for the particular application as specified by the industrial customer. The choice of microprocessor is discussed elsewhere in this journal[11, 12].

6   RANGE OF APPLICATIONS

The advances in microprocessor and associated microelectronic technology have been such that they have penetrated most sectors of industry, business and leisure. It would be invidious to attempt to give a comprehensive survey of application areas, since it is becoming more difficult to find places where they have *not* been utilised.

The Microprocessor Engineering Unit has had fruitful association with more than 40 companies and concerns, ranging from small business organisations with only one or two employees to the very large multi-national corporations. The objectives of individual application projects vary, with combinations of cost reduction, flexibility, enhanced products, increased productivity considerations, etc. Projects under investigation cover the spectrum from intended large-volume, low-cost markets to the special, purpose-built, one-off multi-microprocessor system. Usually there is a cost/performance trade-off in most systems. However, it is not uncommon to find application areas where cost is not paramount. Reliability and a high system operational integrity often take precedence in areas where human beings or essential services are being maintained.

Microprocessors are also being considered in application areas considered hitherto unsuitable for conventional computer involvement, on the grounds of space, cost, performance and environmental considerations.

The vast majority of microprocessor system applications involve some form of measurement, instrumentation and pertinent, individual implementation. Such is the scope of microprocessors that problems and techniques encountered in one field of application often lead to the alleviation of difficulties in totally unrelated disciplines.

Microprocessors and computer techniques are being applied in areas, via such interrelationships which inject a greater degree of quantitive assessment, where previously qualitative judgements were made, e.g. medical observation and correlation of drug efficacies and treatment methods.

Table 1 gives a non-exhaustive list of microprocessor permeation into industry experienced by the Microprocessor Engineering Unit, with two sectors amplified as illustrations to underline this fact and demonstrate the versatility of such devices.

The literature[4, 5, 6, 7, 8, 9, 10] abounds with articles on microprocessor applications where interested readers can keep in touch with current hardware, software and design methodology developments.

TABLE 1

Sector

Electrical and Electronic Engineering	
Mechanical	
Building and Civil	Engine Mapping
Chemical Engineering	Ignition Control
Textile	Exhaust Emission
Medical	Gearbox Control
Food Processing	Distributed Wiring and Control
Automotive ———————	Heating and Ventilation
Home and Leisure	Fuel Injection
Paper	Instrumentation and Warning
Polymer and Chemistry	Load Distribution/Axle Weight
Computer	Braking/Anti-skid
Oil	Jack-Knife Prevention
Transport	Security/Theft/Protection
Commercial	
Aviation	
Communications	
Machine Tool	Machine Tool Control
Measurement and Instrumentation ———	Automatic Test Equipment
	Shoe Gauge
	Washing Machines
	Balance
	Blood/Fluid Flow
	Auto/Cross Correlators
	Wave Shaping
	Process Control
	Sequencers
	Motor Control
	Traffic Lights
	Protection
	Precision Instruments
	etc.

7   CONCLUSION

The foregoing is a brief survey of the rôle which an engineering department can play in the research, teaching, retraining and particularly the application of the very important field of microprocessor technology. The resources are wide and varied, both in terms of capital equipment and human effort. Close co-operation with technological, scientific and business departments having resident, specialist expertise in many different disciplines, married to the particular skills in microprocessor system evaluation and design techniques, provides a centre of knowledge and experience not found in many industrial establishments.

The cross-fertilisation of the university, via the Microprocessor Engineering Unit and industry ensures that there is a steady but continuous transfer of knowledge and expertise in both directions. Important to both parties is the fact that industrially sponsored research and application projects bring in real problems to the university environment. It is on such projects that students and engineers are trained alongside permanent staff with the immediacy, awareness and relevance to current industrial needs. Without a group functioning as does the Microprocessor Engineering Unit, such activity is moved back one step in the training and education circle. Thus the Microprocessor Engineering Unit serves the immediate demands of both industry and university, each benefiting from the complementary activity of the other partner.

8   REFERENCES

[1]   Terrell, T. J. and Simpson, R. J. 'Microprocessor short courses for industry', *this volume*.

[2]   Cahill, S., 'A laboratory experiment on microprocessors' *this volume*.

[3]   Hartley, M. G., 'An example of an M.Sc. course — Digital Electronics at U.M.I.S.T.,' due to appear in IJEEE 17, No 1.

[4]   Powner, E. T., Depledge, P. G., Escuder, M. A. and Best, P. J., 'Introduction to micropro-cessors, structure, design and application', *Int. J. Elec. Eng. Educ.* **14**, pp. 73–80, pp. 173–186, and pp. 269–279, (updated version in *The Challenge of Microprocessors*, Manchester University Press, 1979).

[5]   Powner, E. T., 'Medical and measurement applications of microprocessors'. *IEE Symposium on Microprocessor Application*, Manchester 1978.

[6]   Depledge, P. G., 'Fault-tolerant microprocessor systems for aircraft', *IERE Conference on Computer Systems and Technology*, (1977).

[7]   Dagless, E. L. and Aspinall, D., *The Microprocessor and its Applications*, Pitman, (1977).

[8]   Betteridge, D. and Dagless, E. L., 'Application of Microprocessors to Chemical Analysis', *Analyst*, **101**, pp. 409–420, (1976).

[9]   Altman, L., (editor), *Microprocessors*, McGraw-Hill, (1975).

[10]   Altman, L. and Scrupski, S. E., (editors) *Applying Microprocessors*, McGraw-Hill, (1977).

[11]   Depledge, P. G., 'A review of available microprocessors', *this volume*.

[12]   Waterfall, R. C., 'Choosing the microprocessor for the job', *this volume*.

BIBLIOGRAPHY

Microprocessors: Fundamentals and Applications Lin, W. C. (editor), I.E.E.E. Press, distr. J. Wiley, (1977).

Microprocessors: New Directions for Designers, E. A. Torrero. Hayden Book Co., (1975).

A review of microcomputer journals and magazines is given elsewhere in this volume.

MICROPROCESSOR TEACHING IN NEW ZEALAND[1]

D. A. PRICE
Auckland Technical Institute, New Zealand

INTRODUCTION
A knowledge of the operation and use of microprocessors is becoming essential for electronic technicians and engineers. Such work is now being introduced into courses on digital electronics, computer engineering and control technology ensuring that forthcoming technicians and engineers will be familiar with microprocessors.

COURSE AT THE AUCKLAND TECHNICAL INSTITUTE
Courses are run at the introductory, basic and the advanced level. The introductory courses are only attended by students with little knowledge of current digital electronics. A large proportion of the students already hold qualifications such as New Zealand Certificate in Engineering or Science, Bachelor or Master Degrees in Engineering or Science and go directly to the basic course. Direct entry to the advanced courses is possible but most students complete the basic course before embarking on the advanced course. The first three courses, comprising of Digital Techniques, Microprocessor Basic, and Microprocessor Applications, are offered as one week full-time (35 hours) or twelve week part-time (3-hour sessions) courses.

MICROPROCESSOR BASICS COURSE (35 HOURS)
The time is fairly evenly divided between formal lectures and 'hands on' experience. The lectures describe the hardware arrangement used in microprocessor systems before introducing various number systems and programming at the machine language level.

Hardware topics covered include the interconnection of functional blocks of a typical microprocessor system, the concept of buses, tristate devices, clocks and timing requirements. Address lines, decoding of, types and operation of various types of memory. Extra MPU functions such as hold, interrupt, reset and wait, I/O techniques, latches, LEDs, UARTs. Software topics include binary, octal and hexadecimal numbers, two's complement numbers. Architecture of typical MPU and of Motorola 6800. Instruction set of the 6800, addressing modes, branching, subroutines, programming parallel output ports. The use of flow charts and coding forms to manually assemble programs.

The students are generally at home with the hardware topics but have some difficulty with the concept of stores programs at the machine level and are unfamiliar with the terminology (jargon?) in use. The use of a logic analyser on the data and address buses can aid understanding. The practical part of the course is presently based on the Motorola 6800 D2 kit, in common with many other institutions, but an alternative version of the course based on the Intel 8080 is being offered in 1979.

MICROPROCESSOR APPLICATIONS COURSE (35 hours)
About one third of the time is spent in formal lectures, the rest being spent working on one of a number of projects using microprocessors. Instruction covers the use of interrupts, parallel and serial data transmission, ASCII code, operation of terminals, the use of more sophisticated microprocessor systems which include monitors and assemblers, the use of PROM programmers, cross-assemblers and simulators. Completed projects include the control of a titration process, stepper motor control from data switches, paper tape reader and punch handlers, dot matrix printer interfacing (alphanumeric and graphics), use of conventional oscilloscopes for graphical display, the collection and display of data using analogue to digital and digital to analogue conversion.

OTHER COURSES
Short courses on specific topics such as the projects mentioned above are being offered for 1979. A course completely devoted to hardware has been organised for 1979. In this course a collection of chips is connected up to produce a simple microprocessor system during the course, in step with lectures explaining the design of the bus system, timing signals, etc.

PROJECT WORK
Students and staff at the Auckland Technical Institute have been involved in a number of projects. These have ranged from simple projects such as designing and building a 2K memory board, a fuseable link PROM programmer, a basic 6800 system directly from components through to converting dot matrix printers (ex calculators) to general alphanumeric and graphic units, a Tarbell (phase encoded) cassette interface. Two more ambitious projects, undertaken for outside organisations, were a simulated carpark charging system and a lift floor indicator using a SC/MP Microprocessor and a large dot matrix display, requiring only a change of PROM to convert to a different set of floor labels.

EQUIPMENT USED
The Motorola D2 kit is used for the basic microprocessor course and the institute has five of these. On the advanced courses the students have the choice of the following systems:

EVK200 (6800)	COSMAC (RCA 1802)
SDK80 (8080)	Intersil 6100 (12 bit)
H8 (8080)	D2 kits with MIKBUG

Each of the above systems operate in conjunction with a terminal and the following terminals are used:

ASR33 teletype	2 VDUs
2 LA43s	Tektronix 4010 graphics

Anciliary equipment used for practical work in the courses presently include the following items:

8 bit switch registers	conventional and storage oscilloscopes
2 digit hexadecimal displays	fuseable link PROM programmer
stepper motor	audio cassette tape recorders
A to D converters	paper tape punch (50 char/s)
D to A converters	paper tape reader (300 char/s)
digitally controlled tap	7 by 5 dot matrix printer
model electric train	floppy disk

A PDP-11 minicomputer is used for running 6800 and 8080 cross assemblers and direct communication between microprocessors and the PDP-11 via serial interfaces can be made. The EVK200 system has a resident assembler but it only has a limited range of features. A resident assembler for the SDK80 has recently been acquired.

COURSES AT OTHER INSTITUTIONS

Wellington Polytechnic have been running courses for three years. Courses are run as one or two week full-time blocks, and comprise microprocessor fundamentals, applications and appreciation. The latter course is a non-technical description of microprocessors for management. Courses usually centre around the 6800 and 8080 microprocessors but a large range of microprocessors are available. These include Cosmac 1802, Pace, SC/MP, F8, 6100 and the 6502.

Waikato Technical Institute have just started running courses and are using the Motorola D2 kit exclusively. At present they have little in the way of ancillary equipment but will build this up as courses progress. Christchurch Technical Institute will run their first microprocessor course next year. Their staff spent several months visiting a number of firms that work with microprocessors to gauge industries training requirements. Otago Polytechnic are keeping abreast of developments and should run their first course in 1980.

The University of Auckland teaches microprocessors in both the Physics and the Engineering Departments at the fourth year level in courses on digital electronics and on microprocessors and minicomputers. Microprocessors are being used in several research projects including the on-line processing of underwater acoustic signals. The 6800 and 8080 are both used.

Victoria University (Wellington) teaches microprocessors to senior-level Physics students and has laboratory experiments based on the Motorola D2 kit. The Engineering School at Canterbury University have a National SC/MP microprocessor kit with additional hardware for several projects including the testing of a bulk stock of RAM chips and the driving of a display console for teaching purposes. They feel that the SC/MP is not the best machine for teaching purposes.

NOTE

[1] This paper was first presented at the *Pacific Region Conference on Electrical Engineering Education* at the South Australian Institute of Technology, Adelaide, Australia, in December, 1978.

PLANNING MICROPROCESSOR COURSES AND A LABORATORY IN A UNIVERSITY ENVIRONMENT

V. V. ATHANI

Department of Electrical Engineering, Indian Institute of Technology, Bombay

INTRODUCTION

The microprocessor emerged as a result of rapid developments in large scale integration (LSI) technology. Ever since its introduction in 1971, the micro-processor has gained tremendous popularity and is finding application in such diverse areas as indicated below:

(i)   Dedicated application in data acquisition and process control systems forms a major area of microprocessor application.

(ii)   Use of microprocessors has given rise to a new breed of 'intelligent' instruments like digital processing oscilloscopes, automated test equipment, etc.

(iii)   Similarly, 'intelligent' computer peripherals like graphics terminals, keyboards, etc. have emerged as a result of introduction of microprocessors.

(iv)   Special microprocessors have been developed for dedicated use in electronically-switched telephone exchanges, computer networks, distributed processing, etc.

(v)   Automotive electronics has assumed an important position in micro-processor applications. They are used for controlling emission from automotive engines, and increasing fuel economy.

(vi)   Microprocessors have permeated even power systems, and are finding use in power system protection, energy economy, etc.

(vii)   Microprocessors have introduced the concept of personal computer for home accounting, TV games, kitchen, etc.

The potentialities of microprocessors were grasped by American universities who started offering microprocessor courses from 1973. Since then, regular as well as short-term courses have proliferated with the IEEE, microprocessor manufacturers and computer consultants joining the fray. Microprocessors made an entry in the IEEE Computer Society's CompCons in 1975. Since then, microprocessors are the centre of attraction at CompCons, Asilomer Workshops, an International Conference hosted by the IEE, etc. Several issues of the IEEE Computer Society's journal, COMPUTER, have been devoted to microprocessors[8]. The IEEE Proceedings have brought out two special issues on microprocessors[5, 6].

184

All this goes to show that there is a tremendous interest in microprocessors, and that this interest is growing with time. That is why the time has come for computer and electrical engineering educators to realize the importance of microprocessors and to include them in computer science and electrical engineering curricula. A beginning in this direction has already been made in I.I.T.-Bombay. This paper gives the details of microprocessor activities in I.I.T.-Bombay.

MICROPROCESSOR COURSES

As a first step in the introduction of microprocessor courses, they have been included as important topics in two of the existing courses:

EE 506: Digital Computer Design and Microprocessors

This is a compulsory course in 5th year second semester of our 5-year B.Tech. degree program, with 3 lectures/week. Its syllabus includes the following topics:

> Introduction to micros and classification; selected micros and supporting chips; programming aspects and software support; micros and minis; micro applications.

CS 641: Microprogramming and Microprocessors

This is an elective course at M.Tech level, with 3 lectures/week. The syllabus of this course includes the following:

> Introduction to micros and classification; micro architecture: bit-slice micros, supporting chips, I/O interface, bus transceivers; floppy disk and cassette systems; microprogram sequences; software support; case studies in micro applications.

Besides this, a full-fledged course on microprocessors is being planned. This will be offered as an elective course at the senior-graduate level in the first instance. It will be a 3 lectures/week course and will comprise the following topics:

> Micro development and classification; micro architecture: fixed instruction set and bit-slice architectures, supporting chips, I/O interface, DMA control; software aspects: microprogramming, assemblers, loaders, compilers for PL/M and BASIC, simulators and cross assemblers, etc; Micro applications illustrated by case studies.

MICROPROCESSOR LABORATORY

The so-called 'hands-on' approach to microprocessor education has been advocated by authorities like Imsong Lee[1]. In the light of this expert opinion, it has been decided to set up a microprocessor laboratory at I.I.T.-Bombay. The considerations in planning such a laboratory in a university environment have been discussed by Carey[2]. Our attempts at organizing a microprocessor laboratory have been guided by these views. The following objectives have been kept in view in laboratory development:

1   *Instructional*: The primary objective of the micro lab is to support courses at senior-graduate levels. This will also enable short-term courses with 'hands-on' experience to be organised for teachers, researchers, practicing engineers, etc. and thus spread the 'microprocessor culture'.

2   *Research*: An equally important objective of the laboratory will be to undertake research at B.Tech., M.Tech., and Ph.D. levels.

3   *Consultancy*: It has been the experience of the author that many industries have ordered LSI chips since they are inexpensive. However, lack of hardware and software development aids, which are very expensive, has been the chief factor hampering the use of microprocessors in industry. With its hardware and software debugging facilities, the proposed laboratory will be able to help industry in its microprocessor-based product development work. In return, the laboratory can become self-supporting.

4   *Sponsored research*: The minimum facilities being established can serve as a nucleus to attract sponsored research projects from various funding agencies. This will enable substantial research projects, having social relevance, to be undertaken. This will also contribute towards further laboratory growth.

The following rationale has been evolved with a view to achieving the above objectives:

(a) In view of newer, more versatile, and sophisticated products being continually introduced, it would be inadvisable to get stuck with any one microprocessor, however good it may be at present.

(b) For regular laboratory experiments, it would be better to have a few full microcomputer systems, complete with a minimum of 8K RAM, peripheral and software support. Radioshack's TRS-80, PET-2000 by Commodore, Heathkit's H-8 or H-11 systems could be considered for this purpose.

(c) Test equipment for hardware as well as software debugging is a must for research. This includes Tektronix 8002 microprocessor lab, 7D01F logic analyzer, Explorer digital storage oscilloscope, PROM programmer, in-circuit emulator, etc.

(d) Microprocessor kits; supporting LSI chips like EPROMs, RAMs, PICs, SIOs, UARTs, DMAs; microperipherals like TTY, CRT terminal, LED displays, minifloppies, diskettes, cassettes; would be needed for research work. This would enable the researcher to select a configuration commensurate with the complexity of his project.

A typical list of components for the microprocessor laboratory has been drawn up and is given in Table 1 for ready reference.

RESEARCH WORK

The importance of research in a university environment is already well-established, so that this point need not be laboured here. Recognizing its importance, research work on microprocessor-based systems was initiated long before courses in microprocessor were thought of. Fourteen projects at

TABLE 1   *Typical microprocessor laboratory equipment.*

Item no.	Item	Estimated cost (Rs.)
1.	Radioshack TRS-80, Commodore PET-2000, HeathkitH-8, or H-11 Microcomputers	24,000
2.	IMSAI 8048 Control Computer Board (EROM version plus 2K byte RAM)	7,000
3.	Tektronik 8002 Microprocessor Lab	1,20,000
4.	Tektronix 7D01F logic analyzer	70,000
5.	Explorer-II digital storage oscilloscope	60,000
6.	PROM programmer	32,000
7.	In-circuit emulator	12,500
8.	Teletype ASR-33	30,000
9.	Paper tape reader-punch	6,000
10.	Full ASCII keyboard with LED display	3,000
11.	Video monitor	6,000
12.	Datapoint alphanumeric printer	6,000
13.	Microprocessor kits	12,000
14.	LSI chips like EROMs, RAMs, I-O interface, DMA, A/D and D/A cards, etc.	12,000
15.	Digital cassettes with interface cards	9,000
16.	Dual floppy disc drives with interface	15,000
17.	Other items	30,000
	Total:	4,54,500

M.Tech., DIIT (Computer Science), and B.Tech. levels employing microprocessors have been completed. These have been listed in Table 2. Microprocessor-based research has gained momentum, with the result that one Ph.D. level project and as many as 24 M.Tech., DIIT, and B.Tech. level projects are being carried out. These are shown in Table 3. This trend is likely to continue in future as good students vie with each other to get microprocessor projects.

TABLE 2   *List of microprocessor projects completed.*

(1) Software support for F-8 microprocessor
(2) M6800 microcomputer system
(3) Design of homogeneous microcomputer network
(4) Design of microprocessor-based patient monitoring system — systems aspects
(5) Design of microprocessor-based patient monitoring system — hardware aspects
(6) Design of microprocessor-based patient monitoring system — software aspects
(7) Simulation of 8080 microcomputer system
(8) 8080-based automated digital IC tester
(9) Microprocessor-based data acquisition system
(10) Use of microprocessor in thyristor control of DC motor
(11) Thyristor firing circuits using microprocessors
(12) Microprocessor application to static excitation control system

TABLE 3 *Details of microprocessor projects initiated.*

 (1) Microprocessor application in automotive electronics (Ph.D. project)
 (2) M6800: hardware extensions and system software
 (3) IBM 1401 machine design using microprocessor
 (4) BASIC language compiler for MCS-8080
 (5) Microprocessor-based data processing computer
 (6) Communication terminal for a microprocessor
 (7) Hardware and software development for microcomputer network
 (8) Designing TDC-316 using AMD 2900 family
 (9) EC 1030 CPU design using the AMD 2900 family
(10) Intel 8080-based patient monitoring system
(11) Design and simulation of multi-microprocessor system
(12) Multi-microprocessor system for Monte Carlo solution of PDEs
(13) Continuous system simulation using multiple microprocessors
(14) Problem-solving with multiple microprocessors
(15) System identification using a microprocessor-based correlator
(16) Use of microprocessor in process control
(17) Microprocessor control of three-phase inverter
(18) Microprocessor-based stepper motor drive circuits
(19) Application of microprocessors to protective relaying
(20) Microprocessor-based ADM switches
(21) Test programs for 8080 microcomputer
(22) Microprocessor application to overcurrent relay simulation
(23) Minicomputer-based PROM programmer

CONTINUING EDUCATION PROGRAMS

Microprocessors have become so popular that not only students but also teachers, researchers, and practicing engineers are curious to know what they are and how they could be employed in their applications. It was on persistent demand from students that the very first short-term course was run here in November 1976 under the auspicies of the IEEE Students Branch. This course on 'Introduction to Microprocessors' is being repeated in September 1978. An appreciation course on microprocessors for teachers and research scholars was organized in the summer of 1978. A six-week course on 'Microprocessors and their Applications' was arranged for officers from the defence services. This course proved to be so popular that it had to be repeated in the summer of 1978.

A QIP Summer School in microprocessors is planned for the summer of 1979. A short-term course for practicing engineers may also be arranged in the near future.

CONCLUSIONS

This paper has established the need for microprocessor's inclusion in computer and electrical engineering education. It has summarized the activities in the microprocessor area being carried out at I.I.T.-Bombay. This includes course work, laboratory development, research projects, and continuing education programs.

REFERENCES

[1]   Lee, Imsong, 'Hands-on approach to microprocessor education', *Proc. IEEE*, **64**, No. 6, pp. 1002–1007, (1976).

[2]   Carey, B. J., 'Microprocessor laboratory for a university environment', *Computer*, **10**, No. 1, pp. 40–46, (Jan. 1977).

[3]   Wakerly, J. F. and McCluskey, E. J., 'Microcomputers in the computer engineering curriculum', *ibid*, pp. 32–38.

[4]   Rony, P.R. and Larsen, D. G., 'Teaching microcomputer interfacing to non-electrical engineers', *ibid*, pp. 53–57.

[5]   *Proceedings of the IEEE, Special Issue on Microprocessors*, (June 1976).

[6]   *Proceedings of the IEEE, Special Issue on Microprocessor Applications*, (February 1978).

[7]   *Scientific American, Special Issue on Microelectronics*, (September 1977).

[8]   *Computer, Special Issues*, (July 1974, January 1976, April 1976, February 1977, etc.).

THE CYBERCOM MULTIMODE EDUCATION COMMUNICATION SYSTEM

DONALD LOMAX
Plato Education Division, Control Data (PTY) Ltd., Johannesburg, South Africa,
formerly of the Education Department, The University of the Witwatersrand,
Johannesburg, South Africa

> 'We are on the threshold of an exciting and revolutionary period, in which the scientific study of man will be put to work in man's best interests. Education must play its part. It must accept the fact that a sweeping revision of educational practices is possible and inevitable.'
>
> B. F. Skinner, 1954.[1]

Modern education systems are increasingly placed under stress by technological developments which are rapidly changing the distinctively human contribution to social and economic growth. Future societies will need more people with higher levels of training and education who are able to make creative contributions in the fields of work and leisure. Education systems, therefore, must expand, become more flexible and be quicker to adapt to new pressures than in the past[2]. The most rapidly changing environment to which our species has ever been exposed challenges us to make a constructive response.

Confronted by the explosions of knowledge and of population, educators are now seriously challenged to recognise the vital needs for universal popular education, a new distribution of knowledge, a changing structure of educational authority, changes in the role of the teacher and new insights into the nature of the teaching-learning process[3].

If education systems with the capacity to accept these future challenges are to be evolved, then new concepts must be applied in those decision making processes which control planning and innovation[4]. In industrialised countries the costs of education and training now account for a large proportion of national expenditure. As a consequence there is more concern that educators should be accountable for their performance and that education systems should attain the targets which have demanded such high investment. Some economists and social scientists now question whether we can afford the high costs of instruction which are associated with apparent low productivity. Too often in the past our attention has been centred upon teacher performance to the neglect of pupil learning. Fortunately, there has emerged in recent years a new technology of training and education which promises to provide the needed conceptual framework for the orginisation and control of learning resources. This technology is characterised by a systematic approach to the problems of teaching and learning. Given the relatively undeveloped state of the science of instruction and learning, it is not surprising to discover that some

190

problems have hindered the growth of this important technology. One serious
problem has been the emergence of two differing interpretations of what is
meant by educational technology[5]. The first of these interpretations is essentially a hardware approach that emphasizes the mechanisation of instruction
by the introduction of increasingly sophisticated aids which enhance teacher
performance. The ideal aim of this technology might be expressed as increased
learning efficiency at reduced cost. The second interpretation is essentially a
software approach[6] and is based upon the belief that it will prove to be possible to distil general propositions about teaching and learning from fundamental research. The development of mechanical aids is believed merely to facilitate
presentation. Although doubts exist about the way in which the behavioural
sciences should influence educational programmes, it may be argued that the
main problem in applying psychological principles is one of engineering, which
plays a vital part in the application of scientific principles in many fields[7]. If we
are to advance our understanding of the instructional process it is necessary to
reconcile these divergent interpretations. It seems possible that this recon-
ciliation may be encouraged by the application of a systems approach to
education. From this third point of view we shall now define educational
technology as the development, application and evaluation of systems, techniques and aids to improve the process of human learning[8].

In industry the systems approach has proved to be useful in solving many
complex design and development problems.

'The process involves the accurate identification of the requirements and
problems, the setting of specific performance objectives, the application of logic
and analysis techniques to the problems, the development of methods for the
solution of the problems and the rigorous measurement of this product against
the specific performance objectives'[9]

Thus, the systems engineering concepts which have been usefully employed
in the development of hardware may also be applied to the development of
educational and training programmes.

Although these procedures may lack the elegant precision and predictive
power of the physical sciences, they bring us closer to the science of education
upon which our future prosperity may be built[10].

It may be argued that the technological advance which promises to make the
greatest contribution to the wider distribution of effective individualized
instruction within the developing science of education is computer-based
instruction. This form of instruction requires more than the provision of
hardware, software and courseware. It demands the creation of a complete
educational environment which is characterised by the specific applications of
educational and computer technologies to aid the learning process. An interesting example of a recent attempt to create this type of educational environment
is provided by the development of the *Cybercom Multimode Education
Communication System*. This system facilitates a systems approach to education
by recognising that teaching and learning involve a range of methodologies
and strategies. A brief outline of the hardware components may serve as a

helpful introduction to discussion of the educational implications of the system.

The Cybercom system is modular in construction (a macro unit having a maximum of 256 terminals), see Fig. 1. It consists of the following basic components with appropriate operating systems and interfaces in each case.

(i) The student terminal (Fig. 2) has a full alphabet, numerals and other symbols to provide a total of 64 characters with a layout similar to that of a typewriter. The panel, which operates in a full duplex mode, is flat and therefore does not obstruct vision. It is robust in construction, quiet in operation, and may be built into an existing desk or conference table. The panel operates by touch, has no visibly moving parts, and incorporates a window which presents a twelve-character alphanumeric display. Messages concerning the evaluation of responses are conveyed to the student by flashing lights in the window. In making his responses the student may use numbers, groups of words or complete sentences. There are procedures by which the student may backspace to change or cancel a response. Should the student wish to review his response, the required information is presented in the window. Other messages are also displayed to control the learning procedures. For example, the student may be informed that his response exceeds the required length or that an option he has chosen (such as a request for help) has not been allowed by the teacher. It is also possible to fit various overlays on the panel to facilitate the use of different alphabets, pictures, symbols or diagrams.

(ii) A console, (Fig. 3), which is operated by the group supervisor or instructor contains a video display unit that shows all student responses as they are made, and also provides such other data as the percentage of students who are responding and the percentage who are correct in their responses. This

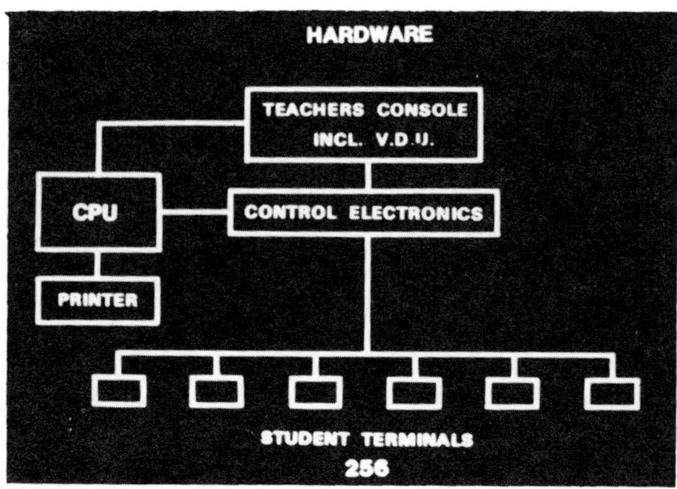

FIG. 1 *Block diagram of the overall system of student-response monitor.*

FIG. 2 Student 'keyboard' and display panel.

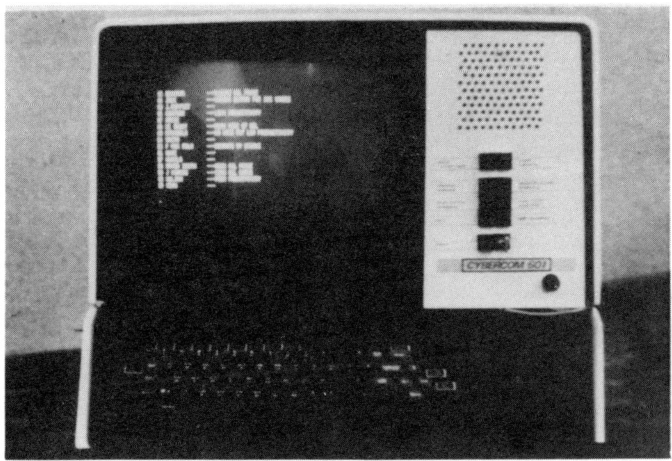

FIG. 3 View of VDU monitor at lecturer's desk.

constant feedback is a major advantage for the group leader and preserves his central creative role. A typewriter keyboard in the console enables the supervisor to interact with the whole group whilst selecting various teaching strategies by means of a number of push buttons. For example, the group leader may choose several different schedules of reinforcement to convey knowledge of results, may work with students individually, in one large group, or in eight different groups. He may allow students to erase incorrect answers, or may decide to limit them to a single response.

Students may receive help from their terminals in answering or may be required to work without assistance. Sometimes exact answers may be required whilst on other occasions it will be sufficient to produce a sentence answer containing certain key words.

(iii) A printer, which incorporates a paper tape punch and reader is linked to the system to enable the group supervisor to obtain a printed record of all that appears on the video display. Statistics referring to either group or individual performance are thus readily available for private use or for wider distribution.

(iv) A mini-computer is housed in a separate cabinet alongside a disk storage unit and the central electronics. The disk storage system provides long-range mass recording of individual responses to a large number of questions for research purposes, and also facilitates the rapid loading of different programmes.

The additional optional features which may be added to the system include extension video display monitors which may present information to individuals, a single large group or a number of separate groups. Audio-visual device interfaces may also be utilised in conjunction with various audio-visual aids, which thus become an integral part of the complete interactive system[11].

As a full Cybercom unit contains 256 student panels which may, if desired, be assigned to as many as eight groups, each working on different material, and as the system provides instant feedback to individuals, interesting possibilities exist for the development of personalized systems of instruction based upon a mastery learning model. Fig. 4 shows a group of students at work. It is possible, for example, whilst teaching a large group to identify failing students and to transfer them temporarily to a number of remedial groups, enabling them to acquire the desired mastery of material before returning to the main group. The feedback, which is a fundamental feature of the Cybercom system, is also an essential characteristic of effective learning procedures. This information comes to the teacher in the form of a battery of reports at the end of a test session, or, alternatively, may be available during a teaching session if the teacher wishes constantly to monitor student performance. If student performance is monitored throughout a teaching period, the student input to the system is displayed upon the television screen which forms part of the teacher's console. At any moment during the lesson, the teacher may call for a variety of reports from the computer, which analyses group or individual performance. The reports, which are obtained at the end of the session, may be displayed upon the television screen and, if necessary, may also be obtained in printed form from the teleprinter.

The nature of the responses which may be obtained by this system clearly depends upon the kind of questions which are asked. At the most simple level the student is given either a verbal or written statement and asked to indicate whether he agrees or disagrees. During the lesson or at the conclusion of a

FIG. 4   Students using the system.

teaching period, the teacher may thus get feedback on the percentage of the class who agree with chosen statements, and may, if he wishes, modify his teaching accordingly. If a more sensitive method of measuring attitudes is required, students may be asked to respond to statements on a seven-point scale which ranges from strong agreement through neutral to strong disagreement. The computer report on this test provides a measure of the mean performance of the group for each question and the standard deviation. If further information is required, then a detailed report provides an analysis of each student's response to each question.

A group supervisor may employ the system in four basic activities. He may interact with the trainees by transmitting additional knowledge and by evaluating their understanding of this material. As students respond to his presentation they may, if the supervisor so decides, receive reinforcement. Secondly, the group may discuss a model performance or demonstration which they have observed. In this discussion, in which all participate by entering comments through their personal terminals, the supervisor may play a number of roles, such as discussion leader or neutral observer. Another alternative activity allows students to engage in a self-paced learning sequence, working with printed materials, which may be programmed, and respond individually through their terminals, receiving reinforcement as they do so.

Fourthly, the group may be examined on their knowledge or on their attitudes. The system thus recognises that a variety of strategies and methodologies may be available to the teacher, and permits him to make a choice. The emphasis is placed upon making the education process more humane by improving communication between members of the group and by enabling a large number of students to express themselves simultaneously, privately and independently to a single group leader. These various activities may serve to provide a focus upon the essential elements of the material being studied.

The vital distinction between efficiency and effectiveness in terms of 'doing things right' and 'doing the right things', Davies[12] points out, focusses our attention upon the two roles which educational technologists may play. Emphasis placed only upon efficiency assigns a peripheral and sometimes trivial role to the technologist. Emphasis upon effectiveness, however, assigns to the technologist a central role in the development of education in which he is able to strive to create a total learning environment which is humane and not mechanistic. 'People may thus', he says 'be given an opportunity for influencing both the content and process of education, as well as being treated as human beings with complex sets of needs'.

As the number of students entering education systems has increased, the retention in many institutions of conventional patterns of organisation and traditional teaching methods has produced some unfortunate consequences. For many students the learning experience has become cold and impersonal. Feedback to the individual learner about his performance is reduced, and takes longer to reach him. The course instructor also experiences reduced feedback on student performance. The result of these deficiencies is that neither the student nor the instructor has sufficient information upon which to base educational strategies. There is therefore a danger that both participants in the enterprise may be exposed to a cumulative and destructive sense of failure. If, as Davies argues, students must have the chance to influence the content and process of the learning system in ways which ensure that their personal needs are met, then educational technologists must confront several challenges. The egalitarian concern to extend educational opportunities to a wider range of people means that more attention must be paid to the individual differences which are found in more heterogeneous learning groups. If most students are to reach the intended terminal performance level, then consideration must be given to differences in learning styles, abilities and attitudes, on entry to the study programme. Instructional resources must be organised so as to motivate diverse groups of individuals to learn effectively. The new distribution problems created by the need to serve large numbers of people, sometimes in widely isolated locations, will require that these resources are portable, flexible and readily accessible. Students and instructors will require quick and adequate feedback to enable them to correct or improve their performance.

It seems unlikely that traditional systems will be able to meet the challenges which have been described above[13]. In general such systems tend to be characterized by; vague objectives, emphasis upon teacher performance, a learning speed determined by the teacher, inadequate feedback on performance to the student, a high level of teacher talk, and a low level of interaction between teachers and those taught[14, 15]. These failings have prompted the development of humane individualized study programmes which recognize that individual differences require sensitive and varied courses designed to enable a majority of students to succeed in their learning endeavours[16, 17].

It was argued at the beginning of this article that the technological advance which promises to make the greatest contribution to the wider distribution of humane and effective personalized instruction is computer-based education. The term 'computer-based education' (CBE) has come to mean virtually any teaching or learning procedure which uses a computer system. In seeking to create a complete educational environment characterised by the principles of computer and educational technologies, the modern educator has the opportunity to use increasingly sophisticated hardware in the form of computer systems and associated communications equipment. The software (the coded instructions to which the hardware responds) includes two types: machine and user. 'Machine software' refers to the instructions which control computer activity, whilst 'user software' refers to the instructions which are available to people who are using the system. The hardware and software must be carefully integrated with the curriculum content (courseware) within the embracing instructional strategy. One of the important forms of CBE, which is known as computer-assisted instruction (CAI), involves direct interaction between the learner and the study programme by means of a terminal which allows him to receive and to send information. The student thus interacts with the computer in a way similar to that found in the typical one-to-one tutorial setting[18]. Another important form of CBE is computer-managed instruction (CMI) which is a series of evaluative and prescriptive processes involving interactions between students, instructors, administrators and the computer. Paulson describes this procedure as one in which the student is guided through a course of study along a learning path designed for him by the teacher who is managing the learning process. The learning path strategy is based upon a diagnosis of the needs of the individual student whose progress is continually evaluated and recorded.

It will now be clear that the illustrative example of a South African attempt to design a complete learning environment, the Cybercom system, is best described as a computer-based education system as it does not attempt the comprehensive analysis, diagnosis and guidance of computer-managed education systems, and yet is more flexible than many computer-assisted systems. Cybercom is able to go beyond mere efficiency to reach educational effectiveness, and manifests all the main characteristics of personalised systems of instruction. The system is designed to fit into and shape existing educational situations. Multiple users have concurrent access to the mini-computer, whilst each individual functions as if he had exclusive use of the system. The speed and flexibility of the system encourage a number of forms of information presentation.

Zawels[19] suggests that one useful advantage of the Cybercom system is that no programming knowledge is required by the user, as lesson programmes are written in plain daily language. This makes the instructor independent as he is able to write his own lessons or to modify an existing programme to suit his needs without the assistance of a specially trained programmer. He points also to the impressive flexibility of the system, which may allow up to eight different groups of different size, working on different lesson material, to be monitored by one instructor in a central location. In most conventional CAI courses the programmer presents a fairly rigid lesson format but Cybercom gives the student more freedom in his approach to lesson material. The system is also very adaptable and does not demand special communication lines, architecturally designed space, nor specialized furniture. Interesting possibilities, however, also exist for the incorporation of Cybercom terminals into enclosed learning carrels in circumstances in which private study is deemed to be advantageous. Carrels may be designed with varying degrees of sophistication. Cybercom, for example, may be linked in interesting ways to video-replay monitors, microfische projectors, audio replay facilities and synchronised tape-slide presentations. A price has to be paid, unfortunately, for the privacy of the carrel, in that personal eye contact is lost between student and instructor. The flat unobtrusive student terminal used in a classroom or lecture theatre does not place a barrier between the instructor and his class as so many other CAI terminals do. The instructor is thus free to employ a full range of histrionic techniques.

The fact that teachers using the system may employ four broad strategies (presentation of information to a group, group discussion, self-paced learning or individual testing) gives it wide appeal and makes it less likely that it will ever stand idle. This obviously increases its cost effectiveness.

Another attractive feature of the Cybercom system is the way in which it works in close association with books. It is worth noting that the book has been, and remains, excellent educational technology[20]. It is relatively inexpensive and is portable, so that a student may work with it in a variety of different locations. It requires no maintenance, has good print and may be beautifully illustrated. Students may use it in highly personal ways, by underlining the text or by making private notes. It facilitates self-paced work and allows the student to use his personal style of study. It allows the student easy random access to any section of the text and is usually well-indexed and carefully subdivided into logical sections for his convenience. It may be conveniently stored and may also be linked to other printed materials. Little wonder that casual attempts to replace this excellent technology have been doomed to failure. It does not make sense therefore, it may be argued, to store a book inside an expensive computer. Cybercom thus is designed to work with books and not to replace them. Similarly, the system is planned to assist the teacher and not to replace him. Cybercom is not a teaching machine but rather a communication system within which various presentation devices may be linked by the teacher who creates and controls the educational environment.

There appear to be three trends in recent educational developments which suggest that educational systems may be able to make significant responses to the needs of rapidly-growing modern societies. Firstly, there is increasing interest in new ways of achieving a wider distribution of education. Secondly, there is a growing commitment to humane personalized systems of instruction, and thirdly there is the recognition of the significance of educational technology. The Cybercom system, being specifically created to provide individualised instruction for large numbers of students in a systematically designed educational environment, exhibits the influence of all three trends. It thus seems likely that computer-based systems of this type will make an important contribution to future social and economic developments.

REFERENCES

[1] Skinner, B. F., 'The science of learning and the art of teaching', *Harvard Educational Review*, **24**, pp. 86–97, (1954).

[2] Lomax, D. E., *The Education of Teachers in Britain*, Wiley, London, (1973).

[3] O.E.C.D., 'The teacher and educational change. A new role', *Organisation for Economic, Cooperation and Development*, Paris, (1974).

[4] Lomax, D. E., *European Perspectives in Teacher Education*, Wiley, London, (1976).

[5] Davies, I. K., *The Management of Learning*, McGraw-Hill, London, (1971).

[6] Lumsdaine, A. A., 'Educational technology, programmed learning and instructional science', in *Theories of Learning and Instruction*, H. G. Richey, ed., University of Chicago Press, (1964).

[7] Anderson, R. C., Faust, G. W., *Educational Psychology: The science of instruction and learning*, Dodd Mead, New York, (1973).

[8] Department of Education and Science, *Central arrangements for promoting educational technology in the United Kingdom, H.M.S.O.*, London, (1972).

[9] Butler, F. C., *Instructional systems development for vocational and technical training*, Educational Technology Publications, Englewood Cliffs, N.J., (1972).

[10] Lomax, D. E., 'A review of British research in teacher education', *Review of Educational Research*, **42**, 3, pp. 289–326, (1972)

[11] Zawels, J., *The Cybercom Multimode Education Communication System*, Mimeo, Department of Education, University of the Witwatersrand, Johannesburg, (1976).

[12] Davies, I. K., 'Educational technology at the crossroads: Efficient message design or effective communication', in *Aspects of Educational Technology VIII*, J. P. Baggaley, G. H. Jamieson and H. Marchant, Pitman, London, (1975).

[13] Lomax, D. E., *Teaching for Tomorrow's World*, Witwatersrand University Press, Johannesburg, (1978).

[14] Goldschmid, B., Goldschmid, M. L., *Modular Instruction in Higher Education: A Review*, Centre for Learning and Development, McGill University, Montreal, (1972).

[15] Cooper, J. L., 'Learning theory and effective instruction', *Journal of Higher Education*, **44**, pp. 217–34, (1973).

[16] Bloom, B. S., 'Learning for mastery', *UCLA, Evaluation Comment 1*, No. 2, (1968).

[17] Block, J. H., *Mastery Learning: Theory and Practice*, Holt Rinehart and Winston, New York, (1971).

[18] Paulson, R. F., *Control Data Plato*, C.D.C., St. Paul, (1976).

[19] Zawels, J., *The Cybercom Conference and Decision Making System*, Mimeo, Department of Education, University of the Witwatersrand, Johannesburg, (1977).

[20] Zawels, J., *The Cybercom Educational Television System*, Mimeo, Department of Education, University of the Witwatersrand, Johannesburg, (1978).

A REVIEW OF MICROCOMPUTER JOURNALS AND MAGAZINES

The vast increase in the number of available microprocessors and microcomputers over the past five years has recently been matched by a similar expansion in the publishing of new journals and magazines relating to these devices. Many such new publications originate from the United States and to some extent reflect a greater awareness, particularly in the small business environment, of the public in that country to microprocessors. Furthermore there are vigorous developments in the home computer or 'hobbyist' market in the U.S.A. Many of the journals published are thus aimed, not at the professional engineer or computer scientist but rather at amateurs with very limited electronics or computer knowledge. We thus have a spectrum of publications covering three broad areas; research, hobbyist/small business systems and industrial/engineering applications. The last area is already covered by existing trade journals such as *Electronics, EDN, Electronic Design, Computer Design, New Electronics, Systems International*, etc., which, in the main, have sections dedicated to microprocessor developments and applications. We shall concentrate in this review on the new research and hobbyist/business journals.

Only one journal is totally dedicated to the theoretical and research aspects of microprocessors, this being the *Euromicro Newsletter* or, more formally, *The International Journal of Microprocessing and Microprogramming*. This publication is a vehicle for papers on all aspects of theory, design and research in both hardware and software for microprocessors and will be of value to anyone with interests outside the straightforward application of microprocessors to relatively simple tasks. *Microprocessors and Microsystems* also covers this area although at a lower level, concentrating mainly on new systems and advanced devices. Both these journals are, in my view, expensive as will be seen from the list below.

The large number of hobbyist/business microprocessor journals prohibits even a brief description of individual characteristics. However, an indication of their broad area of coverage can be given. Typical of the business end of the spectrum are *Personal Computer World* and *Practical Computing*, which are European and *Interface Age* and *Calculators and Computers* which are American. These journals tend to include a good deal of information on applications software, particularly programs written in BASIC, and details on the user aspects of microcomputer systems. The hobbyist journals generally cover both software (in BASIC and assembly language) and hardware in similar detail. Typical of this class are *Creative Computing, Byte, Kilobaud, 73, Personal Computing, Peoples Computers* and *ROM*, all published in the U.S.A. These journals are often of great interest to beginners since introductory articles appear with some regularity. Finally, two journals are available which fall into the specialist hobby category. These are *Dr. Dobb's Journal of Computer Calisthenics and Orthodontia* and *Computer Music Journal*. The coverage of the latter is fairly obvious. *Dr. Dobb's* consists almost entirely of program listings provided by readers. Programs are usually in BASIC or assembly language and cover applications in games, arithmetic and systems software.

Some problems may be found in obtaining the American hobbyist journals, although specialist companies do provide U.K. subscription services to the majority of publications listed here. For example L.P. Enterprises of 313, Kingston Road, Ilford IG1 1JP, Essex and Computer Workshop, 38, Dover St., London W1X 3RB both stock many of the magazines and journals reviewed.

Byte: Byte Publications Inc. U.S.A. £21 p.a., 12 Issues.
Calculators and Computers: £10 p.a., 7 Issues.
Computer Music Journal: Peoples Computer Company, Box E, 1263 El Camino Real, Menlo Park, California 94025, U.S.A. £8.50 p.a., 4 Issues.
Creative Computing: Creative Computing Press, U.S.A., £8.50 p.a., 6 Issues.
Dr. Dobb's Journal of Computer Calisthenics and Orthodontia: Peoples Computer Company, Box E, 1263 El Camino Real, Menlo Park, California 94025, U.S.A., £13 p.a., 10 Issues.
Euromicro Newsletter — International Journal of Microprocessing and Microprogramming: North Holland Publishing Co., P.O. Box 211, Amsterdam, The Netherlands. D.fl 90.00, 4 copies p.a.
Interface Age: McPheters, Wolfe and Jones, 16704 Marquardt Ave., Cerritas, California 90701, U.S.A. £20 p.a., 12 Issues.

Kilobaud: 1001001 Inc., Peterborough, N.H. 03458, U.S.A. £20 p.a., 12 Issues.

Microprocessors and Microsystems: IPC Science and Technology Press, Westbury House, Bury St., Guildford, Surrey GU2 5AW £23 p.a., 6 Issues.

Peoples Computers: Peoples Computer Company, Box E, 1263 El Camino Real, Menlo Park, California 94025, U.S.A. £8 p.a., 6 Issues.

Personal Computer World: Intra Press, 62A Westbourne Grove, London WC2. £8 p.a., 12 Issues.

Personal Computing: Benwill Publishing Corp., U.S.A. £17 p.a., 12 Issues.

Practical Computing: EEC, 2 Duncan Terrace, London N1. £6 p.a., 12 Issues.

ROM: ROM Publications, U.S.A., £1.75 per Issue.

73: 1001001 Inc., Peterborough, N.H. 03458, U.S.A. £20 p.a., 12 Issues.

P. G. DEPLEDGE, *Microprocessor Engineering Unit, Dept. of Electrical Engineering and Electronics, U.M.I.S.T.*

BIBLIOGRAPHY

All the books listed have been reviewed in *I.J.E.E.E.*, and the volume and page number of the review is given with each book.

Aspinall, D. and Dagless, E. L., *Introduction to Microprocessors* (Pitman, 1977) **16**, No. 2 and 3, p. 268.

Aspinall, D. (ed.) *The Microprocessor and its Applications, an advanced course* (Cambridge University Press, 1978), **16**, No. 2 and 3, p. 269.

Bibbero, J., *Microprocessors in Instruments and Control* (Wiley, 1977) **16**, No. 2 and 3, p. 270.

Cluley, J. C., *Computer Interfacing and On-Line Operation* (Edward Arnold, 1975) **16**, No. 2 and 3, p. 276.

Hartley, M. G. and Healey, M., *A First Course in Computer Technology* (McGraw-Hill, 1978) **16**, No. 2 and 3, p. 271.

Healey, M., *Minicomputers and Microprocessors* (Hodder and Stoughton, 1976) **13**, No. 4, p. 380.

Lesea, A. and Zacks, R., *Microprocessor Interfacing Techniques* (Sybex, 1977) **16**, No. 2 and 3, p. 268.

Lin, W. C., *Microprocessors: Fundamentals and Applications* (IEEE Press, distr. J. Wiley, 1977) **15**, No. 4, p. 380.

Lippiatt, A. G., *The Architecture of Small Computer Systems* (Prentice/Hall, 1978) **16**, No. 2 and 3, p. 272.

McCracken, D. D., *A Guide to PL/M Programming for Microcomputer Applications* (Addison-Wesley, 1978) **16**, No. 2 and 3, p. 270.

McGlynn, D. R., *Microprocessors: Technology, Architecture and Applications* (J. Wiley, 1976) **14**, No. 4, p. 382.

Sanderson, P. C., *Minicomputers* (Newnes-Butterworth, 1976) **13**, No. 4, p. 301.

Sawin, D. H., *Microprocessors and Microcomputer Systems* (Lexington, 1977) **15**, No. 4, p. 380.

Soucek, B., *Microprocessors and Microcomputers* (J. Wiley, 1976) **14**, No. 2, p. 192.

Ward, B., *Microprocessor/Microprogramming Handbook* (Foulsham Tab, 1975) **15**, No. 1, p. 13.

Zacks, R., *Microprocessors: from Chips to Systems* (Sybex, 1977) **16**, No. 2 and 3, p. 268

Zissos, D., *System Design with Microprocessors* (Academic Press, 1978) **16**, No. 2 and 3, p. 269.